# THINKING THROUGH
# THE DEATH OF GOD

SUNY series in Theology and Continental Thought
Douglas L. Donkel, editor

# THINKING THROUGH THE DEATH OF GOD

## A CRITICAL COMPANION TO THOMAS J. J. ALTIZER

*Edited by*

LISSA McCULLOUGH

*and*

BRIAN SCHROEDER

STATE UNIVERSITY OF NEW YORK PRESS

Published by
State University of New York

© 2004 State University of New York

For information, address State University of New York Press,
90 State Street, Suite 700, Albany, NY 12207

Production by Marilyn P. Semerad
Marketing by Susan M. Petrie

**Library of Congress Cataloging-in-Publication Data**

Thinking through the death of God : a critical companion to Thomas J. J. Altizer / edited by
   Lissa McCullough & Brian Schroeder.
       p. cm. — (SUNY series in theology and continental thought)
   Includes bibliographical references and index.
   ISBN 0-7914-6219-6 (alk. paper) — ISBN 0-7914-6220-X (pbk. : alk. paper)
     1. Death of God theology.   2. Altizer, Thomas J. J.   I. McCullough, Lissa.   II.
Schroeder, Brian.   III. Series.

BT83.5.T48 2004
230'.092—dc22

                                                                    2003067306

                              10 9 8 7 6 5 4 3 2 1

# Contents

v

# Preface

*Forward to a Future Thinking*

BRIAN SCHROEDER

In the present age, marked by an unprecedented conservatism on multiple registers, it is increasingly rare to find any truly radical thinking occurring, especially in the area of theological reflection. And even if the phrase has grown cliché in certain circles, surely there is no more radical idea than the death of God. Heralded by Nietzsche and others after him as the "greatest event of the age," recognized and even celebrated periodically in late modern and postmodern thinking, the death of God has nonetheless remained largely unthought in its full signification. This death implies not only that the transcendental ground of truth, value, and meaning is called into question (the more radical forms of twentieth-century thought have indeed done this), but so too is the *future* of thinking itself, having now exposed itself to what is arguably the gravest threat of the age—nihilism. Yet, as Nietzsche reminds us, only in such exposure is a "consummate" or "ecstatic" nihilism finally revealed as a genuine possibility, a creative and resourceful nihilism that overcomes its previous "passive" and "active" forms and does not subsume and neutralize pure thinking under the shadow of impossibility, but rather dissipates that shade by transfiguring it into the high noon of *new* horizons.

It is surely ironic that any present thinking about God should assume the form of the impossibility of such thinking. Nowhere is this more manifest than in contemporary philosophical discourse, which has become the new voice of what remains of theology, even if it is largely unaware of this. Ironically still, much contemporary philosophy continues to be a reaction to dialectical thinking, the language of our most progressive theologies, and in particular to the philosophy of German idealism. Two centuries ago, Hegel could announce the death of God at the end of his *Phenomenology of Spirit* by declaring historical time the "Golgotha of Spirit." The transcendent deity, having emptied itself (*kenosis*) of its being as the purely abstract idea (*Idea*), is now actualized as historical spirit (*Geist*), and fully realized and known as such in and through the concept (*Begriff*). Given that, as Hegel famously notes in the *Phenomenology*, "the real is the actual and the actual is the real," whatever is must be, and indeed is able to be, articulated in language—in other words, *named*. Thus one finds in Hegel the last fully systematic philosophical attempt to generate a rational theology, and according to his interpretation, Christianity alone is able do this, hence it is the absolute religion.

If the traditional task of theology has been the naming of God, however, this naming has been reduced to a virtual silence in our day. Assuming the charge relinquished by theology, it is philosophy, for the most part, that now names this silence, doing so as the "death of God." Responding to Hegel, Nietzsche and Heidegger, foremost among other philosophical thinkers, disclose or name the "ground" of all God-thinking as groundless, thereby calling forth the absolute darkness left by the deity's demise as the horizon for future thinking. Borrowing the term from Kant's *Critique of Pure Reason*, Heidegger identifies such naming as ontotheology and further identifies the flight or abandonment of God as the withdrawal of being (*Sein*) from beings, from the horizon of the world. But in this retreat, being itself is made manifest, such that now it is possible not only to fully name the impossibility, that is, being as objective presence, but also to name the appropriating event, or "enowning" (*Ereignis*), of "be-ing" (*Seyn*), that is, being (*Sein*) no longer thought metaphysically. This is the move that Heidegger makes in his posthumously published and recently translated *Contributions to Philosophy: From Enowning*, undoubtedly his most theological venture, even if it advances his most theologically critical thinking, the genesis of which occurs as he is most under Nietzsche's influence, whose thought courses throughout the work, albeit largely unacknowledged. The actual historical enactment of being's withdrawal occurs, to use Heidegger's language in the *Contributions*, in the "going under" of the "ones to come," those who "constantly question" and through this questioning are oriented toward the future, belonging therein to the "last god."

The dark void or emptiness of nihilism is henceforth revealed as chaos itself, as both the impossibility of possibility and the possibility of impossibility. That is to say, the groundless ground of chaos, the actual body of the now ghostly God, is the standpoint of nihilism's refutation through the will's affirmation of its necessity, though conversely, it is also the moment wherein the negativity of the abyssal nothing threatens to swallow not only all existing meaning and value but the possibility of its being created anew. This dilemma is the challenge for humanity posed by the death of God, the meaning of which event must be thought through in order to overcome and transfigure the threatening paralysis of No-saying into a liberating Yes-saying to our actual historical future.

Now it is also ironic that the theological depths in which the above-mentioned philosophers are immersed, and out of which they formulate their respective philosophies, is, with few exceptions, all but absent from the philosophical thinking occurring today. This is truly a recent phenomenon, and one that testifies to the impossibility of naming God, and perhaps even of naming the death of God. Even so, the death of God, on the one hand, is now often assumed as a general starting point for other reflections, seemingly embraced by a whole generation of "continental" thinkers who largely interpret its meaning in a decidedly *non*theological manner as the simple thesis of God's nonexistence. Construed thus, the death of God loses all power as an absolute naming, and the correlated themes of the death of the subject and of Yes-saying to the earth are likewise rendered impotent. Indeed, this is arguably the crux of the so-called postmodern dilemma, namely, how to confront the problem of nihilism. Yet, on the other hand, this recent theological naiveté indicates the emergence or birth of a new consciousness, one perhaps untainted by the stigma of previous metaphysics, and so open to the future in a way never before possible. Here the imagination now holds full sway, enabling not only the revitalization of philosophy and theology but opening wholly new paths of thinking, conjoining these disciplines with literary traditions, where perhaps the most radical expressions of Western consciousness have emerged and flowered.

This conjoining is the great legacy bequeathed to thinking by Thomas J. J. Altizer, arguably the most visionary contemporary thinker of the death of God, whose thought the essays of this volume engage critically. This collective critical response, drawn from a number of leading voices in theology, philosophy, and literary studies, not only acknowledges the enormous debt that thinking owes to Altizer, but also, true to the spirit of his lifelong project, advances the task of thinking through the death of God by pressing beyond the framework of his radical theological vision. As these essays testify, just when theology has seemingly given up the proverbial ghost, when philosophy seems increasingly to embody the endless play of hermeneutical games, and literary studies are often construed as floundering in the sea of deconstruction, the advance of thinking continues, charting new seas, mapping future possibilities. Like Nietzsche, who declared his vision of the eternal recurrence "a prophecy," Altizer too is prophetic. And if it is the case that a prophet is commonly not recognized among his or her own, and is "untimely" in this sense, then surely this is true of Altizer.

Well over a century has passed since the proclamation of Nietzsche's "madman," and the shock of the death of God movement of the 1960s has long since worn off, virtually forgotten by the general populace and most academics. Yet all things, all events, have a beginning, whether timely or untimely. If the contemporary state of theology demands an awakening, even a "rude awakening" (a phrase associated with the Kyoto school of comparative religious philosophy, recognized by Altizer years ago as identifying the perilous condition of our present nihilism) from our current cultural slumber, induced by an uncritical conservatism, then the present work is truly timely. Yet it is also untimely in being both too late and too early. That radical theology has been all but completely marginalized in mainstream academic discourse (one need not even consider the churches at this point) only indicates that the level and range of critical reflection found in these pages ought to have been more sustained over the years. Thus is this work too late in its arrival. Still, if one holds to the principle of Eleatic metaphysics, made familiar in its medieval rendering as *ex nihilo nihil fit*, then any truly new parturition must emerge out of what has come before, oftentimes only after an extended gestation. Certainly the essays presented herein by such distinguished scholars as Edward Casey, Janet Gyatso, Ray Hart, David Jasper, D. G. Leahy, Alphonso Lingis, Carl Raschke, Walter Strauss, Mark C. Taylor, and Edith Wyschogrod are the fruit of many years of sustained engagement with the themes and questions raised by the death of God, including Altizer's pioneering theological interpretation of it. It may well be, though, however cliché the phrase "God is dead," that this event is *still* years away from being recognized as such. In this sense, this work perhaps arrives too soon.

Nietzsche wrote that it would take possibly a hundred years before his readers would understand him. Altizer is one of those few readers. Hopefully such a length of time need not pass before we are able to understand

Altizer's apocalyptic vision. This collection not only pays tribute to the theological originality with which Altizer interprets the prophetic pronouncement of the death of God but advances its promise as well by thinking it through more fully, thus embodying the impossible possibility of a joyous affirmative future *willing*, now needed more than ever given the dark times that confront us all.

# Acknowledgments

This volume was initially conceived, as destiny would have it, at the annual meeting of the American Academy of Religion in November 1997. We editors, who were only briefly acquainted with each other through a meeting with Tom Altizer the year before, found ourselves crossing paths. In the course of our discussion we mused that the time was ripe for a collaborative critique of Altizer's mature thinking, and from that moment we began to draft an outline for the present volume. We are grateful for the overwhelmingly positive response we received from the contributors to this work, not to mention their abiding spirit of patience and support. We are also indebted to the State University of New York Press staff members for their labor in bringing it forth; we owe particular thanks to Nancy Ellegate, senior acquisition editor at the Press, and Douglas Donkel for enthusiastically including this volume in his series Theology and Continental Thought. Most of all we wish to acknowledge our gratitude to Tom Altizer, who has enriched both our lives deeply these many years through his theological vision, critical responsiveness, and personal friendship. From the depths of our hearts we offer this work to you, Tom, by offering it to others.

# Historical Introduction

## Lissa McCullough

From the beginning, and throughout its course, Thomas J. J. Altizer's theological stance set him apart from the other figures associated with the so-called death of God movement, which achieved its peak from 1965 through 1967, then subsided in the late sixties and early seventies. In truth, it was not organically a movement at all, but was generated as such by the media treatment. William Hamilton and Paul van Buren were the fellow travelers most often cited, while mention was made here and there of Richard Rubenstein, Gabriel Vahanian, Harvey Cox, and Langdon Gilkey.[1] In the media coverage, which often failed to make finer distinctions among their disparate positions, a number of outlooks were corralled together that did not have much in common. Some were using the phrase as a cipher for the secularization of society (Cox, Vahanian), others were concerned to examine the vacuity and impossibility of God language (van Buren) or the impossibility of believing in God in the wake of the Holocaust (Rubenstein), while others wanted to develop Bonhoeffer's notion of a "religionless Christianity" focused on ethics and Jesus as the man for others, pulling the mind of the age away from the God question as moot metaphysics (Hamilton).

Only Altizer among them was intent to focus on God and nothing but God. His concern lay not primarily with human existential need or the condition of society, but with *what God has done in history*. Beginning with his earliest writings, Altizer's position was theocentric and metaphysical. Far from intending, along with the secularists, to resolve all divine values into a human ground, Altizer sought as a pure theologian to resolve all human values into a divine ground. In a sense, this gets to the heart of Altizer's project: unthinking the "God" of Christian history as a way of releasing Godhead qua actual reality from the "dead body of God" remaining to a collapsed Christendom. And this "releasement" of Godhead qua actual reality from Christendom's God would constitute, as Altizer understands it, a renewal of Christianity in its original form.

For as Altizer analyzes the early history of Christianity, the Christian church radically reversed the prophetic ground of original Christianity, giving it a wholly new identity, one radically discontinuous with its earliest manifestation. Christianity was born as an apocalyptic movement grounded in the prophetic and apocalyptic traditions of ancient Judaism; its leading figure envisioned an imminent transformation of the world by God, a transformation that would draw forth the full power of Satan in the process of realizing the Kingdom of God. The early church rapidly reversed this original manifestation of Christianity, essentially converting a radical prophetic faith into a neopagan mystery religion, a priestly religion focused on otherworldly salvation and sacerdotal participation, rather than on this-worldly apocalyptic transformation. In its most primitive form, original Christianity conceived salvation in an entirely different sense than did the mystery religion generated by the church, for this is a salvation event wholly committed to enacting the divine kingdom *here*, transforming this actual world, rather than one anticipating the transport of the "soul" into a "spiritual body" in a heavenly realm. For prophetic faith, salvation or salvific wholeness is achieved partly by present participation, which is actual, and partly by pure faith, which is eschatological and future-oriented. But both elements of faith—present participation and future expectation—are forward movements toward the divine transformation of history and world. Rather than transporting elements of earthly existence (the "soul") toward the divine (in "heaven"), this is a vision of the divine breaking in and enacting itself on earth, effecting an apocalyptic transformation of the earthly realm itself into a kingdom of God.

As European Christendom has collapsed in the modern period, so has the transcendent and otherworldly God of that collapsed Christendom 'died'—that is, become no longer real as a center of value and generative source of life and light. Precisely by virtue of this collapse, Altizer posits, the post-Christian reality of God, qua *actual* and *present* reality, is being released from the "heaven" generated by the Christian mystery religion to become all in all in the world through an eschatological process of *kenosis*.

The death of God is "good news" because God is no longer regarded from the point of view of a sacerdotal faith as the transcendent Other, alienated from the world, an object of religious worship, a Father and Judge infinitely distant from the world, but through the kenotic realization of death is experienced now by a prophetic faith as increasingly incarnate in our very midst as the "flesh," or active embodiment, or actual eventfulness of the world. Altizer is not a simple atheist, then, but a post-theist—one for whom the metaphysical reality of God (theism) is dialectically and historically indispensable—for it is truly *God* who is overcome and transfigured by death, which is to say, by absolute self-sacrifice.

In his historic debate with Rev. Dr. John Warwick Montgomery in Rockefeller Chapel at the University of Chicago on the evening of February 24, 1967, speaking ex tempore to an audience of thousands (the chapel was so crowded to overflowing that loudspeakers were arranged for the throngs on the lawn), Altizer affirmed:

> 'God is dead' are words recording a confession of faith. Let me be clear in emphasizing that as far as our intention is concerned, we intend to be speaking in faith. We do not intend to be speaking as unbelievers . . . I think that, if any attention at all is given to these words, it will be seen that they do not represent ordinary atheism. The ordinary atheist, of course, does not believe in God, does not believe that there is now or ever has been a God. But we are attempting to say that God Himself is God, and yet has died as God in Jesus Christ in order to embody himself redemptively in the world. In saying that God is dead we are attempting to say that the transcendent Ground, the ultimate final Ground of the world, life, and existence has died . . . to make possible final reconciliation of Himself with the world.[2]

To his credit, in confronting Altizer on this occasion, Montgomery, who was then professor of church history and history of Christian thought at Trinity Evangelical Divinity School, recognized more clearly than did the general public of the period that he was debating not a "secularist" or "atheist," but a passionately convinced *heretic*—someone laying claim to the title of "Christian" and advocating publicly a highly unorthodox reconception of the Christian faith. Montgomery therefore fought Altizer's heterodoxy with all the power of orthodoxy he could muster, and perceptions of who "won" the debate depended entirely on which side you were on.

While Montgomery took Altizer seriously as an enemy of the faith, at least a handful of others were taking him seriously as a major religious thinker of our time. In 1970, as the death of God media blitz ebbed into yesterday's news, a book emerged entitled *The Theology of Altizer: Critique and Response*, edited by the prominent process theologian John B. Cobb Jr. of the School of Theology at Claremont, which acknowledged the abiding importance and influence of Altizer as a systematic theologian. The volume dubbed Altizer "the most original and creative American theologian of this period," whose writings offer "a coherent vision of great power." Of all American theological writing of the period, it went on to assert, "it is Altizer's that embodies the most vigorous and passionate faith," making him the "boldest evangelical theologian of our time." The volume also acknowledged Altizer as the "most influential" theologian of the day, although unfortunately that influence was almost solely a response to Altizer's negations, not to his affirmations, for his influence encouraged the emergence of "an ethical Christian humanism" that is far removed from his own theological project.[3] This well-executed volume sought to address critically the significance of Altizer's affirmations, and as such it remains to this day an excellent and valuable resource for understanding the early phase of Altizer's career.

Another who took Altizer's affirmations seriously was Mircea Eliade, the distinguished historian of religions at the University of Chicago. In 1967, at the height of the media furor, the subject surfaced in Eliade's journal. Eliade comments on the death of God theme as it appears in Heidegger's work: "Have I noted these lines from Heidegger's *Holzwege* [Frankfurt: Klostermann, 1950, p. 186] that Tom Altizer should meditate on? In any case I'm recopying them here: 'Hier stirbt das Absolute. Gott ist tot. Das sagt andere, nur nicht: es gibt keinen Gott.' (This is where the Absolute meets death. God is dead. And this means everything except 'There is no God.')"[4] As noted by Eliade, Heidegger's reflection is crucial: "God is dead. And this means everything except [*andere, nur nicht*] 'there is no God.' If Heidegger is right in this claim, then the death of God does not mean the end of theological inquiry, but rather a new beginning in earnest, for there is still "everything" to be comprehended as a consequence of this absolute death. What is this "everything" (*andere*), positively analyzed? For Altizer this question was to become his vocation, and he went on to write a dozen theological books making his case for an answer: "God is dead" acknowledges a historical transformation of consciousness marking the end of Christendom and Christendom's God, not the end of Godhead apprehended qua ultimate reality. The theologian's task is to speak of the ultimate reality now dawning in and through the death of God.

Eliade explores the subject more closely in a conversation with his colleague Claude-Henri Rocquet. In their exchange, Rocquet infers that atheism, just as much as theism, constitutes a part of the history of religions, and Eliade replies: "The theology of 'the death of God' is extremely important, because it is the sole religious creation of the modern Western world. What it presents us with is the final step in the process of desacralization. For the historian of religions its interest is considerable, since this ultimate phase shows the 'sacred' reaching a perfect state of camouflage or, more accurately, becoming wholly identified with the 'profane.'"[5] Is the death of God theology truly the *sole* religious creation of the modern Western world? Is it the dark and restless heart of modern religious creativity? What does it mean to take what Eliade called "the final step in the process of desacralization"? Eliade goes on to point out that theologians of the death of God—and here he has Altizer primarily in mind—still hope, thanks to a dialectical *coincidentia oppositorum*, that this new awareness of the radically profane nature of the world and human existence can become the foundation for a new mode of religious experience; that the death of "religion" is not the death of faith, but its purification and revitalization. Some years later Altizer, responding to Eliade's work, construes this point explicitly: "What could be a greater camouflage for the incarnation than the death of God? Remembering that for Eliade the sacred hides itself in showing itself, we can only conclude that in the supreme theophany God is totally hidden, and totally hidden precisely in that theophany itself."[6]

It is significant that Altizer's own academic training was in the history of religions at the University of Chicago, where he later befriended Eliade, for his lifelong development as a theologian has shown the distinct impact of this formation. His outlook on Christianity—and on the death of God as a culminating event in the history of that religion—has always been fundamentally informed by a comparative perspective on religions, Eastern and Western; see *Oriental Mysticism and Biblical Eschatology* (1961) and *Mircea Eliade and the Dialectic of the Sacred* (1963). This comparative perspective emboldened him to explore Christianity's enormous cultural power and impact outside the bounds of traditional Christian institutions and teachings, which is to say, in disregard of the purview of the church. Taking a long and broad history-of-religions view of Christianity, Altizer grasped that no ecclesiastical theology would ever be capable of recognizing the death of God as an event intrinsic to Christian history, whereas a radical theology taking its stand in the secular world—not constrained by the conservative and sectarian God traditions of the church—would be able to appropriate the death of God so widely attested in modern culture after 1789 (by Blake, Hegel, Nietzsche, Dostoevsky, Heidegger, Sartre, Joyce, Beckett, etc.) as the embodiment of a revolutionary new theological meaning and motive in Christian history, a meaning inescapably manifest in the most creative cultural developments of late modernity. It was his study of William Blake's prophetic vision, *The New Apocalypse: The Radical Christian Vision of William Blake* (1967), that set Altizer decisively on this path. Judging by the gauge of cultural creativity, the "dead God" demonstrated as much power to inspire creative vision as "God alive," for negative experience of the sacred is nonetheless real and often overwhelming experience.

Assimilation of a highly creative secular theology was to become the heart of Altizer's systematic project. In the crisis of modern theology brought on by the critical dissolution of "God," Altizer discerned an either/or emerging, a decisive fork in the road that demanded radical decision: Either theology would make a forward movement into uncharted regions of heterodoxy, and in so doing embrace *becoming* as an act of God that transforms the Godhead itself, or theology would entrench itself in a conservative orthodox reaction, clinging to the God traditions of absolute transcendence, immutability, and impassibility, presumed secure on the basis of the two millennia (Kierkegaard's "1800 years"), thus preserving the transcendent God of Christendom. This fork in the road was articulated by Altizer as "A Wager" in the final chapter of *The Gospel of Christian Atheism* (1966), which he hoped would communicate this either/or challenge to a popular audience.

What even now distinguishes Altizer's voice among late modern theologians is his appropriation of the death of God theme in modern culture to effect a radical renewal of systematic theology, producing a fully systematic theology entirely liberated from allegiance to God traditions of the church, and above all the church's essentially conservative claims to special authority in the knowledge of God. With the decisive fall of Christendom (occurring roughly from the early sixteenth century through the French Revolution, when the church was violently ejected from the political establishment), the question of who has the "authority" to speak of God becomes entirely open. Altizer's theological stance presses the Protestant Reformation to its radical conclusion and emancipates theology from the domain and authority of the church once and for all. Technically, this is how Altizer defines the term "radical theology"; it is a theology whose "authority" stems from visionary witness alone, and not at all from validation by institutional authority or the established mandate of tradition. Radical theology is a totally free witness in living apprehension of the sacred, self-authorizing; it is a witness that unthinks every established theological ground in order to rethink the fundamental ground of theology anew.[7] Not only does it unthink every established ground, but by its radical nature it resists being established as a ground. It speaks its affirmations with an intrinsic authority, and by its essence as free witness, this "authority" cannot be captured in transferable forms or sealed in dogmatic propositions. The apocalyptic Jesus provides a prime model of this radical witness, for when the spirit speaks in him it speaks with power, and its intrinsic "authority" can be heard (Mark 1:22, 27), but efforts to establish that authority transform it into something alien to its original form.

Altizer has always been serious about the implications of *death* in the phrase "the death of God," and what this death does to transfigure the gospel or "good news" as a Word of life and light. His own criteria for recognizing the kenotic Word focus on the crucifixion to the virtual exclusion of resurrection. To know the death of God is to know crucifixion and the descent into hell. It is to encounter the consuming nothingness that is so acutely manifest in the full reality of our world—in its darkness and evil, its ungodly holocausts, its all too brutal and unaccountable forms of sacrifice. If theology does not have the power to illuminate and redeem *this* world's evil, Altizer believes, it is not genuine theology but a form of escapism or wishful illusion, an evasion of reality.

This is above all so in the shadow of the Holocaust, where theology has no shelter from darkness. Altizer's death of God theology has always been implicitly a Holocaust theology in its open-eyed witness to the inescapable reality of evil and horror in our world and the relationship of this evil to an ultimate divine responsibility. In a thirty-year retrospective article of 1996, Altizer reflects on the influence of human mass extermination on the genesis of the death of God theology: "History now first appears to the modern theologian as an arena of darkness and horror, and of ultimate and final horror and darkness. Although this may not be due to the Holocaust alone, it is the Holocaust alone that openly embodies such horror, and we may presume that the Holocaust was a generating cause of the death of God theologies, as it certainly was for this theologian."[8]

Whereas earlier Christian theology could affirm a providential God, a God who acts providentially and even redemptively in history, the Holocaust blows the doctrine of providence out of the water. After the Holocaust, it is no longer possible to affirm providence, Altizer maintains, unless one affirms that God wills or effects ultimate evil; that is, unless evil itself is providential. "How can one accept the reality of the Holocaust and not accept the reality of an ultimate evil? And how can the Christian accept the reality of an ultimate evil and wholly divorce it from reality or God? . . . If the Christian knows that God is the ultimate origin of every event, then God is the ultimate origin of the Holocaust, even if we follow Augustine and orthodox Western theology and speak of God's 'permission of evil.'"[9] The omnipotence and omniscience of God do not permit us to imagine that God is not ultimately responsible for the Holocaust, even if human evil is accepted as the proximate cause. For if the traditional attributes of omnipotence and omniscience are granted, then God knew it would happen and "permitted" it, and the Holocaust is of a piece with God's providence. "Certainly the God of Christendom died in the Holocaust," Altizer concludes, "or became theologically unthinkable and unimaginable," and this means that "the God of every church dogmatics is now unthinkable."[10] So, as Altizer articulates it, the unprecedented theological challenge of our time becomes: Is a theology possible today that is not at bottom an erasure of the Holocaust?[11]

Opposing the established religion of his day, Luther advocated a "theology of the cross" in opposition to any and every "theology of glory"; for similar reasons, Altizer has advocated in our age what we might call a "theology of darkness" in opposition to every "theology of light." Virtually all Christian theologies, by Altizer's rigorous standard, have to some degree or other given in to the temptation of light; that is, they deny the full reality of evil and embrace a "salvation" or "heaven" that is essentially an escape from suffering and darkness into a transcendent "happy" realm. Whereas the death on the cross, for Altizer, is the unique formula for taking the sacrifice of God with absolute and final seriousness. All that our natural being says "no" to is symbolized in the cross as that which we must pass into with Christ in the flesh, for this enacts the divine "yes" to incarnation, and this "yes" itself is crucifying.

This journey into flesh is what Altizer means by the "descent into hell" in his book by that title, *The Descent into Hell* (1970); it is a divine movement into a real earthly body, which in this theology of darkness displaces the offensive "ascent into heaven" of the quasi-Gnostic "spiritual body." This descent implies a total compassionate solidarity with the suffering body of the victim, who often cannot actually experience a light in the darkness but can believe in faith that it exists in the mercy of God (Job 19:25–26) or Christ (Mark 15:34) and can therein embody the light by faith alone. This theology refuses to abandon the suffering body in a quest for "heaven" and "light" but stands by the body in crucifixion, abiding with the crucified flesh as a flesh willed by God, a flesh actually loved by God into a condition of crucifixion.

This correlation of incarnation and crucifixion brings us to the core of Altizer's mature understanding of God as an apocalyptic dichotomy: God as at one and the same time self-incarnating and self-annihilating. His fully apocalyptic understanding of God comes to birth in a highly compressed form in *The Self-Embodiment of God* of 1977, published when Altizer was fifty years old. Only with this work does Altizer break through to the pure dialectical ground of his theological vision and press it into a tight, terse, powerful, self-contained, seemingly airless capsule of a book—a book that acts as a primal seed for his later thinking, germinating many times over to express new dimensions of the same fundamental idea; each of his works thereafter systematically expands one aspect or another of the synthesis compressed in this book. By analogy, this was Altizer's *Phenomenology of Spirit,* and indeed the spirit giving it birth was now far more Hegelian than Blakean. It remains the purest expression of Altizer's vision, and truly to *read* this book is to read Altizer straight up, but for that very reason it is perhaps the least accessible of his works. Here a biblically grounded apocalyptic voice enacts the movement of spirit into flesh as a kenotic self-emptying of the primordial God into the full actuality of the body of the world; in so doing, it enacts genesis, exodus, judgment, incarnation, and apocalypse as an integral series of self-embodying transfigurations of the Godhead itself. The whole traces out a revelation history.

Just as a jazz musician may play for years before finding his signature "voice," a voice that is purely his own because it speaks directly, one might say "bodily," out of the inspirational source of originality and authenticity, so Altizer finds his theological voice in *The Self-Embodiment of God,* and suddenly in retrospect all his earlier books, however creative and thoughtful they may be, sound juvenile. Whereas all his published writings from 1958 forward set out to prosecute the same fundamental theological project with a truly remarkable consistency and tenacity, the earlier books are written in a talky, external, academic tone that simply disappears after 1977. One hears in the early Altizer certain phrasings and cadences of the voice to come, but only in midcareer does the voice become whole and pure, no longer speaking *about* what it means to say, as if from outside, but now *enacting* what it means to say as it says it, unfolding a current event.

In this newfound oracular voice, the medium is the message, for voice is the medium of apocalypse. Now speech is event, uniting interiority and exteriority. And precisely as event, speech is shattering: an apocalyptic breaking in upon silence. The act of creation is this breaking in upon the silence of God. God before creation cannot be heard, for the primordial God constitutes a silence so pure, so total and quiescent that it has no voice. Creation shatters the primordial silence, annihilating it as silence so that for the first time it can be heard. Thus the "speech" of God in genesis is the genesis of a self-revealing God, a God revealing Godhead by embodying Godhead in actual event. The body of the world is "spoken" by God as the only way possible for the original silence of God to be heard, for "it is silence itself that passes into speech" (*The Self-Embodiment of God* 5). To be heard, the primordial reality of God must be sacrificed, must be shattered by the "speech" of creation. So it is that in every moment of actuality God is both embodied (posited in incarnation) and annihilated (negated in crucifixion) simultaneously; God *is* this dichotomy. God *is* this inbreaking occurrence, this apocalyptic shattering of quiescence, this ongoing transformative eventfulness of the world, in which Godhead continually negates Godhead in order to enact and embody Godhead.

Envisioning this negativity in the Godhead means that the absolute positivity of Godhead, or the plenitude of Being, is self-consumed in the act of creation; in turn, this self-consuming negativity releases God to every freedom of becoming. God is not constrained to an original or primordial form but is freed to change revelatory forms or epiphanies, and here again it seems likely that Altizer's history of religions background influences his theological reading of Christian revelation history. Why should not ultimate reality reveal itself historically and progressively by means of changing epiphanic forms, forms distantly analogous to the *avataras* of the Hindu gods—but radically more comprehensive and absolute because they are identified with the ground of reality or actuality per se?

Altizer's later works meditate on this dialectical ground of actuality— that is, the apocalyptic ground of eventfulness or actuality as the revelatory manifestation of the will of God—both historically and constructively. *Total Presence* (1980) examines the apocalyptic speech of Jesus in the parables of the New Testament as an enactment of the Kingdom of God. *History as Apocalypse* (1985) explores the Christian epic tradition, from its historical and biblical origins through its ending in *Finnegans Wake,* as an apocalyptic revelation history. *Genesis and Apocalypse* (1990) articulates Altizer's most comprehensive systematic theology (making it *my* personal favorite), while *The Genesis of God* (1993) focuses more intently on the historical-dialectical logic of the relationship between apocalypse and genesis, a logic according to which only the genesis of God can make possible the death of God. *Godhead and the Nothing* (2003) ventures further into the eye of genesis as the sacrificial origin and primordial ground of creation. Finally, "Altizer on Altizer" should be mentioned here as a valuable reflection by the author in retrospect upon his own intentions in writing each of his major books up through *The Contemporary Jesus* (1997).[12]

Looking back on his own theological voyage as reflected in these writings, Altizer encapsulates his overall project thus:

> The intention throughout this voyage is to seek a truly radical and yet nevertheless fully Christian theology, a theology with a genuinely Biblical ground but one nonetheless fully open to our world, a world here understood as embodying what Blake envisioned as the "Self-Annihilation of God." Moreover, and perhaps most deeply, there is the intention of renewing an original apocalyptic Christianity, and doing so with the recognition that Christian theology itself has truly reversed that origin, and only the most radical transformation of our theology can recover it.[13]

For all his controversial radicalism and heterodoxy, Altizer is a systematic and biblical theologian of an utterly classic type: one committed to systematically rethinking the core visionary truths of the Christian faith—creation, fall, incarnation, crucifixion, resurrection—as these are historically transformed and radically reinterpreted from the point of view of late modern consciousness in a thoroughly "revolutionized" and "holocausted" world, an apocalyptic world of unprecedented beginnings and endings. The Christian vision is revealed as bearing a wholly new meaning that is actively generated by the death of Christendom's God and the savage extermination—forevermore—of human innocence. In our time, as we move out of the twentieth century toward who knows what kind of unprecedented global world order or world chaos, we have a pervasive new knowledge of Death and an unshirkable new acquaintance with the Nothing, hence our theology of the future, if there is to be one, and if it is to be genuine, must contend with a dark exterior history and a dark interior history in terms that speak the whole truth of our devastation, including the new light that shines on that devastation.

This is what makes Altizer's "theology of darkness" one of the few live options, in my own view, for a reflective contemporary person of faith. It is a theology that fully engages the world we actually inhabit, the world to and for which we are called 'bodily' to be responsible. In repudiating false light, in boldly foreswearing every extrinsic or established "ground" validating theology—objective, rational, historical, institutional, scientific, scriptural, or otherwise—and in theologizing passionately and creatively on the basis of a groundless but deeply erudite and reflective Christian vision, Altizer has ushered theology out of the age of Newton and into the age of Einstein and beyond. Here theology realizes a new freedom from the "law" or *nomos* of extrinsic authority and a new liberty to respond spontaneously to intrinsic authority. If incarnation is the actualization of energy, and energy is eternal delight, it is at least possible we have a new and unfamiliar epiphany of Godhead emerging in our midst.

## NOTES

1. No history of the death of God controversy has yet been published that would put the movement in critical perspective. The existing resources are relics from the period, many of which contain bibliograhies: Charles N. Bent, S.J., *The Death of God Movement* (New York: Paulist Press, 1967); André Gounelle, *Foi vivante et mort de Dieu* (Tournon: Cahiers de Réveil, 1969); Lonnie D. Kliever and John H. Hayes, *Radical Christianity* (Anderson, SC: Droke House, 1968); William Robert Miller, *The New Christianity* (New York: Delacourte, 1967); Thomas W. Ogletree, *The Death of God Controversy* (Nashville: Abingdon, 1966); *The Death of God Debate*, ed. Jackson Lee Ice and John J. Carey (Philadelphia: Westminster, 1967); *Radical Theology: Phase Two*, ed. C. W. Christian and Glenn R. Wittig (Philadelphia: Lippincott, 1967); *The Meaning of the Death of God*, ed. Bernard Murchland (New York: Random House, 1967); *The Death of God Debate*, ed. Gabriel Vahanian (New York: Bobbs-Merrill, 1967); see also, Deborah Scerbicke, "A History of the 'Death of God' Theology in America, 1955–1969" (doctoral dissertation, Bowling Green State University, Department of History, 1994).

2. *The Altizer-Montgomery Dialogue: A Chapter in the God Is Dead Controversy* (Chicago: Inter-Varsity Press, 1967), 7–8. For those seeking an accessible introduction to Altizer's theology as a radical expression of faith, this spontaneous statement made in Rockefeller Chapel is as helpful as any. Audiotapes and transcripts of the dialogue are available from the Canadian Institute for Law, Theology, and Public Policy, ciltpp@cs.com (which, for the record, supports Montgomery's stance against Altizer's). I wish to thank Will Moore, president of CILTPP, for generously donating copies for my use.

3. *The Theology of Altizer: Critique and Response*, ed. John B. Cobb Jr. (Philadelphia: Westminster, 1970); quotations are from the introduction by John B. Cobb and Nicholas Gier, 13–16.

4. Mircea Eliade, *Journal II: 1957–1969*, trans. Fred H. Johnson Jr. (Chicago: University of Chicago Press, 1989), entry of April 4, 1967, 297–98.

5. Mircea Eliade, *Ordeal by Labyrinth: Conversations with Claude-Henri Rocquet*, trans. Derek Coltman (Chicago: University of Chicago Press, 1982), 151.

6. Thomas J. J. Altizer, "Mircea Eliade and the Death of God," *Cross Currents* 29, no. 3 (Fall 1979): 267.

7. Thomas J. J. Altizer, "Doing Radical Theology," unpublished manuscript, 1.

8. Thomas J. J. Altizer, "The Holocaust and the Theology of the Death of God," in *The Death of God Movement and the Holocaust*, ed. Stephen R. Haynes and John K. Roth (Westport, CT: Greenwood, 1999), 19. The editors of this volume are mistaken in asserting (p. xiv) that the *Time* cover story, "Toward a Hidden God," in the Easter issue of April 8, 1966, which is reprinted in their volume, was the first major stir of the controversy; rather, the matter surfaced five and a half months earlier in an article in the *New York Times* on October 17, 1965, and it was the October 22, 1965 issue of *Time* magazine, containing the article "Christian Atheism: The 'God Is Dead' Movement," that set off the flurry.

9. Ibid., 21.

10. Ibid., 20.

11. Ibid., 22.

12. Thomas J. J. Altizer, "Altizer on Altizer," *Literature and Theology* 15, no. 2 (June 2001): 187–94.

13. Ibid., 187.

# Abbreviations

# CHAPTER 1

# Rending the Veil of the Temple

*The Death of God as* Sacrificium Representationis

CARL A. RASCHKE

> If there is one clear portal to the twentieth century, it is a passage through the death of God, the collapse of any meaning or reality lying beyond the newly discovered radical immanence of modern man, an immanence dissolving even the memory or the shadow of transcendence.
>
> —Altizer, *The Gospel of Christian Atheism*

> The madman jumped into their midst and pierced them with his eyes. "Whither is God?" he cried; "I will tell you. *We have killed him*—you and I. All of us are his murderers."
>
> —Friedrich Nietzsche, *The Gay Science*

Thomas J. J. Altizer has been called the "prophet of postmodern theology." As the gray eminence and source of intellectual luminescence for various postmodern theologians, particularly Mark C. Taylor, Altizer stands at the threshold between modern religious thinking and the kind of writing that has surpassed it. The debate in contemporary

circles over what constitutes "modernist" and "postmodernist" styles of religious reflection has not been adequately resolved. One of the reasons may
be that discussants have rarely had a genealogy, or a historical reference
frame, for settling much of the argument. The postmodernist turn has its
origins in death of God theology. It is "the death of God put into writing."
As the prime force in the death of God movement, Altizer gave impetus to
this set of trends. Over a generation later it is perhaps time to decipher
more of what has been meant by the "death of God" from the theological
standpoint. The death of God, as Altizer himself has insisted, signifies the
culmination of the apocalyptic vision of the West. Apocalypticism is the
eschatology of the modern, insofar as it is imaginative apprehension of
"total presence," the parousia of what has not yet been realized in the
thought of Calvary.

What do we mean by such a parousia? The death of God, according
to Altizer, is something far more momentous than the fatality of the
West's premier theologoumenon. For Nietzsche, who first proclaimed
*mors Dei*, it is a moment of deicide, the most capital of all capital crimes.
In contrast to the two-millennium-old canard, it is not a *gens*, a people,
or as the anti-Semitic vitriol runs, the "Jews," who have killed God in
Nietzsche's picture of things. Deicide is an act of "mass slaughter." So
long as we heed the proviso that it is the masses who have perpetrated
the slaughter, the "we" does not seem at all problematic; we have, as the
Christian confessional goes, all in some manner of speaking cried, "Cru-
cify him." One can imagine the historical episode, the curious mise-en-
scène, when the even stranger prophecy of the dying and rising "Son of
man" becomes instantiated in the passion narrative. Stranger still remains
Pilate's quandary concerning the justice of exchanging Jesus for Barrabas.
The regulative metonymy in what René Girard calls the "surrogate victim" of the blood sacrifice is at a stroke dissolved. The crucified Messiah
no longer "signifies" by the thaumaturgy of symbolic exchange those
who are destined to be redeemed from the violence of that historical site
and figuration. The savage act of torture and execution can no longer re-
distribute the elements of cultural economy that invariably align the
"sacred" with death, the "sacrificial" or "sacred-making" with crime. Pilate's protestation of the man's innocence bespeaks this terrible realization. Ecce homo, "behold the man." It is a homicide that conceals the
apophatic expanse of deity!

The founding event of "Christian theology" resides in this very
enigma. Catholic tradition has called it the "mystery of the Incarnation."

But the mystery reaches far deeper than the logical paradox that befuddled the early church councils. How does the death of a man, the Son of man, manifest the eternal nature of God? The first-generation Christian community resolved the issue by the testament of the Risen One. God died, but he rose again. Yet it was God's death that fascinated the Conciliar movement and compelled resistance to such heresies as Docetism, Patripassionism, Montanism, and even Arianism. The affirmation that God had died, and not merely taken on the "appearance" of mortality, penetrated to the marrow of both pagan and Hebraic thinking. And it served as the setting for a convulsion in Western thought that would be felt as late as the dialectical philosophies of the nineteenth century—the transformation of the classical theory of representation into the idea of "sacred history," of ontology into narratology, of metaphysics into soteriology, of the doctrine of essence into the romance of existence. Nietzsche's "murderers of God" are all of us, precisely because by embracing dialectical thought we have acceded to the abolition of the boundary between the two signs of thinking itself: presentation and representation, immediacy and mediacy, intimation and articulation, *ousia* (in the Heideggerian sense of that which simultaneously shows and hides itself) and parousia, temporality, and eschatology.

Apocalypticism is impossible within the limits of a metaphysical ideology. The signifying dyad of metaphysics, which enables the novelty of dialectics, is that of permanence and change, stasis and kinesis, time and eternity. The linguistic sign is schizoid, as is the case with Derrida's grammatology; it emerges out of the incision of the text. The sign of the "eschaton," however, is plenipotentiary; it gathers and fuses all forms of signifying praxis into itself; it draws them all in itself at the same time it shatters them and breaks them down into what they "are" before the judgment throne of deity. Apocalypticism means the effacement of all double sentences, the unmasking of every duplicitous system of representation. It is "allness" and "nothingness" in the same instant.

It is to Altizer's credit to have used dialectics to turn eschatology on its very cranium. The apocalyptic reversal of eschatology for modern thought is far more significant than the Marxist upending of reason, of bringing "heaven down to earth." Hegel's "Golgotha of Absolute Spirit," an eventuality that can only be described as a genuine philosophical apocalypse, the great speculative moment of silence in heaven, is the precondition for the movement from divine transcendence to radical immanence, to the event of "total presence" that is at the same time

God's self-presence as complete divine self-reference, secular theology that has become secular eschatology, the eschaton that is once and for all saeculum. As Altizer has written, "Despite the Nicene formula, the Word cannot be fully God and fully man, if, on the one hand, it continues to exist in an eternal form and, on the other, it is unable to move into the present and the full reality of history" (*GCA* 41).

In this peculiar volte-face, this transposition of millennial revelation, in this strangest of "scenes" where mythic construct of "the end of time" signifies time itself as end, the dialectical drama of history, which Hegel envisioned as culminating in the abolition of limited consciousness, can no longer come to fruition. The death of God intimates something far more epochal than any triumphal "humanism," as theologians a generation ago suggested.[1] The orthodox formula for "incarnation"—that curious, doxological compromise of the church fathers between the Hebraic reverence for the unspeakably "beyond" and the pagan valorization of the senses—is also upended in the Altizerian world of metadoctrine, transforming itself into a rhapsody of pure immanence, a Dionysian *sparagmos* of theological limbs and entrails where hitherto there had been some kind of coherence in the ecclesiological idea of the corpus Christi.

We must begin to understand the death of God, as perhaps even Altizer himself has not understood it, as the disclosure of the end times, as a time of dismemberment and sacrifice. So much of the so-called death of God theology derives from the glory, as well as the bathos, of Hegel's phenomenology. The Hegelian stamp is evident as well in Altizer, not to mention the influence of Eliade and Nietzsche's notion of "eternal recurrence." But the thought of Altizer carries us beyond the now obsolete "modernist" controversy between theism and pantheism into the more complex, and fateful, biblical problem of Jesus' death as divine sacrifice. The work of Girard, of course, has alerted us to the intimate correlation between the semiotics of the sacred and ritual sacrifice. What Altizer seems to suggest, perhaps without a recognition of the dramatic implications of his own thought, is that the Nietzschean metaphor of the "murder of God" points to the profound analogy of the death of God as sacrificial slaying. What could such a metaphor mean in terms of the secular theology Altizer's work has spawned?

The relationship between Christology and the cult of sacrifice is evident in the Letter to the Hebrews—a segment of Scripture that is usually ignored, or overlooked, by modern theological authors. Hebrews is a strange document; it is attributed to Paul but most likely composed by the Levite Barnabas. It is a treatise on soteriology that deconstructs by a miscellany of metonymical transpositions the rhetoric of the already defunct sacrificial system of the Jewish temple priesthood. More than any other "work" in the New Testament, Hebrews follows through with the theo-logic of "God's death," but it does so in a way that is bereft of the cant of theological modernism.

The Letter to the Hebrews begins with the assertion that God's "speech" in these "last days" is no longer direct, but "by his Son." The Son is the "radiance of God's glory and the exact representation of his being (*character tes hypostaseos*), sustaining all things by his powerful word" (Heb. 1:1–3). On the face of it, there is nothing remarkable about this statement insofar as it prefigures the kind of orthodoxy that for two millennia would be the ideological staple of Western Christendom. But the subsequent unfolding of its soteriological implications in Hebrews is indeed remarkable. Although Hebrews affirms the Pauline as well as Johannine proposition that Jesus through his death "shared in [our humanity]" (Heb. 2:14), he transports it to a more radical site of interpretation; the "humanity of Jesus" is revealed in his concurrent role as hierophant, or sacrificial priest, and sacrificial victim. The Son that is the hypostasis, the full but particularized signification of God's Being, sacrifices himself in order to leap the chasm between Being and representation itself.

The theological framework for this move is found in the ninth chapter of Hebrews. The author of Hebrews employs the symbology of the Hebrew tent of meeting. The presence of God dwells in the inner sanctum, the Most Holy Place, the location of the ark of the covenant. The presence is mediated only dimly through animal sacrifice. "But now Christ has come, high priest of good things already in being. The tent of his priesthood is a greater and more perfect one, not made by men's hands . . . the blood of his sacrifice is his own blood, not the blood of goats and calves; and thus he has entered the sanctuary once and for all and secured an eternal deliverance" (Heb. 9:11–12). Christ, the writer of Hebrews argues, is a "spiritual and eternal [*pneumatos aioniou*] sacrifice."

Christ's self-sacrifice elsewhere in the New Testament characterized as God's self-emptying, or *kenosis*, is something far more profound than what is suggested in the Chalcedonian formula of God becoming "man." It points to what in Hegelian terms is the abrogation, the *Aufhebung*, of God's eternal self-diremption, the negation of the divine self-negation, which in turn fulfills the concept of the Son as hypostasis. The metaphysical conundrum of co-eternality of Father and Son now becomes explicable in terms of what the author of Hebrews calls "a new and loving way opened for us through the curtain [of the Holy of Holies] that is his body" (Heb. 10:20). The evangelical shibboleth of "blood redemption" entails an astounding form of theological semiotics—namely, that the unity of divine essence and simulacrum, of presence and re-presentation, is not achieved by any kind of transcendent synthesis of the religious imagination. Rather, it manifests itself in the movement when God's own "blood" is shed, when the sacrifice from below to above is transferred into the literal "dying of the Lamb" on the cross of Calvary. Incarnation only makes sense at the site of pure divine carnality, the irruption of flesh and blood. Any "death of God theology" must take into account the butchery and grandeur of the sacrificial moment, the resolution of holy as profane, the "carnivalesque" character of Christian experience in its sheer primality.

The connection between Dionysian symbolism and christological speculation, therefore, is not accidental. Hegel's phenomenology of "Spirit" mirrors a more primitive phenomenology of religion that is pretheological, pre-Chalcedonian, prespeculative. Again, it can be found in Hebrews. "This is the blood of the covenant, which God has commanded you to keep" (Heb. 9: 20). If the death of God is grounded in such a blood covenant, the suggestion is staggering. Anthropological theories of blood sacrifice rest on the premise that the "life" of the victim is in the blood and that the spilling of blood conjoins the sacrifice with the ontological source from which all emanates. Ancient theology, of course, was confounded by the paradoxical quality of this relationship. The gradual elimination of the practice of human sacrifice in the archaic world underscored the perception that the shedding of human blood in the sacrificial ceremony was not an act of consecration but a incidence of "barbarism" that mistakes the sanguinary for the liturgical. The movement from human to animal sacrifice, particularly as manifest in the evolution of Hebrew ritual, however, resulted only in a heightening of the paradox and the incapability of the archaic complex of religious signification and representation to encompass it.

The difficulty of making intelligible the notion within ethical monotheism of an all-loving, entirely holy, and merciful God whose worship must still be based on ritual slaughter must have seemed to ancient devotees to have been weighted quite precariously. The theology of Hebrews, which some scholars believe was composed after the destruction of the temple in Jerusalem as a means of explaining to early Jewish Christians how the act of "making sacred" could be accomplished without sacrifice, attests to the final resolution of this quandary. It is not the transfiguration of the dead victim into a form of divine life that matters. It is the dying of God himself on the "altar," the redemption of all things through the eschatological shedding of blood, "God's blood."

But the issue of the semiotics of blood sacrifice, which remains ultimately an anthropological question, must not obscure the basic and most original problem of God's death as the "end" of representation itself. The end of representation, the overcoming of the inherent ontological dualism of the West, is what the death of God is truly all about. The key to this intricate hermeneutic of divine semblance can be found in the opening verse of Hebrews, which we have already referenced. The realization of the nature of the Son as the "exact representation" of God through death on the cross bespeaks a type of radical theology—or "fundamental ontology"—that the formalism of Greco-Roman thought could never articulate. The orthodox conception that God "sacrificed" his Son to redeem fallen humanity transfers into the ontological insight that the infinite divine presence, and its reproduction in the sacrificial victim, is overcome once and for all in the moment of crucifixion. The victim as representation, or surrogate, is abolished—not momentarily as in the sacrificial system—but decisively and irrevocably. Presence and representation are no longer terms of difference but of identity within difference. Heaven and earth, word and flesh, are equalized.

The "blood covenant" between God and humanity in Christ's death becomes a root metaphor for the erasure of the boundary between God and the *imago Dei*. The boundary, metaphysically expressed as "sin," is washed away in the blood. There is but a temporal, not a logical, gap between God's presence (*ousia*) in Christ and parousia. For parousia itself can be deciphered as the full, postrepresentational expression of what the troped concept of 'God's son' truly entails, namely, as philosophical idealism understood, the "taking up" of finitude as speculative infinity, of the concretization of "Absolute Spirit." Such a vision is already labored in the main writings of Altizer. We must therefore pose the question if the death of God in all truth signifies the sacrifice of God. The analogy of sacrifice, of course, was prominent in Nietzsche. The cry of the madman that the divine murder is bleeding "under our knives," a translation to a "higher history than all history hitherto," betokens the phenomenology of the ritual sacrifice.

But the theory of sacrifice as applied to any theological dialectics must first take into account Georges Bataille's economics of expenditure and excess. As Bataille observes, a theory of religion cannot in any way be derived from a doctrine of utility. Indeed, the opposite is true. The experience of the sacred arises out of what Nietzsche described as the joy of self-expenditure, the "overflowing" of power, an economy that like a swollen watercourse overruns its banks. Only economies of consumption and excess are capable of sacrifice. Sacrality requires death, a "creative destruction" in Schumpeter's terms. The element consumed, the victim, the ensign of excess, is Bataille's "accursed share," and it is in this accounting "accursed" that the production of the sacred becomes possible.

The centrality of the sacrificial motif in the Christian doctrine of atonement underscores the importance of Bataille's hermeneutics of excess. We can begin to understand the Nietzschean parable of the murder of God and the classical dogmatic formula of God's sacrifice of himself as a kind of obversity within a theological double sentence, a semiotic divide for all forms of religious discursivity. Here theology truly becomes anthropology, because the theological and anthropological are envisioned as commensurate. The death of God therefore can be comprehended as a kind of controlling catachresis, as the distension of the dialectics of sacrifice to the point where the "paradox of incarnation" is no longer a linguistic stumbling block. But the structure of the catachresis, wherein the expenditure of what is "all too human" logically communicates at the same time the idea of divine self-exteriorization, cannot be resolved by any Hegelian juggernaut of the negative. The catachresis remains an impenetrable membrane through which yet sift hints of divine presence.

Theological dialectic must become the "deconstruction" of the cross in the most radical sense. Here we surpass all forms of "secular" as well as "negative" theologies—the metonymy of the divine *ousia* expressed in the horror and mystery of sacrifice, both anthropologically and theologically. In Hebrews, and then overtly in Altizer, we cross over the semiotic threshold into the postmodern. Postmodernism is frequently, but wrongly, understood as an exergue, as a discursive "supplement" to the textuality of the modern. If we systematically reread Altizer's writings, we discern the way in which his visionary statement of God's death, and its cultural apocalypsis, offers a profound, and previously unthought, relationship between variant epochs, divergent semiologies. There can only be "writing" in a theological sense after the death of God, because the commencement of the grammatological era and the apocalypsis are one and the same. As Altizer says, "the real ending of speech is the dawning of resurrection, and the final ending of speech is the dawning of a totally present actuality. That actuality is immediately at hand when it is heard, and it is heard when it is enacted. And it is enacted in the dawning of the actuality of silence, an actuality ending all disembodied and unspoken presence" (*SEG* 96).

Taylor picks up on this theme more explicitly in his seminal essay of religious postmodernism entitled "Text as Victim." "If sacrifice and sacrificer are one, then victimizer is also victim. A death of God (a)theology, which is really a radical Christology, finds its completion in the crucifixion of the individual self and the resurrection of universal humanity. This end (or beginning) is realized through the dissemination of the Word."[2] And such a motif is "resurrection is not a movement from flesh to Spirit, but is rather in some sense a movement from Spirit to flesh" (*DH* 116). Divine totality and text/flesh are symmetrical with each other. As in the Flemish masterpieces of the late Middle Ages, the roseate, unspeakably wounded flesh of the sacrificed God serves as its own hieratic wonder. It is a hierophany of the modern, theologically speaking, inasmuch as it manifests what in the argot of an older, pious religious liberalism we would call the "humanity of God." But this humanity—Taylor's "universal humanity"—constitutes an apocalypse of representation as sheer surface, as an iconography that has shifted from vertical to horizontal, as the dissolution of the logical space between immanence and transcendence. Total presence becomes the utter finality of the text. The veil that is rent in the tent of meeting with the murder of God is not so much between this world and "the other world"; it is between subject and alterity, between the phenomenal and the "intelligible," between the Sinailike presence of God and the myriad representations of theological discourse through the ages. The death of God as total presence means the "taking up" of all forms of representation into the singularity of the Word itself, the Word made flesh, the Word qua flesh. That is perhaps Joachim's "third age," the age of fire that consumes the interpreter, as Derrida would have it, the age of the Spirit.

The blood was spilled long ago. The shedding of the blood is now spoken over all of us. The universal murder is a universal redemption, for the sacrifice is of that which was always incomplete, inessential, idolatrous, "representational." The text discloses that speech. It reveals the concealed absence, which is at the same time parousia, the fullness of presence.

After Altizer, nothing can remain hidden.

## NOTES

1. See for example the following statement: "History is moving toward the ultimate dissolution of the distinction between God and man and a merging of the two in the new godmanhood of the eschatological age" (Theodore Runyan Jr., "Thomas Altizer and the Future of Theology," in *The Theology of Altizer: Critique and Response*, ed. John Cobb Jr. [Philadelphia: Westminster, 1970], 49).

2. Mark C. Taylor, "Text as Victim," in *Deconstruction and Theology*, ed. Carl Raschke (New York: Crossroad, 1982), 73.

CHAPTER 2

Betraying Altizer

MARK C. TAYLOR

Thomas J. J. Altizer is, perhaps, the last theologian. As such, his words are haunted by the impossibility of theology. It is precisely this impossibility that Altizer writes and rewrites endlessly. In one sense, he has realized this impossibility from the beginning; in another sense, his refusal to accept this impossibility is what allows him to speak and prevents him from falling silent. It only becomes possible to move beyond Altizer when one realizes that there is no beyond to which to move. What Altizer refuses to acknowledge is that the death of God is incomplete apart from the end of theology. To remain faithful to the course Altizer follows, it is necessary to betray him by ceasing to speak theologically.

Surveying the remarkable body of work Altizer has produced during the past five decades, one is struck by the extraordinary consistency of his theological vision. It is no exaggeration to insist that Altizer's entire corpus is a sustained meditation on themes that are already apparent in his earliest writings. Though his style changes until its distinctive rhythms and cadences become unmistakable, his ideas and obsessions remain constant. In the opening pages of the book that established his theological persona, *The Gospel of Christian Atheism*, Altizer defines the coordinates that orient all of his work.

Today a new theologian is speaking in America, a theologian who is not so confident of the truth or certainty of faith, yet a theologian who is willing to discuss the meaning of faith. From

11

the perspective of the theology of our century, the strangest thing about this new theologian is his conviction that faith should be meaningful and meaningful in the context of our world. . . . Refusing either to deny the Word or to affirm it in its traditional form, a modern and radical Christian is seeking a totally incarnate Word. When the Christian Word appears in this, its most radical form, then not only is it truly and actually present in the world but it is present in such a way as to be real and active nowhere else. No longer can faith and the world exist in mutual isolation, neither can now be conceived as existing independently of the other; thus the radical Christian condemns all forms of faith that are disengaged with the world. A given autonomous faith here reveals itself to be nonincarnate—and is judged to be a retreat from the life, the movement, and the process of history— with the result that faith must now abandon all claims to be isolated and autonomous, possessing a meaning or reality transcending the actuality of the world, and become instead wholly and inseparably embedded in the world. (*GCA* 16–17)

This text is fraught with paradox. On the one hand, Altizer claims to present a distinctively contemporary American theology, but on the other hand, his thinking is consistently indebted to European traditions and is thoroughly grounded in the eighteenth and nineteenth centuries. Far from elaborating or establishing an American theological tradition, Altizer extends European lines of thought that stretch back from Nietzsche through Hegel to Blake. Contrary to the French Hegel popularized by Derrida, Deleuze, Foucault, and Bataille, Altizer realizes that in matters theological Nietzsche and Hegel's similarities are more important than their differences. Nietzsche brings to completion the notion of the death of God identified by Luther and developed by Hegel. Blake's imaginative poetry and art capture this theological vision in visual and verbal images. Remaining preoccupied with European modernism, Altizer nowhere engages American theologians, writers, or artists. For reasons that will become apparent in what follows, he never even seriously considers the presuppositions and implications of American culture.

While Blake's poetic vision and Nietzsche's aphoristic style have profoundly influenced Altizer, it is Hegel's systematic philosophy that provides the substance and overall structure of his theology. Hegel's dialectical rendering of Christian theology captures the radical notion of incarnation that defines Altizer's gospel of Christian atheism. This is not to suggest that Altizer simply repeats Hegel's insights; to the contrary, significant differences distinguish their work. Most important, while Hegel insists that philosophy brings to completion the truth represented first in art and then in religion, Altizer translates Hegelian philosophy into religious language, which, he believes, is prefigured in modern art. Schematically formulated:

Hegel:  Art → Religion → Philosophy
Altizer:  Philosophy → Art → Religion

Altizer maintains that from a twentieth-century perspective, this reversal perfects rather than overturns the Hegelian dialectic.

In order to appreciate the depth of Altizer's Hegelianism, it is helpful to consider two complementary works: *The Self-Embodiment of God*, Altizer's best but most abstract book, and *Total Presence*. While in the former work he presents the bare dialectical structure of his position as a drama in five acts (Genesis, Exodus, Judgment, Incarnation, and Apocalypse), in the latter work, he attempts to make his relentlessly abstract language concrete by suggesting how the Christian Word is embodied in the actual historical process. Falling between his earlier speculative work and his later "historical" analyses, *Total Presence* is a transitional work that anticipates the argument developed more fully in *History as Apocalypse*. The movement from abstract speculation to concrete analysis is made possible by an exploration of the problem of language. The subtitle of *Total Presence* is, significantly, *The Language of Jesus and the Language of Today*. An analysis of Altizer's account of language in this book clarifies the conclusions he reaches in *History as Apocalypse*. The language of Jesus, we are told, *is* the language of today, and the language of today is the language of the here and now.

According to Altizer, "there is virtually unanimous scholarly agreement that the parabolic language of the Gospels is closest to the original language of Jesus" (*TP* 3). Furthermore, the language of Jesus is the language of *presence*, which must be verbal rather than visual. "Pure parable embodies an auditory as opposed to a visual presence, an immediate sounding which commands and effects a total attention. One hears a parable, and does so even in reading, for the parable sounds or speaks an immediate presence" (*TP* 6). The eschatological presence incarnate in parabolic speech is the perfect union of God, self, and world. In the word of the parable, "world speaks in voice itself, a speech wherein and whereby world is totally actual and immediately at hand. The speech is world and world is speech at once." The immediacy of the here and now present in speech erases "every trace of a beyond which is only beyond" (*TP* 7–8). The absence of every beyond realizes the total presence of the Kingdom of God here and now. For Altizer, the Kingdom of God is nothing other than the enjoyment of a presence that is total and as such is undisturbed by any absence. This pure presence becomes actual *in* speech *as* speech.

But of course, Jesus' parabolic speech is never present as such but has always already disappeared in the written text of scripture. Altizer acknowledges that "the very act of writing deeply transforms a purely parabolic language." Within his dialectical scheme, the transformation of speech into writing is, in effect, the fall that sets history in motion.

> For the pure parable so centers the attention of its hearer upon its enactment as to end all awareness of a meaning or an identity beyond its immediate arena of speech. In this sense parable, or pure parable, is present only in its enactment, only in its telling or saying. Therefore, it can pass into writing only with a loss of its original immediacy, a loss which occasions a reversal of itself, a reversal effecting its fall into the language of simile and metaphor, a fall culminating in its full reversal in allegory. (*TP* 16, 4)

In this telling remark, Altizer appropriates Hegel's threefold dialectical structure to interpret the development of biblical language, which can be read in different ways: union, division, reunion; birth, death, rebirth; assertion, negation, negation of negation; and garden, fall, kingdom. The "progression" from speech through writing to speech repeats the universal structure of the absolute itself. As such, language or the Word is the self-embodiment of God. Though pure speech is always already lost in impure writing, Altizer is convinced that the origin it embodies is conclusively present in the end even as the end is proleptically present in the origin. The perfect coincidence of Alpha and Omega closes the circle of becoming in a way that makes possible the recovery of pure speech and thus the enjoyment of the total presence of the Kingdom of God.

> To confine the identity of Jesus to words or text is to lose that identity, a loss which has occurred again and again in Christian history, but most obviously so in the modern world. Hence, in

attempting to recover the parabolic language of Jesus we must not confuse that language with the words of the synoptic texts. Nor may we allow the form or forms of the synoptic parables to determine or mold our sense of the original identity of the parable, for it is now clear that these forms or structures are movements away from the original parables. But if we can see that the parable itself is a reversal of all given or manifest meaning and identity, and that the synoptic parables move in the direction of reversing the original parables, then in this movement of reversing reversal we can apprehend a decisive returning to an original parabolic language. (*TP* 15–16)

So interpreted, the language of Jesus can be understood *only* as the language of today. But what *is* the language of today? In *History as Apocalypse*, Altizer maintains that the language of today, which reverses the reversal of the biblical text, is literature. More precisely, the Western epic tradition embodies Jesus' parabolic speech here and now. "Literary language," Altizer argues, "has returned or become open once again to its original oral source, and voice itself has become reenacted in the text, even if such a reenactment gives the text the form of antitext" (*TP* 18). A text that is an antitext presupposes writing that is "truly" speech. In Altizer's epic vision, the fullest realization of such a nonwriterly antitext is Joyce's *Finnegans Wake* in which the fallen Word is resurrected as the voice of "pure speech."

If, however, *Finnegans Wake* is the incarnation of the Word, then the voice of the author is not only Joyce's own. The uniqueness of "the Joycean epiphany," for Altizer, "lies not in the interior individuality of the artist, but rather in the fullness of a language that unites an exterior totality with a cosmos of interior and immediate centers" (*TP* 81). The unity of interiority and exteriority in modern literary language brings to completion the identity of God, self, and world declared but not totally realized in the parabolic speech of Jesus. When voice is "totally present," it transcends its individuality and is grounded in a universal presence that is completely anonymous. Is it possible, Altizer asks,

to conjoin an understanding of the actual advent of a universal hand and face and voice with a realization of the actual disappearance of an interior center of self-consciousness? By this means we could realize that the negation and transcendence of an individual and interior self-consciousness goes hand in hand with the realization of a universal humanity, a humanity that can neither be named nor apprehended by an interior and individual voice. We might also thereby see that it is precisely the individual conscience and the individual consciousness that are the deepest obstacles to the realization of a universal humanity, a humanity that can be born only by a negation and transcendence of every previous historical configuration and voice of consciousness. (*TP* 86–87)

The birth of universal humanity, in other words, is impossible apart from the death of the individual self. The death of the self, in turn, brings to completion the death of God and issues in the birth of a universal humanity, which is the resurrection of the divine.

The self whose death marks the advent of the Kingdom of God was initially conceived in Pauline Christianity. Though Greek and Jewish culture prepare the way for the individual subject, self-consciousness, Altizer contends, first emerges in the letters of Paul. As Paul makes clear, the self is born guilty. In the Hegelian language that Altizer borrows to explicate Paul, self-consciousness is unavoidably "unhappy." "Thus self-consciousness as such initially appears as a dichotomous consciousness, a doubled and divided consciousness which is itself only insofar as it is not itself, which is for itself or manifest to itself only insofar as it is against itself, only insofar as it is a pure and total negativity" (*HA* 66). The subject becomes itself in and through a process of *inner* division in which otherness is initially posited as difference and finally returned to the sameness of self-identity. It is *as if* the self-conscious subject were two. This apparent duplicity, however, is a condition of the possibility of a more profound unity. The unity and identity of the subject are secured by the purity and totality of its own self-negation. Pure negativity is *doubly* negative. While self-consciousness achieves its initial articulation in the negation of immediacy, the divided self is itself negated through a dialectical process in which opposites are reconciled.

When pure negativity passes into the very center of consciousness, it realizes itself as the consciousness of itself, as a doubled and divided consciousness, a self-alienated consciousness whose alienation lies at the very center of itself. Then self-alienation becomes manifest and real as the source and ground of consciousness itself, and the otherness of death and guilt becomes real as the otherness of consciousness itself, an otherness which knows itself as its own "I." Now absolute otherness is "I" myself, it is wholly internalized and interiorized as the integral otherness of itself. Finally otherness is itself only insofar as it is within itself, only insofar as it is finally irrevocably within. Thereby a within is fully actualized which is its own otherness, an otherness which is itself, which is "I." The actualization of this dichotomy is the actualization of a pure internal and interior dichotomy, a self-dichotomy which is self-consciousness. For consciousness can be conscious of itself only by being other than itself, only by realizing itself as its own otherness, an otherness which is the subject of consciousness, but simultaneously the subject as well. (*HA* 76)

Within this structure of self-consciousness, otherness is always the subject's own other. Difference, therefore, is an inward difference, which, in the final analysis, is identical with the subject itself. The other to which the self becomes reconciled is not only another subject but is the entire cosmos, which now is manifested as the self-embodiment of God. The subject's self-realization is, paradoxically, at the same time its self-negation. In negating its own other, the self simultaneously negates itself and gives birth to universal humanity, which is present in complete anonymity. "The anonymity of humanity" is the real presence of "the anonymity of God" (*TP* 19–36). In the presence of this anonymity, difference disappears in speech. Describing apocalypse in *The Self-Embodiment of God*, Altizer writes:

Hence difference, as difference becomes unsaid when it is fully spoken. But it is unsaid only in being actually unsaid. The silence of the unsaid is now actually spoken, and when it is fully spoken it passes into total speech. Total speech can only be the disembodiment, the actual negation, of difference. When speech is fully embodied in pure voice, it is disembodied from difference, or disembodied from all difference which is only difference. But that disembodiment from difference is also the full actualization of difference. Now difference is fully actual by having come to an end as difference, by having come to an end as a difference which is other and apart. (*SEG* 82)

The self-sacrifice of the subject extends the Christian drama of incarnation, crucifixion, and resurrection by repeating it. The death of the individual self who is only himself completes the death of the transcendent God who alone is God. The divine is emptied into the human, and the human is emptied into the divine. This doubly kenotic process can be described both abstractly as the negation of negation, which issues in absolute reconciliation, and concretely as the death of death, which brings life eternal. When negation is negated and death gives way to life, apparent loss is turned to actual gain.

The "total and actual presence" of the resurrection presupposes the reversal of the fall of speech into writing. This reversal cannot occur apart from the emergence of a form of writing that is essentially speech. Altizer is convinced that precisely such a speech event takes place in the "liturgical language" of *Finnegans Wake*.

> The wholly worldly or fleshly language of the *Wake* is also a language which at least by intention never strays from an actually spoken speech. Writing or scripture finally ends in *Finnegans Wake*, for this is a text in which a written or writable language has wholly disappeared as such, and disappeared to make way for or to awake that primal and immediate speech which is on the other side of writing or text, and on the infinitely other side of that writing which is Scripture or sacred text. (*HA* 237)

But, of course, Joyce does not have the last word; Altizer does. Literature gives way to theology in speech that remains writing. In the wake of Joyce, Altizer's words, like Hegel's before him, become the self-embodiment of God. These words, however, are not his own but are also the words of (the) all, which is incarnate in everyone. "Here Comes Everybody" . . . "H.C.E." . . . *Hoc est corpus meum* . . . Take, read, this is my corpus, broken for you.

To read is to hear, and to hear truly is to hear the "pure voice," which, once having been present in the parabolic language of Jesus, now returns in the poetic language of Joyce. The words of *Finnegans Wake* do not merely repeat the original language of Jesus but extend the incarnation by actually re-presenting the presence of the divine in the human.

> The language of the *Wake* is not only human and divine at once,
> it is totally guilty and totally gracious at once, for our final epic
> language is a cosmic and historical Eucharist, a Eucharist cen-

tered in an apocalyptic and cosmic sacrifice of God. Now a primordial chaos and abyss is indistinguishable from the Godhead, just as an original chaos has passed into the center of speech. But now, this ultimate chaos is fully and finally present, and present in and as this apocalyptic and liturgical text." (*HA* 234)

The eucharistic festival unleashed by devouring this antitext issues in a *missa jubilaea*—an all-inclusive mass that encompasses the entire cosmos. "Therein and thereby the conjunction and coinherence of cosmos and chaos become actual and real, and actually and fully present in a *coincidentia oppositorum* wherein the opposites are real and opposing opposites even as they are united in a radically new and immediate *coincidentia*" (*HA* 234).

This immediate coincidence of opposites is the total presence of a universal humanity, which is at the same time fully divine, and an incarnate divinity, which is at the same time fully human. In the *missa jubilaea*, incarnation is crucifixion, which is resurrection, and resurrection is crucifixion, which is incarnation. In the end, three are one: "An actual end is an actual ending, a real ending of the voice of 'I AM.' That real ending is the silencing of 'I AM,' the self-silencing of 'I AM,' a self-silencing whereby "I AM' passes into 'I am'" (*SEG* 92). The "I" that seemed to disappear before the beginning returns at the end not merely as itself but as the I AM of Being. At the end of history, the speaker who hears the Word discovers that his voice is the voice of God: I am I AM. This *missa jubilaea* is a "bacchanalian revel in which no member is sober."[1]

This new Dionysian redemptive way is nothing more and nothing less than the proclamation of the dance of Eternal Recurrence. Yet this is a uniquely modern or postmodern identity of eternal recurrence, for it reverses the archaic symbol of eternal return by both apprehending and creating an Eternity or "Being" which *is* the pure imminence of a present and actual moment. That pure imminence dawns only when the Eternity and the Being of our past have been wholly forgotten, only when God is dead. Then and only then is that center everywhere whereby and wherein: "Being begins in every Now." (*HA* 230)

In the eternal return of this "Now," Joyce becomes Nietzsche becomes Blake becomes Hegel becomes Altizer becomes Joyce, and so on ad infinitum.

But is this "Now" the now that is today? Is the language of Joyce re-sounding in the speech of Altizer the language of *our* world? Or do their words echo a time that is now and perhaps always has been past? Might Altizer's antitexts enact, which is not to say embody, an interminable mourning that refuses to accept the impossibility of the presence of the "Now"?

Altizer, it would seem, has not carried his analysis far enough. While claiming to be a theological radical, he remains *malgré lui* a cultural con-servative. It should now be evident that, for Altizer, the incarnation is not a once-and-for-all event but is an ongoing process in which the di-vine becomes increasingly embodied in nature, history, and, most im-portant, culture. The culture to which Altizer is religiously committed is the "high" culture of the European modernist tradition. Moreover, he is persuaded that the truth of this culture can only be articulated in the language of Christian theology. As we have seen, Altizer rewrites Hegel's dialectic (Art → Religion → Philosophy) as Philosophy → Art → Reli-gion. From this point of view, religion or more precisely, theology brings to conceptual clarity the implicit truth that gradually unfolds throughout nature and history. Without denying their force, it is difficult to escape the impression that Altizer's words are tinged with a nostalgia that suggests a negation rather than an affirmation of the world. To negate this negation, it is necessary to reformulate Hegel's dialectic in yet another way. As the new millennium begins, it is becoming apparent that the course of mod-ern culture might more accurately be plotted: Religion → Philosophy → Art. Moreover, the art that brings this course of development to closure is not merely verbal but is inescapably visual. In contemporary media culture, image is reality and reality is image.

As a devotee of high modernism, Altizer abhors popular culture. This is one of the reasons his theology can never be truly American. Further-more, Altizer's aversion to media and hostility toward what Clement Greenberg labels "kitsch" prevent him from following his own argument to its logical conclusion. We have already noted that from the outset Al-tizer insists: "No longer can faith and the world exist in mutual isolation, neither can now be conceived as existing independently of the other; thus the radical Christian condemns all forms of faith that are disengaged with the world." Nonetheless, his own theological revision undeniably remains "disengaged with the world." Protests to the contrary notwithstanding, Altizer does not allow the process of *kenosis* to run its course and thus short-circuits what he so effectively describes as "the self-embodiment of

God." If the incarnation were ever to become complete, high would have to become low as the sublime is manifested in something as mundane as "a red wheel barrow glazed with rain water beside the white chickens" (William Carlos Williams, "The Red Wheelbarrow"). The artist who most effectively traces the trajectory that Altizer refuses to pursue is Andy Warhol. While from one point of view, Warhol betrays everything Altizer holds dear, from another point of view, this betrayal is actually a realization of Altizer's most important theological insights.

Though rarely acknowledged, Warhol's aesthetic vision extends the European avant-garde tradition, which can be traced to Schiller's *Letters on the Aesthetic Education of Man*. Elaborating Kant's analysis of the beautiful work of art in the Third Critique, Schiller argues that *l'oeuvre d'art* is not an aesthetic object to be placed on a pedestal or hung on a wall but is fully actualized in a vital sociopolitical community. Accordingly, the artistic challenge is to transform the world into a work of art. The means to this end is the aesthetic education that artists provide. As the artist displaces the religious prophet, the Kingdom of God is transformed into an aesthetic utopia. From Wagner's *Gesamtkunstwerk* and Marinetti's futurism to experiments conducted in the Bauhaus and by Russian constructivists, this understanding of the function of art has inspired many of the most important artistic innovations in this century. But European dreams of sociopolitical transformation were shattered by two world wars. As the ashes of Europe smoldered, the site of the Kingdom seemed to drift westward toward America. Contrary to expectation, postwar American consumer culture realizes the avant-garde project of transforming the world into a work of art. Warhol was the first to realize the rich irony of this unanticipated development.

In a 1963 interview with G. R. Swenson, Warhol provocatively announced: "I think everybody should be a machine. I think everybody should be like everybody."[2] When humans become interchangeable cogs in the industrial or postindustrial machine, the anonymity for which Altizer longs becomes frightfully real. Though the distance separating the factories of Russian constructivists from the Factory of Andy Warhol Enterprises seems to be more than geographical, there are surprising similarities between the practices of some of the leading members of the Russian avant-garde and the strategies Warhol devised. In many ways, Warhol's activity in his Factory inverts the relation between art and industry in 1920s Russia. While Rodchenko, for example, takes his artistic skills into the factory to produce advertising and packaging for

everything from beer, candy, and biscuits to pacifiers, cigarettes, and ga-
loshes, Warhol brings ads for everything from shoes, telephones, and
televisions to soup cans, scrubbing pads, and cars into his Factory to be
transformed into works of art. Like many leading artists of his generation, Warhol began his career as a commercial artist who did drawings for
newspaper and magazine ads and display windows for department stores.
Having become adept at using his skills in fine arts to promote consumer
products, Warhol reverses his tactics and uses consumer products—or,
more precisely, their images—to create art. When Warhol reproduces
Brillo boxes and displays them in a gallery, he asks not only "What is
art?" but also "What is not art?" and "Who is not an artist?" One need
only consider Duchamp's "Fountain," Picasso's collages, or Schwitter's
*Merz-Werbezentrale* to realize that the line between art and world had
been eroding for decades. Completing this process by erasing the difference between art and nonart, Warhol stages the death of art, which had
already been proclaimed several decades earlier.

In September 1921, Moscow's Institute for Artistic Culture
(INKhUK) mounted a controversial exhibition, entitled "5 × 5 = 25,"
which marked a decisive turning point in the emergence of a distinctively
Russian constructivism. Rodchenko, whose abstract formalism had long
made him suspect for many Russian artists, displayed monochromatic
paintings done in the three primary colors. Even as the show was opening,
Rodchenko realized that this work signaled an end rather than a beginning. Echoing Nietzsche's declaration of the death of God, Rodchenko
declared: "Art is dead! . . . Art is as dangerous as religion and as an escapist
activity. . . . Let us cease our speculative activity and take over the healthy
bases of art—color, line, materials, and forms—into the field of reality, of
practical construction."[3] But just as the death of God is not a simple negation but a complex process in which the divine becomes incarnate when
the profane is grasped as sacred, so art ends not because it disappears but
because it appears everywhere. Art, in other words, dies when everyone
becomes an artist and the world is finally transformed into a work of art.

Rodchenko's future becomes Warhol's present. Rejecting the romantic myth of the creative artist as a lonely genius who produces original
works, the artist in Andy Warhol Enterprises was more like a supervisor
who oversees workers on an assembly line or an administrator who manages data entry clerks. As Campbell's soup cans and Brillo boxes roll off
the assembly line and screened images quickly flash on video screens like
faces and scenes on television, the identity of the artist becomes as obscure

as the difference between art and nonart. The transfiguration of art into nonart and nonart into art culminates in late twentieth-century consumer capitalism. In Warhol's Factory, art becomes business—big business. The work of art in the age of mechanical and electronic reproduction holds up a mirror in which the world sees itself reflected. The business of art is the inverted image of a consumer culture in which the consummate art is the art of the deal. Explaining his philosophy in 1975, Warhol writes:

> Business art is the step that comes after Art. I started as a commercial artist, and I want to finish as a business artist. After I did the thing called "art" or whatever it's called, I went into business art. I wanted to be an Art Businessman or a Business Artist. Being good in business is the most fascinating kind of art. During the hippie era people put down the idea of business—they'd say, "Money is bad," and "Working is bad," but making money is art and working is art and good business is the best art.[4]

Warhol's prescient remark overturns the notion of art that informs modernist theory and practice. From the time of Kant's Third Critique, art is defined by its uselessness. What differentiates high or fine art from popular art or craft is its inutility. Greenberg offers the decisive formulation of this point in his classic definition of kitsch.

> To fill the demand of the new art market, a new commodity was devised: ersatz culture, kitsch, destined for those who, insensible to the values of genuine culture, are hungry nevertheless for the diversion that only culture of some sort can provide.
>
> Kitsch, using for raw material the debased and academicized simulacra of genuine culture, welcomes and cultivates this insensibility. It is the source of its profits. Kitsch is mechanical and operates by formulas. Kitsch is vicarious experience and faked sensations. Kitsch changes according to style, but remains always the same. Kitsch is the epitome of all that is spurious in the life of our times. Kitsch pretends to demand nothing of its customers except their money—not even their time.[5]

When Warhol turns to pop culture for artistic inspiration, he collapses the distinction between high and low art and insists that art does not lie outside economic networks but is a commodity like any other commodity.

Warhol's art makes money—both as a product and as a process. "I don't understand anything except GREEN BILLS," he declares.[6] At one point he goes so far as to suggest that "the real thing" should replace his silk-screened sheets of money. "I like money on the wall. Say you were going to buy a $200,000 painting. I think you should take that money, tie it up, and hang it on the wall. Then when someone visited you the first thing they would see is the money on the wall."[7] This characteristically ironic remark expresses an important insight: not only has art become com-modified, but money has been aestheticized. As art becomes money, money becomes art. Money, in other words, is a matter of image.

The recognition of the pervasive power of images marks the inter-section between industrial and postindustrial capitalism. Warhol's Fac-tory is a TV stage or film set as well as an assembly line. Long before others, Warhol realized the far-reaching implications of media culture. In turn of the twenty-first century consumer capitalism, the token of exchange is not the thing itself but an image. Use value increasingly gives way to exchange value in an economy that tends to consume the thing itself. As products proliferate, markets expand by deploying images to create desire where there is no need. People buy and sell images: the shoe, the car, or the watch is not valuable because of the function it serves but because of the image it projects. In the world of simulacra created and sustained by complex networks of exchange, differences be-come indifferent until it seems that nothing is special. Warhol's econ-omy of consumption realizes Altizer's dream of anonymity and the equality it implies. This equality and the economy that makes it possible are distinctively American accomplishments.

> What's great about this country is that America started the tradi-tion where the richest consumers buy essentially the same thing as the poorest. You can be watching TV and see Coca-Cola, and you can know that the President drinks Coke, Liz Taylor drinks Coke, and just think, you can drink Coke, too. A Coke is a Coke and no amount of money can get you a better Coke than the one the bum on the corner is drinking. All the Cokes are the same and all the Cokes are good. Liz Taylor knows it, the President knows it, the bum knows it, and you know it.[8]

Deliberately ignoring new hierarchies created by consumer capitalism, Warhol envisions a world in which identical commodities create social equality. This social leveling harbors important cultural implications. The distinction between high and low implodes, leaving the extraordinary ordinary and, conversely, making the ordinary extraordinary. Just as there are no better or worse Cokes, so there are no better or worse paintings. "You see," Warhol explains, "I think every painting should be the same size and the same color so they're all interchangeable and nobody thinks that they have a better or worse painting. And if the one 'master painting' is good, they're all good. Besides, even when the subject is different, people always paint the same painting. In the absence of master artists and masterpieces, art is 'just another job.'"[9] When everyone is an artist, there is nothing that is not art. This conclusion marks the death of art.

The artistry of Warhol's specular economy indirectly reflects the machinations of Hegel's speculative philosophy. If everyone is an artist, and everything is a work of art, then everyone is, in some sense, a work of art. In this artistic interplay, object and subject pass into each other. Warhol exhibits this complex reflexive process by explicitly turning himself into a work of art. In the final analysis, Warhol's art is about himself; his *Gesamtkunstwerk* is nothing other than "Andy." Extending the work from canvas to skin, "Andy" becomes his own production. To create "Andy," Warhol must become nothing. "I'm sure I'm going to look into the mirror and see nothing. People are always calling me a mirror and if a mirror looks into a mirror, what is there to see? . . . Some critic called me the Nothingness Himself and that didn't help my sense of existence any. Then I realized that existence itself is nothing and I felt better. But I'm still obsessed with the idea of looking into the mirror and seeing no one, nothing."[10] Emptying himself of himself, "Andy" mirrors a world in which image is real and the real is image. *This* is the Now that is today. By lining the Factory with reflective foil and taking up the electronic prostheses of tape recorder and video camera, Warhol screens a world in which nothing is hiding since all is on display. In this world, everything once believed real is slipping away, and *nothing can be recovered, absolutely nothing.*

In the end, it all comes down to a question of nothing—or a question of different nothings. Though difficult to distinguish, not every nothing is the same. The nothingness of Warhol and the world it reflects is not the nothingness that obsesses Altizer. Faced with the nothingness of contemporary culture, Altizer turns away in horror and utters a Munch-like scream: "NO!" He simply cannot accept the utter banality of media culture and the consumerism it promotes. While insisting that "the radical Christian condemns all forms of faith that are disengaged with the world," Altizer turns away from the world that has become our own and toward a world imagined by the patron saints of modernism where "authentic Christianity" remains possible. Far from a celebration of an apocalyptic faith that now is possible "for the first time," his obsessive writing and rewriting enact an endless work of mourning for the impossibility of faith as well as theology. It is as if contemporary culture is *too* nihilistic for this self-proclaimed nihilist. Protests to the contrary notwithstanding, Altizer cannot bear the prospect of a nothingness that is merely nothing. As a committed Christian, he firmly believes that there is no crucifixion without resurrection. In the abstract language of Hegelian philosophy, since negation inevitably is negated, nothingness always harbors being. Concluding *History as Apocalypse*, Altizer describes this process by translating what he understands to be the shared apocalyptic vision of Joyce and Hegel into his own unmistakable theological idiom.

> Soon we will be "Nomon," but only because we were first "Nomad," and nomads who strayed or fell from "prefall paradise peace." This "felicitous culpability" is the "archetypt" of our destiny, a destiny which is fully and finally realized in a purely immediate speech. That speech is the real presence of resurrection, and its full enactment is the total presence of Apocalypse, a presence in which the dark and negative passion of God becomes immediately at hand. And it is immediately at hand insofar as it is actually spoken. Then the total silence and emptiness of an original abyss becomes an immediately present chaos, but a chaos which is cosmos when it is resurrected in language and word. This cosmos is the resurrection of Christ, but a resurrected Christ who is inseparable and indistinguishable from the crucified Christ, for now the Christ of glory *is* the Christ of passion. So it is that the body of this Christ can only be a dark and broken body, but it is a body which is present in all the immediacy of an unformed and primordial matter, as a totally fallen body that now realizes itself in the pure immediacy of the word. In that immediacy death is life, and "Lff" is all in all. (*HA* 254)

But, of course, this is not the end. In 1977, Altizer had concluded his magisterial *Self-Embodiment of God* by declaring the victory of silence and repeating the final words of the crucified Jesus.

The real ending of speech is the dawning of resurrection, and the final ending of speech is the dawning of a totally present actuality. That actuality is immediately at hand when it is heard, and it is heard when it is enacted. It is enacted in the dawning of the actuality of silence, an actuality ending all disembodied and unspoken presence. Then speech is truly impossible, and as we hear and enact that impossibility, then even we can say: "It is finished" (*SEG* 96). In the many books that have followed this proclamation of the end, Altizer repeats his conclusive claim again and again and again. As the pages accumulate, the words grow more and more alien. This *is not* the language of today but the language of a bygone era. No one thinks like this; no one speaks like this, no one writes like this here and now—no one, that is, but Altizer, and he *cannot* do otherwise. The "Christian atheist" whose name is synonymous with the death of God is actually our most God-possessed theologian. Irrepressibly dialectical, Altizer believes but does not believe, does not believe yet believes. The repetition compulsion that keeps him writing is a symptom of profound doubt he cannot quite overcome. Living the solitude he so powerfully describes, he does not write for others but to persuade *himself*. As the circle of his antitexts gradually closes, his passionate *cri de coeur* becomes more desperate. Thomas J. J. Altizer *cannot* avoid writing theology. If the Word is life, then to cease to write is death. Paradoxically, by refusing to let go of theology, Altizer betrays his own theological vision.

What, then, would it mean *not* to betray Altizer's vision? The only way to remain true to his most important insights, it seems, would be to betray Altizer's betrayal of himself. The death of God remains incomplete as long as theology continues. Theology does not end when it is no longer written but when it is forgotten. More precisely, theology ends when we forget that we have forgotten God. As long as the specter of God haunts the world, the kenotic process that Altizer, following Hegel, charts remains unfinished. The nostalgia of mourning and faith in apocalypse are ways of holding on to what will not let us go. To betray Altizer's betrayal of himself, it is necessary to let go of faith by forgetting that we have forgotten God. Like everything else, this betrayal is duplicitous: on the one hand, it turns against many of Altizer's most cherished convictions; on the other hand, it discloses the implications of his insights that he himself resists. For the "No" of world negation to be negated and nihilism to be complete, we must say "Yes" to the nothingness and emptiness hiding in the utter ordinariness and banality of contemporary culture. Perhaps then it will be finished.

## NOTES

1. G. W. F. Hegel, *Phenomenology of Spirit*, trans. A. V. Miller (Oxford: Oxford University Press, 1977), 27.

2. Andy Warhol, "What Is Pop Art? Answers from 8 Painters," *Artnews* 62 (November 1963): 26.

3. Quoted in Camilla Gray, *The Russian Experiment in Art, 1863–1922* (New York: Henry Abrams, 1962), 249.

4. Andy Warhol, *The Philosophy of Andy Warhol* (New York: Harcourt Brace, 1975), 92.

5. Clement Greenberg, "The Avant-Garde and Kitsch," in *Perceptions and Judgments, 1939–1944*, ed. John O'Brian (Chicago: University of Chicago Press, 1986), I: 12.

6. *The Philosophy of Andy Warhol*, 129.

7. Ibid., 134.

8. Ibid., 100.

9. Ibid., 178.

10. Ibid., 7.

CHAPTER 3

∾

# Theology as the Thinking of Passion Itself

LISSA MCCULLOUGH

God Appears & God is Light
To those poor Souls who dwell in Night
But does a Human Form Display
To those Who Dwell in Realms of day

—William Blake, "Auguries of Innocence"

I feel that the Godhead is broken up like the bread at the Supper, and that we are the pieces.

—Herman Melville, Letter to Hawthorne

This chapter attempts an exposition of the "God-obsessed" center of Altizer's work. This a daunting task, for as Schopenhauer noted, it is far easier to point out the faults and errors in the work of a great mind than to give a clear and complete exposition of its value, of that in it which is unfathomable and inexhaustible.[1] Schopenhauer's observation is readily applied to the case of Altizer. Those who read Altizer "academically," with the critical scrupulosity of the scholar, will balk again and again at the massive, sweeping generalizations that characterize his work and will be provoked to cavil at almost every line. But it

29

is too rarely noted that scholarly caution also has a price, as it forestalls the audacity of original thinking. In Altizer's case, hedging qualification is traded for a bold, original, visionary thinking that covers vast intellectual territories across historical periods and cultures and does so at a bracing clip. A host of scholars would be needed to expose the flaws and introduce nuance where it is lacking, but no scholar who is not a genuine thinker will grasp the integral whole that Altizer sees, with its breathtaking power and sweep.

There is an essential systematic core to Altizer's theological thinking, and unless that core is grasped, the import of his work cannot be absorbed except partially, in bits and pieces, not fundamentally. Once that core is grasped, the wide-ranging elements of his work in historical and modern theology, philosophy, history of religions, Christian epic, New Testament research, and so on, can be grasped in their systematic coherence. To read Altizer well we need to discern the vision as a whole in its integrity; otherwise that in it which is "unfathomable and inexhaustible," in Schopenhauer's phrase, will be lost on us. This kind of reading demands a sustained labor—in Altizer's case, a dark and "satanic" labor of the negative—one averse, even perverse or pathological, to the healthy-minded sensibility. Truly to grasp Altizer's radical theology is to be grasped oneself by synthetic insight, a pure dialectical insight into a "darkness fully visible" (*GA* 166), and while such insight is not in our control exactly, it does hinge on our power of attention as readers, so we bear responsibility in the venture insofar as we aspire to partake.

For Altizer, as for Hegel, to be conscious is to participate in a visionary history of consciousness, and that history as such is "spiritual," not historical in any narrow empirical or positivistic sense. Hence only a fully theological understanding of Western history can do justice to the centrality of God vision that imbues its development, and this is a fortiori true of what Altizer calls "the uniquely modern world," which can only be understood in terms of its revolutionary negations and transmutations of an earlier premodern theological history. This makes Altizer's project Hegelian at heart, as "it is only in the wake of Hegelian thinking that Christian thinking has become historical thinking, or that the Bible itself became manifest and real to theological thinking as a truly or fully historical revelation" (*GG* 37). Because an evolving relationship to the biblical God has generated Western consciousness and historical identity, to abstain from naming God is to abstain from naming our own deepest identity, our actual becoming, our destiny *coram Deo*—and this is no less true if our identity and destiny are evolving in a purely negative relation to God *post mortem Dei*.

So, even if postmodernity is now realizing a new ahistorical consciousness, one that consumes its history by "forgetting" it (*CJ* 196), it nonetheless remains the case, in Altizer's view, that "we have irretrievably lost that innocence which makes possible the nonnaming of God" (*TP* 35).[2] To abstain from naming ourselves in relation to the horizon of our theological history is to retreat into an disingenuous innocence, since what has happened in our actual history is the comprehensive ground for everything we are, the matrix of what we are becoming, giving rise to the most fundamental possible questions: *Who are we? What has happened?*[3] Altizer's ultimate seriousness with regard to theology derives from his conviction that only theological-historical reflection can address these essential identity questions at the deepest level at which they are asked: ultimately, comprehensively, with an absolute and universal horizon. As God thinking is the only thinking that pursues an absolute origin and an ultimate destiny, no other mode of inquiry challenges theology with respect to comprehensiveness of vision. This is to say that theology even now has a fundamental role to play in Western culture, one that is perhaps more crucial after the death of God, with the full apotheosis of the Nothing in modernity, than it was before, since nothing is more opaque to us now than our actual horizon, our actually impending destiny, released as it is from all previous moorings and straying, in Nietzsche's words, as through an infinite nothing.[4] Pursuit of the primal identity questions leads Altizer to attempt a "coinherence of abstract or systematic and historical theology" (*GA* 12) as two pillars, synchronic and diachronic, of a systematic rethinking of the history of modern Western consciousness as the story of the negation of the Christian God.

The least understood premise of Altizer's death of God theology is its central paradox: that death alone makes God "alive." God is "alive" *because* God has died, hence the death of God is the ground of all life and the light of the world. If God is truly God (the absolute primordial), then nothing less than absolute death can transform God into a "living" God, for it is death that grounds and conditions life, or actuality. To become actual, actually to "live," God must "die," must predestine death as an irreversible destiny. As every life lives by the principle of dying or perishing, actually consuming itself, dying away from its first dawning toward its final end, so the advent of death actually inaugurates life qua life. Because of their dialectical unity, to affirm life is to affirm death in equal measure, and any conatus toward life that would dispense with its grounding in death is finally seeking a fantasy image of life, an unreal, inactual illusion; whereas to desire actual life is to desire death as its intrinsic concomitant. So Altizer would purge Christianity of a gnosticized understanding of eternal life by dialectically converting the Christian language of eternal life into the language of eternal death, for the two inherently coincide, intrinsic to one another. "A Christian resurrection," he insists, "is vacuous and unreal apart from the crucifixion, even as life itself is unreal apart from death, and an absolute life wholly unreal apart from an absolute death" (*CJ* 202). As the "living" God can only be a "dying" God, so the Christ who delivers into absolute life can only coincide dialectically with the Satan who delivers into absolute death. In centering on absolute death—that death than which no greater can be conceived—Altizer centers dialectically on absolute life, a life than which no greater can be *actual*. For life is actual as becoming, and becoming is an advent enacted by perishing.

Death lies at the core of original Christianity, Altizer reminds us, for Christianity was born in the first century C.E. in response to a devastating passion and death—an unexpected, shameful, public execution—and this violent and ignominious death came to be apprehended in all its darkness and power of offense as an absolutely redemptive event. Early Christianity provoked offense at the "stumbling block" of its own kerygma, as the unthinkability of a divine death—an actual and real death—generated a paradoxical legacy. If we do not sense the extraordinary power of this offense, it is because we fail to recover a sense of its original impact. Altizer points to the transformative power that is centered in Jesus' death in the actual record of this history, the extraordinary energy that is released by it, a power and an energy that not only gave birth to a dynamic new religion, but gave it the explosive impetus to spread across continents. The crucifixion provoked a rending ambivalence between horror and affirmation, between absolute "yes" and absolute "no," such that the early Christian communities generated a powerful new literary form to give expression to this rending ambivalence: the passion narrative. Likewise Paul, the first theologian of the New Testament, centered his proselytizing message on the "stumbling block" and "folly" of Jesus' death.

Paul's theology absorbs the unthinkable thought of the humiliation and crucifixion of one who, being divine, is not subject to suffering or death except voluntarily. For Paul, it is not Jesus as prophet or teacher who is the power of our salvation, but Christ crucified: "I decided to know nothing among you but Jesus Christ and him crucified" (1 Cor. 2:2); "far be it from me to glory except in the cross of our Lord Jesus Christ" (Gal. 6:14). All who are baptized into Jesus Christ are "baptized into his death" (Rom. 6:3), as this divine death uniquely communicates the power of salvation and life. "Christ crucified" is for Paul an inbreaking reality that signals the impending transfiguration of all things, the final judgment of the fallen world and its evil, and the dawning of a new creation released from the power of that evil, "for neither circumcision counts for anything, nor uncircumcision, but a new creation" (Gal. 6:15). By the power of crucifixion the old world is passing away, and a new world is coming to birth, as Christ's death negates the old aeon of fallenness and sin and inaugurates a triumphant new creation of grace and life. So death in Christ is the threshold to a transfigured new world and a transformed new consciousness.

Altizer identifies the ultimate mystery of Christianity as the manner in which divine self-revelation occurs through crucifixion, an act of radical self-negation, a real and actual death that is comprehended as an ultimate death:

> Only Christianity among the world religions enacts the fullness and the finality of a truly actual death, a death that is an ultimate death, and a death inseparable from what Christianity knows as an absolute fall. Paul could know an eternal death that is a consequence of that fall, an eternal death that he could know as actually occurring in the Crucifixion, where it occurs in that second Adam who is an apocalyptically new Adam, and now it occurs as apocalypse itself. (*NG* 27)

Far from being a fringe phenomenon, apocalypticism radiates from Christianity's deepest revelatory center, as this center witnesses to the overwhelming event of death as the *conditio sine qua non* of new life and new creation, as the exterior fallen world and the interior "old Adam" alike are crucified in Christ. This apocalypticism comprises a complex of correlated, in a sense "concentric" actualizations: the actualization of the immanent will of God through the perishing of Jesus Christ in sacrificial death; the actualization of history as the perishing of time, from old aeon to new; and the actualization of Christian consciousness as an interior perishing, "killing" the old Adam and bringing Christ to birth within. Of these correlated forms of perishing, the latter two are grounded in the first, the divine death, as the ground zero of apocalyptic revelation. Crucifixion is that world-shattering act of God that unveils the destiny of things to become absolutely *new*, but only through the negative passage of death and perishing, and Christian apocalyptic consciousness is the manifest awareness of this. Apocalypse is at once absolute judgment *and* promise, condemnation *and* salvation, the full coincidence of a fulfillment that is at hand and an intensifying power of the evil that is being vanquished by it.

By entering it theologically, and thinking it through systematically and conceptually, Altizer seeks to renew this apocalyptic core of original Christianity, centered on an actual and ultimate death, as formally and genealogically applicable to our contemporary consciousness and world in the wake of the death of God. It is Altizer's Nietzschean wager that the spirit of modernity that has "killed God" is not a sui generis phenomenon alien to earlier manifestations of Christian consciousness, but is rather the culmination of a negativity foundational to the Western history of consciousness, having roots as far back as the prophetic revolution of ancient Israel and the apocalyptic faith of an original Christianity.

Altizer wagers that our most powerful resource in contending with modern nihilism, fighting fire with fire, is a fully explicit *theological* nihilism, which would repossess the former genealogically and recognize its *unheimlich* negations as its own. This is to recast modern nihilism in fully theological terms as a negation of God that fulfills the kenotic will of God to be so negated, as "the dissolution of God [in late modernity] is the consummation of the inauguration of the will of God" (GG 184). If we have "killed God," that "murder" fulfills at last the demands of a radical *theologia crucis*, for it is through that "murder" that the kenotic self-emptying of God is truly completed or "finished" (John 19:30). Apprehended this way, the negativity that has enacted the dark night of the annihilation of God, and the correlative annihilation of the subject of consciousness, fulfills a calling intrinsic to the history of Christian consciousness, realizing a sort of manifest destiny, and that destiny may be described as the apocalypse of identity, identity realized in and through apocalyptic fulfillment.

Thinking in a Hegelian vein, Altizer posits the primordial identity of God as absolute plenitude or pleroma, which, because it is absolutely indeterminate, cannot be actual in any sense. It is neither positive nor negative, but a blankness or "nothingness," an utterly inactual potentiality. The absolute unknown, because absolutely unknowable, is absolutely silent or mute, thus not even hearable as "silent." As such the absolute primordial cannot matter—indeed, it *absolutely* cannot matter—for such a pleroma, having no actual division or relation, no actual experience, no actual disturbance of its pure positivity by negativity or evil, can manifest no such thing as life, no such thing as love. In order that there be actual life, in order that there be love, in order that something begin to matter, primordial reality qua absolutely positive plenum must be shattered, must be riven and sacrificed, and if truly sacrificed, then sacrificed irreversibly.

There is only one comprehensive act predestined by God, and this is the decision to become *actual*, giving rise to an actual world or cosmos, that cosmos that has traditionally been named "creation," therein giving rise to everything that we know as act, activity, the actual eventfulness of the world. The primordial will to act, then, is a will to become actual as a pure otherness; it is a willing of self-negation—a willing of the fall[5]—and therein is a self-sacrifice: "Absolute will begins as a negation of absolute plenitude, a negation realizing its own intrinsic other, an intrinsic other which is the pure and actual otherness of a primordial plenitude" (GG 179). When Godhead wills to act, it sacrifices itself, and this sacrifice releases the divine will into actuality. This is the role of the fall, for the fall is the advent of a negativity that sacrifices primordial plenitude. The disruption of primordiality by the fall is an absolute disruption, an apocalyptic rupture of the quiescence of God before any act.

As sound ruptures silence, so the original precreative identity of God is ruptured by the advent of otherness, an absolute otherness that actualizes the will of God as "God." The one unique act of God that grounds all acting and existing, all actuality and event in the world, is an apocalyptic act—the apocalypse of God. That apocalypse is the passion of divine identity and the genesis of everything we know as life and world. Creation itself is this apocalyptic act, inasmuch as genesis or creation entails an apocalyptic transformation of Godhead, a transformation that is the genesis of "God." Through this act, Godhead generates its own transcendence to the world as "God the Creator," for until there is a world, a creation, there is nothing in relation to which God can manifest or reveal God's will as "God." The apocalypse of God is the act of Godhead that generates a "God" who creates and wills creation.

But to create is to act at once creatively and destructively, for to create is to negate, and to create ex nihilo is to negate or shatter the primordial quiescence of the precreative God. This is Altizer's meaning, then, when he speaks of the *genesis* of God, a genesis that presupposes the perishing of the primordial God. Nothing less than perishing—the self-negation of God—can end the stasis of eternity in the primordial God, the perfect aseity, the inactuality and nothingness of God, the eventlessness of God's being God alone. Without perishing, without genesis, there would be "nothing": a nothingness that knows neither generation nor demise, neither time nor place, neither this nor that, a purely inactual reality. The negation of inactuality by actuality is the initial realization of God as the transcendent one, and this realization is the sacrifice of that primordial God who has nothing to transcend, nothing to reveal, nothing to enact except the disenactment of itself in the fall.

As creation generates both the creatureliness of world and the actuality of God as Creator, so the act of creation generates God as "God," rendering God an actual will, the Creator who enacts that absolute will. This act inaugurates "God" as one who acts, disenacting the precreative primordial God: "Now and only now the Creator *is* that which a primordial totality *was*, and even if that 'wasness' is not actual as such until the realization of absolute act, the realization of that act is the realization of a gulf between *is* and *was*, and thus a gulf between the 'isness' of the Creator and the 'eternal now' of a primordial totality" (GG 181). God erupts out of the absolute stasis of nonidentity-nondifference into an actual history of identity-difference, becoming subject as creative will to differential transformation, or transformation by differentiation, within the "nowness" of time and the "hereness" of place. God erupts into a here-and-now actuality that is the incarnation, the being-here-and-now of God, the actual life or Dasein of God effected through the primordial sacrifice of God.

When God acts, the act is an apocalyptic occurrence that is willed eternally, but *actualized* only once. This is the act that grounds and gives reality to all actual events, to existence as such, predestined in this one divine act as the condition of its possibility. Thus God is identified primarily as the God who *acts*, embodying an actual world that is present and real, but that real presence is effected through the negativity of a continual perishing. Creation shatters the eternal now (*nunc stans*) of God, enacting a fall into time, which is the advent of an "antithesis between is and was" generated by the universal perishing of all things. "The 'isness' of absolute will is the absolute otherness of a primordial passivity, and the advent of that 'isness' is the advent of the actuality of time itself, an actuality embodying an antithesis between *is* and *was*, an antithesis that is only possible with the realization of a rift or rupture in that 'eternal now' which is a primordial pleroma" (GG 180). With the advent of perishing, every present moment becomes precarious and ephemeral: only now does the present become manifest as a perishing moment of time that can never return. "Now acts have an actuality that they never had before, and that actuality itself is perishing" (*GA* 54). The full advent of this new actuality is a "total presence," but this total presence is the negative presence of negation or the Nothing. Total presence as an actual presence implies total absence as its dialectical ground and condition, for only continual negation of primordiality makes *actual* presence possible, and makes it possible as a presence that is continually perishing.[6] So presence is perishing, and total presence is a total or universal perishing.

Early Christianity inherited its time consciousness from the ancient Hebrews, for whom God who does not transcend history as *deus otiosus*, but enters history and enacts events in time by way of direct speech, prophecy, and covenant. This is a God who effects a history of determinate and irreversible events, events that not only reveal but "enact" God through time as the God of Israel. To know such a God is to know God's acts as taking place in time, creating the irreversible destiny of a salvation history. The name of this God, generated through unique and determinate acts in the world, is revealed in the speaking of "I AM" (Exodus 3:14). As Altizer understands it, I AM is the speech of God that annihilates the eventlessness and timelessness of God before these acts of revelation, the God who has not yet so spoken, for the speaking of I AM is itself a God-generating event that births the actuality of God even as it births the actuality of history.

> The self-naming of I AM is the fullness and the finality of speech itself, a finality finally ending an original and total silence, and therefore and thereby finally ending an original quiescence. That ending is the beginning of a full and final actuality, an actuality which is perishing itself, and a perishing which we know as history. For the advent of history is the advent of death, and not simply the beginning of a real consciousness of death, but rather the beginning of a consciousness that is inseparable from death, and that not in its periphery, but rather in its center and core. Such death is not only an inescapable actuality, it is far rather actuality itself, an actuality which is the releasement of once and for all and unique events, which themselves are actual and real as the embodiment of death, or as the embodiment of a life that is the other side of death.[7]

The generation of time through the advent of perishing constitutes what Altizer calls "the birth of history." History is the apocalyptic "embodiment of death," for the birth of history is the birth of a time-consciousness of exile and perishing. The forward-moving occurrence of advent and perishing, which we know as the progressive course of history, is comprehended theologically as the passion of God, even as the passion of God enacts itself through this history of advent and perishing. As every moment of actuality is grounded in one unique, eternal-historical apocalyptic act, so every moment of our historical existence participates in the self-negation and self-actualization of Godhead as its ground. This is the deepest ground of our freedom, which is simultaneously a freedom *in* the will of God and a freedom *from* the will of God: we are most free in the will of God when we will this sacrifice of God with God.

Perishing is thus the "metabolism" of God's activity as a God of providence, as a "living" God: perishing is the dichotomized or polarized energy of God's will as it is actually enacted in the eventfulness of the world. This "metabolism" is the energy generated by absolute self-othering, the eruption of an absolute dichotomy in which polar opposites—absolute plenitude and absolute nothingness—are charged with the live dynamic tension of opposition: positivity and negativity, being and nothingness, total presence and total absence.

The actual world embodies that Godhead who is the absolutely passionate one—*passio magna, passio realissimus, passio maximus.* No "return" is possible from this journey of incarnation for Godhead, much less for any creature, for there is no "God" to return to: the primordial reality of God is poured out by the divine will to "Let there be . . ." Alpha is transfigured into Omega by the decision to create, to be incarnated in—crucified by—a universe of mutability and perishing. If an ultimate will has chosen perishing as the means of self-revelation, we cannot hope to escape that perishing. Theology can only find itself in the abyss that the crucifixion opens up, confronted ever again with the truth that divine death (crucifixion) is constitutive of divine life, just as divine life (incarnation) is constitutive of divine death, and it is to contradict and refuse life itself to desire a "life without death," or a "light without darkness," as in Blake's couplet: "God Appears & God is Light / To those poor Souls who dwell in Night." As Blakean theologian, Altizer would have us "Dwell in Realms of day" and realize at last what *incarnation* means, for the glory of actual incarnation is the glory of crucifixion, or perishing. Crucifixion, because it is death, is life—or resurrection. We must understand of the crucified God what King Lear declares of Cordelia, facing the utter finality of her death in order to grasp it himself: "Thou'lt come no more. Never, never, never, never, never!" (*King Lear*, Act V, Scene III, lines 364–65). The God who transcends fallenness and death is no more, will never be restored, unbroken, unfallen, uncrucified—will never be untouched by death again. For the divine will is to be embodied in a totality of real, tragic, passionate, irrevokable, once and for all events constituted by perishing, and this perishing is the light of our life. We are destined unto life by universal perishing, and to refuse this perishing is to refuse this life. Is there any moment of greater beauty than when the precious fragility of life is revealed through its perishing?

The theological doctrine that Altizer most radically challenges is that of divine immutability (*immutabilitas Dei*), the view of God as primordially actualized being, *actus purus*, essentially and perfectly actualized *in se*. Although the doctrine of immutability does not imply inactivity or unrelatedness, it does indicate the already realized fulfillment of being. God *in se*, considered essentially, is not *in potentia* because the inward life of the Godhead is eternally complete and fully realized primordially.[8] Altizer contends that in the doctrine of immutability, and its corollary doctrine of impassibility, Christian theological tradition has reversed and unthought its own deepest apprehension of God—the apprehension of the crucifixion—thereby proscribing the freedom of Godhead to be transfigured in the absolute dichotomy of the divine passion. In Altizer's vision, genesis, which is the genesis of God, shatters divine impassibility and immutability once and for all, and the will of God is realized as a will to absolute passion through absolute mutability.

This apprehension of God shatters the classical *exitus–reditus* model of God's relation to the world, displacing it with a pure and total *exitus*: a final sacrificial exile of God from God, a liberating releasement of Omega from Alpha. In Altizer's vision, an irreversible *exitus* is the true *reditus*, eliminating forever the possibility of eternal return. God is only God *in potentia* until the divine will is fulfilled *in actu* by the sacrifice of the fall, enacting an apocalyptic *exitus* as an absolute self-othering. The theological history of creation, fall, incarnation, and crucifixion are acts not subject to *reditus* or eternal return; they are not subject to resolution back into an immutable Godhead. That outcome would be a work of divine *amour propre*, or self-love. Rather, the Godhead is impassioned and transfigured by its own acts in revelation history, making history the real story of Godhead's "death" for another. In an extremely rare use of the language of love, Altizer writes that if the absolute will of God is "an absolute will of love, that love loves . . . its absolute otherness as its own, a love which is and only could be an absolute act of sacrifice" (GG 179). So it is that the action that most essentially defines Godhead is passion—the kenotic passion of incarnation and crucifixion—for it is incarnation and crucifixion that generate God *in actu*; it is through incarnation and crucifixion that God as Alpha is poured out into God as Omega, its absolute other, in the dichotomous passion of absolute self-othering. The divine *actus purus,* then, is not being but passion, the passion of primordial totality (Alpha) for the actualization of an absolute other, a wholly new totality (Omega).

> If Godhead is totality itself, that totality cannot finally be either an inactual or a passive totality, or cannot be so in the full actualization of Godhead itself. If the full and final actualization of the Godhead is the full and final actualization of apocalypse itself, that apocalypse is inseparable from an absolute sacrifice of the Godhead, and an absolute sacrifice of the Godhead finally inseparable from a total actualization of the Godhead. (*GN*, chap. 3)

As a consequence of this apocalyptic transformation, Omega is not identical to Alpha, as the doctrine of immutability would affirm, but is an absolutely new totality. The crucifixion incarnates Godhead as an absolutely new Godhead (*CJ* xxi).

So God is revealed as love through the passion of self-negation, which is also a self-embodiment, a movement of incarnation. Incarnation *is* crucifixion, and crucifixion is the self-immolation of God that incarnates Godhead in the actual "flesh" of the world. Crucifixion enacts a total and final metamorphosis from disincarnate to incarnate, from dispassionate to passionate. Carrying through to completion the initial *kenosis* of creation, crucifixion effects the final fulfillment, emptying the Creator of transcendence over creation and releasing the will of God into immanence, to the point of realizing a "total presence" in the world. But this total presence of incarnation is a positive presence only insofar as it is a negative presence, for this presence qua presence enacts a negation of the primordial plenitude of being. The final phase of incarnation is the death of God, wherein the full and final incarnation of the will of God effects the Kingdom of God, even as it achieves the full and final dissolution of God as "God."

Above all, should we not now finally recognize that it is no longer possible to speak of God in a classical theological language, or any form thereof, and this means that God can no longer be conceived as transcendent or immanent, either as "above" or "below," in the "heights" or in the "depths," and certainly not as a cosmic power or force of any sort, to say nothing of speaking of God as the cosmological origin or teleological end of the world?[9]

If the dissolution of "God" is effected in incarnation, then no longer is a "return" to primordial or transcendent God possible, and apocalyptic hope depends an enactment *within* history, a redemption transfiguring *this* profane reality—this infinite universe of perishing and death—as sacred in consequence of absolute sacrifice.

As God's will is enacted in time, in history, in fall, so the enactment of redemption hinges on a transfiguration of the fall predestined by God:

> Insofar as Christian theology has understood creation and redemption as the one eternal act of God, it has understood God Himself to be ultimately responsible for the creation, and has even understood the act of creation as an act necessitating the act of redemption. Finally, that can only mean that fall itself is willed by God, and freely willed by God, a freedom that has been known by theology insofar as it has known predestination. But if God freely wills the fall, and freely wills an eternity of Hell as the inevitable consequence of fall, that Hell is absolutely necessary to redemption, for redemption is redemption from eternal death or Hell. Nothing could more clearly make manifest that deep and pure dichotomy which is the dichotomy of the uniquely Christian God. (GG 176–77)

The will of God, in actually willing redemption, therein actually wills fall and damnation (*GG* 178). Altizer contends that Christianity positively embraced this dichotomy in the will of God in the process of defining itself against Gnostic and Manichaean dualism: evil cannot be accounted the work of a lesser god or independent evil principle, that is to say, an agency that is other than the supreme deity. Christianity has repeatedly affirmed that the fallenness of the world is "permitted" by God for the sake of redemption, as redemption of evil finally manifests the greater glory of God, rendering the fall a *felix culpa* or happy fall.[10] However alienating the

evil of the world, however alienated the human situation as expressed in
"sin," the fall into evil is apprehended as working out the providential will
of a redemptive God. "Evil must have a real and actual origin [i.e., in the
fall], for if it is eternal then we must be without an ultimate hope" (*GG*
5). If the origin of evil were independent of the will of God, it would not
owe its existence the will of God but would be external to that will. Only
if the fall into evil is grounded in the absolute will of God can there be
hope for its redemptive transfiguration by the eschatological providence of
that will. If evil is grounded in the will of God, it is primordial as the will
of God is primordial, and therefore evil, and the fall it effects, is providential: "Evil as evil could only be a primordial evil, an evil not only present *from the beginning*, but present 'in the beginning,' in the beginning or
advent of eternity itself, an eternity which is the absolute necessity of
everything whatsoever, and therefore the absolute necessity of everything
which we have known as evil, of everything which has been manifest or
actual as evil to us" (*GN,* chap. 3). Genesis is that apocalyptic fall into evil
"in the beginning" that commences the movement toward final apocalypse as redemption and completion. So, at the systematic core of Altizer's
theology, genesis and apocalypse imply one another in an absolute-iden-
tity-through-absolute-difference that can only be grasped in dialectical
correlation. The dialectical identity of genesis and apocalypse means that
apocalypse now *is* that which genesis *was*, and an absolute future *is* that
which a primordial past or an "eternal now" *was;* yet "that is a dialectical
identity which is inseparable from a dialectical difference, or an ultimate
identity of genesis and apocalypse which is inseparable from an ultimate
difference between genesis and apocalypse" (*GG* 182).

Altizer's affirmation of apocalypse as the fundamental principle of
Christian hope stands against the backward-looking nostalgia for a primordial God "before" or "apart from" the fallenness of creation. That is
a nostalgia for a God who is, in the Nietzschean phrase often quoted by
Altizer, "the will to nothingness pronounced holy": a nostalgia for a
purely quiescent Other, absolutely removed from the crucifying ambigu-
ity, the suffering and joy, the horror and beauty of the world. Altizer's
theology repudiates as a reversal of the movement of incarnation—and
therefore nihilistic—the longings of a world-negating dualism of the sort
reflected in T. S. Eliot's "Choruses from 'The Rock'":

> The endless cycle of idea and action,
> Endless invention, endless experiment,

Brings knowledge of motion, but not of stillness;
Knowledge of speech, but not of silence;
Knowledge of words, but ignorance of the Word.
(Chorus I, lines 6–10).

If the providential will of God is actually revealed in everything that happens, then the Word is revealed in the world's "motion and speech," not in a primordial stillness and silence apart from that world. How else would revelation actually occur? It is time we were released, Altizer maintains, from the expectation of hearing a Word that speaks "apart from" or "above" or "transcendent to" the world. If God wills a world—an infinite universe, a consuming "chaosmos," an anomic Babel of erring, abysmal words—who are we to long nostalgically for a Word that would nullify and silence all this with quiescence and stillness? If the world's very worldliness—its very wordiness—effects the "death of God" in modernity, who are we to refuse this culminating sacrifice of Creator unto creation? For Altizer, the totality of the universe is the totality of the Word that has spoken itself in words and deeds, and it is through the Babel of creation that the silence of God is negatively audible. The din in our ears *is* the Word resounding.

A nostalgic otherworldly, world-negating theology proclaims: God calls us to return to God by way of a negation of the worldliness of the world. Altizer's reversal of this nihilistic *reditus* theology proclaims: God wills the worldliness of the world as a living sacrifice, for our life in this world *is* the sacrificial embodiment of Word: it is the bodily incarnation of God through which we ourselves are embodied. The primordial sacrifice of God affirms the world and the flesh as that which God wills to exist, in all its fallenness and brokenness, in order to love it redemptively. Ours is not to will against that will, not to will against the worldliness of the world, but to realize the Kingdom of God in that world by affirming its fallenness as a work of grace and the condition of an actual redemption.

Thus Altizer thinks the centrality of passion in Christianity: that passion upon which the gospel accounts center; that passion symbolized in the symbol of the cross, "the purest symbol of Christianity" and "the most offensive symbol in the world" (*NG* 27). At the center of this vision is the thought that absolute passion is the mode of divine revelation, a divine revelation that is an absolutely passionate enactment. If Christ crucified is our salvation (1 Cor. 1:21–24), if the "word of the cross" is the power of God (1 Cor. 1:18), this is because the passion of Christ reveals passion itself as the identity of God, and this passion is the source of all that is revealed to us as life and light and joy and hope. The death-of-God kerygma confesses that crucifixion is the actual form of our presence in the world, our here-and-now existence, our actuality in the flesh, and in this sense God has died *pro nobis*. Everything existing is Godhead passion. Everything existing is established in the death of God as the will to actual life of God. Everything existing is the perishing of Godhead in the passionate realization and embodiment of Godhead.

Only through the negative movement of *kenosis* does God become actually immanent and incarnate in flesh, embodying actual life and freedom. Only through death does God transcend God's own transcendence and become embodied in all actuality, disappearing as absolute will into that which it wills absolutely, disappearing as heavenly spirit into the "flesh" of the cosmos. Apocalypse *is* God realized as identity passing beyond identity. Apocalypse is God (Omega) annihilating God (Alpha) in the passion of crucifixion to realize a freedom from self, from identity—to achieve the actual newness of the world, the *novitas mundi*, which embodies the actual newness of God (Omega). This newness and otherness is generated in an act of perishing, and that perishing is the universal passion of God, the metabolic transmutation of absolute being by absolute death to realize absolute life and compassion—"the final life of Spirit" (GG 185). For as death is the ground and condition of life, so perpetually perishing with God, we resurrect God in our very flesh. We live and move and have our existence in the Kingdom of God actually incarnate in us. Altizer confesses in his Apocalyptic Creed, the death of Jesus is "the resurrection of incarnate body, a body which is a glorified body, but glorified only in its crucifixion, which is the death of all heavenly spirit, and the life of a joy which is grace incarnate" (GG 185). But that grace incarnate is a difficult, tragic grace, a grace achieved through the *passio maximus*, the comprehensive finality of sacrifice, yesterday, today, and forever.

To be sure Altizer's is a dark and tragic theological vision, for to know and will the death of God is to undergo and will the correlative perishing of our deepest identity: "an ending of everything that is our own, of everything that we can recognize as being for us and to us in consciousness and experience, and thus of everything presenting us with a human face or voice."[11] If the death of God inaugurates the "triumph" of the Kingdom of God, that "triumph" nonetheless feels like death, a totally consuming darkness, for this is a kingdom in which the Godhead is broken up like the bread at the Supper, and we are the God-bereft pieces, composed of a new groundlessness and nothingness. Our freedom is a *freedom from God*, understood in a dichotomous sense—a freedom deriving from God, and a freedom to be without God. So God's will is done on earth; the kingdom is no longer in heaven but at hand, manifest as a "darkness fully visible" within us and without us. In this comprehensive darkness of a world "unchained from its sun,"[12] we are, God is, the world is united in the passion of identity which is an absolute passion. If divine love is the absolute passion of identity, we are only now, *post mortem Dei,* finding out what that love means.

## NOTES

1. Arthur Schopenhauer, *The World as Will and Representation*, vol. 1, trans. E. G. J. Payne (New York: Dover, 1969), 415.

2. Contra Mark C. Taylor's argument that the purest implication of Altizer's theology is that we should stop doing theology: "What Altizer refuses to acknowledge is that the death of God is incomplete apart from the end of theology. To remain faithful to the course Altizer follows, it is necessary to betray him by ceasing to speak theologically" (see "Betraying Altizer," chapter 2 in this work). To the contrary, to accept the death of God, for Altizer, is to accept the responsibility of an absolute gift, the Incarnation, which remains to be thought theologically in its ultimate import, its sacrality as divine gift, as long as that gift inspires gratitude, compassion, forgiveness, hope, joy, and the like (cf. note 6 this chapter).

3. Adolf von Harnack, under the obvious influence of Hegel, articulates the urgency of knowing oneself in this sense: "Everything which has happened and is still happening in history, *that you are yourself* and everything depends on your appropriating it consciously" (*Adolf von Harnack: Liberal Theology at Its Height*, ed. Martin Rumscheidt [Minneapolis: Fortress, 1991], 57).

4. Friedrich Nietzsche, *The Gay Science*, trans. Walter Kaufmann (New York: Vintage, 1974), 181, §125.

5. Cyril O'Regan rightly notes that Altizer follows his favorite modern visionaries (Boehme, Blake, Hegel, Schelling) in viewing creation itself as fall: "Metaphysically, and perhaps aboriginally, the cosmos is evil; imaginatively, and, arguably, eschatologically, the cosmos is good because it is able to be redeemed" (Cyril O'Regan, *Gnostic Return in Modernity* [Albany: State University of New York Press, 2001], 67–68).

6. Here Mark C. Taylor's criticism of Altizer as perhaps the last ontotheologian, articulated in 1984, merits note: "As a result of his abiding belief in total presence, Altizer is still caught in the web of Western ontotheology that is unraveling around him. Only when one is willing to give up both the nostalgia for origins and the hope for parousia can one discover the affirmation of negation for which Altizer ceaselessly searches" (Mark C. Taylor, "Altizer's Originality: A Review Essay," *Journal of the American Academy of Religion* 52:2 [.1984]: 583). My own response to this criticism would be that it is not Altizer's purpose to affirm negation to the point of a purely irreligious atheism or nihilism. His vision is finally a religious one, affirming that a new apprehension of the sacred is revealed in the "darkness visible," and therefore one can truly rejoice in the death of God as a sacred occurrence. This is an apprehension committed to the continued possibility of the yes-saying of faith, although now it is a yes-saying tried and purified by an equal and opposite no-saying. For to say "yes" to this parousia is to affirm universal perishing, consenting to the irreversible finality of death and the apotheosis of the Nothing.

7. Thomas J. J. Altizer, "The Beginning and Ending of Revelation," in *Theology at the End of the Century: A Dialogue on the Postmodern*, ed. Robert P. Scharlemann (Charlottesville: University Press of Virginia, 1990), 76–77.

8. "Actus purus" and "actus purissimus," in Richard A. Muller, *Dictionary of Latin and Greek Theological Terms* (Grand Rapids, MI: Baker Book House, 1985), 24.

9. Thomas J. J. Altizer, "Satan as the Messiah of Nature," in *The Whirlwind in Culture: Frontiers in Theology*, ed. Donald W. Musser and Joseph L. Price (Bloomington: Meyer Stone Books, 1989), 129.

10. For a historical tracing of this theme in Western traditions leading up to Milton, see Arthur O. Lovejoy, "Milton and the Paradox of the Fortunate Fall," in *Critical Essays on Milton from ELH* [no editor indicated] (Baltimore and London: Johns Hopkins University Press, 1969), 163–81, and Herbert Weisinger, *Tragedy and the Paradox of the Fortunate Fall* (East Lansing: Michigan College State Press, 1953).

11. Thomas J. J. Altizer, "Total Abyss and Theological Rebirth: The Crisis of University Theology," in *Theology and the University: Essays in Honor of John B. Cobb, Jr.*, ed. David Ray Griffin and Joseph C. Hough (Albany: State University of New York Press, 1991), 181.

12. Nietzsche, *The Gay Science*, 181, § 125.

# CHAPTER 4

# Godhead and God

RAY L. HART

[A]ll roads to the mind start in the soul, but none lead back there again.

—Robert Musil, *The Man without Qualities*

I . . . represent to myself a Godhead which has gone on producing itself from all eternity; but as production cannot be conceived without multiplicity, so it must of necessity have immediately appeared to itself as a Second [the Son]; . . . now these two must continue the act of producing and again appear to themselves in a Third . . . as substantial, living, and eternal as the Whole. With these . . . the circle of the Godhead was complete; and it would not have been possible for them to produce another perfectly equal to them. But, since the work of production always proceeded, they created a fourth, which already fostered in himself a contradiction, inasmuch as it was, like them, unlimited, and yet at the same time was to be contained in them and bounded by them. Now this was Lucifer . . . from whom all other beings were to proceed.

—Goethe, *Autobiography*

In a stunningly capacious and varied oeuvre that extends over four decades Altizer has developed his fundamental claims with a remarkable consistency by means of what is effectively a methodological mantra. There is the invocation of the three scions of "pure thinking" in modernity through whose dialectics all theology worthy of the name must now proceed: Spinoza, Hegel, and Nietzsche, with occasional abridgements from Kierkegaard. (It requires some elaborate conceptual footwork, not to mention some fancy shoehorning, to bring these three into coincidence, but Altizer is adept at that.) And there is the invocation of the quaternity of the Western giants of "imagination" in the tradition of epic literature: Dante, Milton, Blake, and Joyce. Thus we have the sacred number of seven, the figural "days" of the creation of Altizer's thought, all 'resting' on and in his foundational theological sources: Paul and Augustine (and not a little in his ancestor Stonewall Jackson's Calvinism). He has many claims to distinction, even uniqueness, not the least of which is that he aspires to be a *biblical* theologian; and I agree with him absolutely that the high literature of the West afterthinks the Bible, especially in its iconoclastic power, with greater fidelity than does the church, whose adoption of it is often adaptation. I am considerably less confident than he that his modern philosophical sources cohere with that imaginative vision, although I am certain that they open afresh the questionableness that motors that vision.

If I say little here about the human quotient in talk of God and Godhead, and all the epistemological conundrums appertaining thereto, that is not to denigrate by implication that quotient in theology but to regret that much of twentieth-century theology has attended to little else. The theologian must sooner or later speak explicitly of Godhead and God or hang up the "Closed" sign in his shop. Nonetheless, however much theologians' heads may be in the clouds of theological abstraction, they must have both feet planted firmly in suffered reality, and here bodily collections and recollections are in order. If so much theological talk "about" God nowadays seems to have come upon diminishing returns, to have extended itself so far from the intensional potencies, is that because such talk "about" is not itself energized by actual speech out of suffered reality "to" or "with" God? Can one think of theological thinking itself as a kind of prayer? One remembers that in both ancient Hebrew and Arabic the word for God was scripted with consonants only, with vowels breathed in with the speaking of the word. In the Hebrew Bible the Tetragrammaton (YHWH) is a form of a verb meaning "to become." *God* is the cardinal instance of a word that is merely potential in its scripted, thus abstract, form. The breathing in of vowels shapes the nuances of meaning.

Yes, God is a word scripted not only scripturally in the world's religious traditions, it is also a word heavily conventioned by history, tradition, and culture, and such is the force of these conventions that a recovery of an aboriginal meaning of the scripturally inscribed word is out of question. Though each scriptural tradition has conventions for its "right" interpretation, scripture at best establishes the range of potency for the word—and the activation of the potencies yielded by multiple scriptural traditions yields yet more potencies. The breach of all conventions is the mark of activating, of energizing the potency harbored in the words *Godhead* and *God*.

'God' is at the apex of words that are simultaneously extremely easy and extremely difficult for the human tongue to pronounce. On the one hand, 'God'—not a "proper" name, not the name of an object, not even the name of a person in any plain sense—flows effortlessly and without stutter from the lips of countless millions daily, has for millennia. Such persons worry little about "about" language, and the ease of their talk to/about God is largely ignored by (shall we say "liberal"?) theologians and other cultured despisers of religion. On the other hand, gathering momentum since the Enlightenment in the West, but really beginning with the Renaissance, talk of/to God has come with increasing difficulty. It does not do to say that both facts are explicable altogether in terms of the human quotient. If the simultaneity of both facts characterizes all times and not just our own, both facts trace 'something' in the divine itself. Have we recovered the complexity of 'God,' or re-covered, covered it over?

Whatever the relation between science and religion, there can be no "science" in any modern sense of God. Science in the modern sense depends altogether on the repeatability of objects, their stability of situated relatedness, and their phenomena, as indeed do all names. Moreover, for the reference to be repeatable, the phenomena of the referend must be representable by many specimens. What is sui generis (thus unique) is not repeatable or susceptible of representation by specimen hence is properly without name.

To which the response might well be: yes, but God did show Godself in creation. Creation—the cosmos itself—might be said to be the multifaceted specimen of deity, mind-bogglingly varied in repeatability and representation. But this response is viable only if the whole of deity is exhausted by, emptied into the temporal cosmos. This claim has been

resisted by the sum total of the Western monotheistic religions: no one
has seen God and lived. Even so, creation has been taken as *some* kind of
epiphany—or, as I prefer to put the matter, God is differently determinate
as Creator and as Redeemer—especially in the light of nonrepeatable
epiphanies (Moses, Mohammed, Jesus). If *indeterminate Godhead* does not
equal cosmos, *determinate God* is not and cannot be a "proper" name. Creation *ab origine*, however sui generis, does not close or exhaust the transformations of indeterminate Godhead; *creatio continua* is the covenant of
epiphantic transformations of the selfsame but redemptive Godhead, the
apocalypse of salvation for both humanity and God.

Godhead and God are to be distinguished. Theoretically and analyti-
cally they are distinct although inseparable. Upon this distinction depends
the intelligibility of multiform historical world religious traditions, particularly what is common and what is diverse among them. Godhead (in the
West, *deitas*) is the sheer indeterminacy of the sacred, the holy. Indeterminate Godhead enfolds the root of all that is and is not determinately, thus
all that is and is not in the cosmos (Eriugena). Godhead pure (indeterminate enfoldment) cannot be manifest because it is unconditioned by any
contingent determinacy, thus cannot be known in any ordinary sense.
Godhead is grasped in (or one is grasped by) an intellectual intuition as
the primordial root, the groundless ground (Böhme's *Ungrund*) of what
there is and what there is not.

Much older than Ockham is the intuition that the higher an entity's
destiny the fewer are the principles of its constitution: hence the nisus toward the divine simplicity. God is One, thus "simple," as the uniquely
princip(a)led determinateness of Godhead; multiform, thus many and diverse, as determinately principled in the temporal visages of creation and
redemption. The principal and principles of the divine economy condition every construal of evil and good—which may be reduced to the
slogan: No cosmogony or anthropogony without theogony. Only late
modernity and postmodernity have been able to think the dying (as in
"death of God") God, hence have positioned Christian theology to take
up where Greek theogony left off (and as otherwise than the Greeks
thought), thus to think the *metaxy* of the living and dying God (to think,
in Robert Scharlemann's phrase, "the being of God when God is not
being God"). If medieval theology "went wrong" in its overdetermina-
tion of eternal creation, late modernity threatens an over*indetermination*
of nonbeing and the death of God. It remains to be seen whether
theogonical theology can now evade both entrapments, can think the

dying God that lives, the living God that dies, and above all whether a religious piety can live the ceaseless dialectic of the indeterminate and the temporal determinate without loss of the metaxic eternal nondeterminate, that is, whether one can be reborn in the totally present aeon of the cosmos of which God is both genesis and apocalypse (rendezvous), be reborn between (living) God and (dying) God.

But for the transformation of Godhead in God the Creator, the 'between' (*metaxy*) of evil and good would be exhaustively internal (to Godhead). But for the transformations of Godhead in God the Redeemer, the 'between' of evil and good in humankind would be exhaustively external. The 'between' of creation and redemption is embodied in the flesh of the human person, in the body of the cosmos, or, as the Christian tradition wished to say, in the 'between' of *in imago* (in the image of God) and *ad imaginem* (toward the image of God). If a religious ethic is always and necessarily subservient to theology, that is so because evil and good have finally to be parsed in the grammar of internal and external relations, the grammar of the 'between': internal to the person, external between persons; internal to Godhead, external between Godhead and God, and between God and creatures.

To be possessed of determinate relations between good and evil is to have a destiny. To be possessed of wholly indeterminate relations is to have a fate. As determinate, God has or is a destiny; as indeterminate, Godhead has or is a fate. Ancient Greek religion venerated fate as sacred; and because fate was thought (rightly) to be unprincipled, the great metaphysical thought experiments of the Greek "axial age" arose to contest fate in the name of "principle." Christian thought experiments arose not to contest fate head-on (Augustine being the incomparably great exception) but rather to reckon with the lived transformations of fate as destiny.

Determinate God is at the apex of the determination process, thus the Creator of the determinate conditions under which the cosmos emerged and emerges, the conditions under which anything at all is and is not. These conditions are solely internal to God Godself and are of God's free deployment. Thus one emends the classical *creatio ex nihilo* (God creates from nothing) with *creatio ex nihilo sive Deo ipse* (God creates from nothing, that is, from God Godself). This claim entails that the nihil, as determinant from which things are *that* they are, is internal to God (although their *what* is external to God), so that the determinate conditions of being *and* nonbeing are internal to God. Without the nihil internal to God, the modern preoccupation with the nihil can only issue in "nihilism."

The relation between Godhead and God is without mundane parallel or instance. This is a relation sui generis obtaining between what is exhaustively internally related (Godhead) and what is both internally and externally related (God) to that 'desert' (Eckhart) of barren (because indeterminate) internality. The sere sirocco of that holy desert, whence arose the monotheisms of the West, is energized by the force and counterforce of indeterminate One and determinate Many, constrained by enfolding internal relations. The name of this energy is *indeterminate Desire* (Böhme, Blake).

The inexhaustible turbic *energeia* of indeterminate Godhead, the primordial force traced in everything that is and is not (whether in determinate God or by creation determinately in the creature) is wholly inchoate Desire: which is why both God and creature are marked aboriginally both internally and externally by turbulence. Wisely did Böhme say that Desire is the mother of being and nonbeing, of something and nothing (an insight not limited to Buddhism). And that is why suffering is at the heart of all that is determinate, whether in God or creature: suffering owes not only to the relation between 'things' but simultaneously to the internality of 'things' themselves. Indeterminate turbic Desire entails inevitable suffering because Desire is intrinsically insatiable. Equally inevitable is the telic force of Desire for satiation in determinate form (William Blake: "Sooner murder an infant in its cradle than nurse unacted desires"[1]).

It was impossible to speak of these matters, not only in philosophy but also especially in the concrete language of religious traditions, without nondiscursive figuration. That holds true cardinally of the rôle of Will in the satiation, frustration, and interdiction of Desire. One thinks of Plato's two horses, one white and one black, and the charioteer whose task it is to make them pull together. In the Christian West (or is it the same everywhere?) it is all but impossible to speak "Desire" without bodily reference, indeed without explicitly sexual metaphor. Only to 'outsiders' can it come as a shock that religious language in respect of God is saturated with sexual reference, above all in the ascetic mystics (cf. John of the Cross, the Song of Songs). Why not and how else, for is not the bodily the most specifically determinate existence known to us? Where is the at once ecstatic and excruciating turba of the 'between' of Desire and Will more determinate than in the life-giving, death-dealing explosions and implosions of consummated sexuality (one hesitates to say: a trace of the Big Bang)? Where else the determinate coincidence of bodily living and dying? Here a rule holds: anthropogenesis recapitulates onto-meontogenesis (of Godhead), tracingly recapitulating theogony.

The primordial 'project' for the satiation of indeterminate Desire in Godhead is the emergence-y of God the Creator, by whom or which there is anything determinate at all, hence determinate 'objects' for the determinate (potential) satiation of Desire. Left to itself, Desire is but an indeterminate raging internality, which can be called the "indeterminate wrath of Godhead" and is traced in the determinate wrath of God. The sheer terror of pure divine wrath is transmogrified as Will, transforming the indeterminate force of Desire into the power (Will) to effect a potential determinate 'object' for its satiation, thus the 'birth' (or 'emanation') of God the Creator. Because no object of Desire exhaustively satisfies Desire, but rather serves to revivify, enhance, and re-form Desire itself, turbic suffering is constitutive of all that is and is not, of Creator (asymmetrically) and creature (symmetrically) alike. In the indeterminate Desire of Godhead vests the 'evolution' and 'devolution' of all being and nonbeing, of all good and evil, of all love and wrath.

The rudimentary task of philosophical and especially metaphysical theology, then, is to think the groundlessly renewing ground at the inmost core of Godhead, thus of the divine God (or gods) of the 'positive' religions, and of all that, qua created, simultaneously is internal and external to God. Theology without theogony is both empty and blind. Although the relation between Godhead and God (gods) is lacking in cosmic or human instantiation, save in "the ground of the soul" activated by the *imaginem ad Verbum* (Eckhart), human life is saturated with intuitions that source symbols of that relation and the relation between the sacred/holy and the human world. Beginning with the Renaissance and climaxing with modernity, all symbols of the sacred have undergone a process of "breaking." Now and for as far as the eye can see, they function intellectually (but arguably not emotively) "brokenly."[2]

From all determinateness, God the Creator's not excepted, follows mutability, hence suffering. Thus eternal creation includes the divine but untested (by temporal creation) determinate parameters of God the Creator's love *and* wrath, light and darkness, good and evil. Were God's suffering redeemable wholly within the scene of eternal creation (*creatio ab*

*origine*) there would not have been the mise-en-scène of temporal creation (*creatio continua*). The suffering of God the Creator is redeemable in,
and only in, the temporal suffering of creatures created *in imago dei et in
imaginem ad Verbum*.

Remarkable advances were made toward a theogonical theology by
nineteenth-century continental philosophy, notably by Goethe, Schelling,
and Hegel, all drawing on Böhme; in a different sense by Kierkègaard
and, even more removed, by Nietzsche; and by twentieth-century Whiteheadian process thought (the latter far less clearly, in respect of the 'divine'
God as internally related to Godhead). Heidegger's assault on the devolution of Being in the West, reaching its apex in technocracy, may be read
as a new chapter in theogony as the 'emergency' of the divine God in a
double sense: the crisis of the emergence of the holy.

Real, lived questions motor and energize a viable theogony, as they
do derivative matters (for example, "theodicy"). The proximate source
of such questions is the palpability of the *nihil* in an existence conscious
of itself. The root question takes both a metaphysical form, "Why is
there anything at all, why not rather nothing"? *and* "Why, given that
there is something, does the *nihil* perdure"?—since everything that is
both is and is not itself comes from nothing (requiring, of course, an
explanation of the classical *ex nihilo nihil fit*). Central to the task of rudimentary theogony, that of conceiving/envisioning the eternal self-
generation of God the determinate Creator (and Redeemer) from the
abysmal indeterminacies of Godhead (for Christian theology, thinking a
radical monotheistic trinitarianism in ontomeontogenesis), is the emergence of "being" and "nonbeing" (or nothingness), their relation, and
their relation to Godhead and God. Without theogony, there is no full
stop to the regressive question, "Why . . . ?" Western ontotheology
reached its full stop in the identification of God and Being (God "the
Supreme Being"). Two extremities of religious passion governing praxis,
one Western and one Eastern, may be mentioned as counting against
such an identification: the stereotypical Western esoteric, as in Eckhart;
burn up the "not" in every created thing as the condition of entering the
desert of Godhead (which latter however is characterized as much or
even more by nothingness as/than being); and a stereotypical Buddhist
exoteric: inflame the "not" to the absolute burn-out of Nothingness.
Neither extreme of religious passion coheres with the metaphysics of ontotheology. A philosophically and theologically warrantable theogony
will accordingly renounce all ontotheology at the outset in thinking

Godhead and God. In thinking the fundamental problematic of one and many, the many cannot be accounted for solely by the self-effusion of a One Being. Any such account renders *a* being as deprived of—and thus a diremption of—Being (thus having only privative being, as in classical Neoplatonism): hence creation as the devolution of Being. And so a sad farewell to all Neoplatonisms (but not to Plato!).

Because inexhaustibly indeterminate, Godhead comprises neither principle nor principal. God, being determinate (and being so both by self-effusion of or emanation from Godhead and by the coeval conditioning of creation), is both principled and a principal in the unity of principles. It was an early argument in Christian theology whether the "principles" comprising deity are that or "persons," an argument reaching orthodox closure in the formula: one substance, three persons. It is no longer possible to think the principality of God through (peripatetic) "substance" nor the internal energies of divine principles through "persons." In truth "substance" and "persons" never did cohere metaphysically. The principality of God is not that of a person (which does not forefend the efficacy of broken personal symbols, used constantly in the rituals of many religious traditions). Here again the *via negativa* is traveled: what God is not is more exactly said than what God is. If metaphysics is the *scientia* of "first principles," itself an inexact account of its full task, and may not commit *petitio principii* in their probative demonstration, it has the perduring problem of the status of the *that* whose *what* the putative first principles comprises. The sheer thatness of God and God's groundlessly renewing ground in Godhead is delivered to religious or theological intuition, as its *what* is accessible (brokenly) symbolically through epiphantic manifestations as received in human experience.

Since its early alliances with metaphysical philosophy Christian theology has been concerned with principle(s) (*arche, archoi*), but, unlike metaphysics as such, there is something anarchic in the way in which (Christian) theology derives its *archoi*, and that for multiple reasons. First is the derived and often faint traces of anarchic Godhead in all determinate 'things,' in God no less (although asymmetrically) than in creatures. Second, if metaphysics has its inception in the afterglow of astonishment (that there is anything at all, etc.), theology originates in the mind's afterglow of epiphantic manifestation, "appearing," showing. No less than metaphysics, theology is bound by the rule of no *petitio principii* in respect of probative argument. But the grammar of demonstrative proof is incommensurable with the grammar of onto/meontogenesis, whether of

God or creature. That something is shown, not proved, which is why the first mark of being is that it appears (as the same is the first mark, or condition, of truth). Theology is exactly Plato's project (he coined the term *theology*) of "saving the appearances"—of divine things (God, the gods), which entails the second mark of truth, coherence (namely, the coherence of epiphantic appearings).

A third reason then may be summarized: Christian theology's concern with 'powers' (*archoi*, principles) is to "save the appearances" of the divine principal. In all the Western monotheisms, spirited being is showing that speaks, in which showing the said and the sayer, the speaker and the spoken, are inseparable. God outstands nothingness by bespeaking manifestation ('speech' extending significantly beyond 'vocables'), which bespeaking includes configurations of the unsaid (as God 'instands' nothingness by silence, by dis-appearing, by *absconditus*). All religions originate and perdure in "showings" (appearances) taken to be paradigmatic (as not just the manifestation of this or that to these or those people, but as a 'pattern' bearing upon any and every showing). No religion, however 'literate,' depends solely upon the inscription once-for-all of its funding/founding showings. Every religion relies constitutively upon ritual (and 'discipline') for the vivification and restoration (indeed aggrandizement) of showings in souls otherwise only sparsely the site of manifestation. In these important respects, theology is a thinking handmaid to religion, and in that sense derivative, funded in and by showings at second, mind's remove. In its Christian ramifications, theology is tasked to speak of the evolution and devolution of "principles" as constituting the living and dying of the principal of creation and redemption, the internal and determinate principles of the divine creativity arising from the indeterminate abyss of Godhead (the divine Wisdom), and the external and determinate principles of all that is not God and not nothing exhaustively, the created itself.

Theology is a theopoetic art that traffics in determinate intelligibles, but determinate intelligibility depends on that which is itself not determinately but only indeterminately intelligible. This may be taken in the quite ordinary way in which the principle or principles of a science cannot be treated within the determinate science itself. Even so, theological art includes a reach that exceeds its discursive grasp: that God the determinate Creator/Redeemer depends upon inexhaustibly indeterminate Godhead. The critical methodological matter centers in the claim that there is a determination *process* more ultimate than determinate things, thus more ultimate than the determinate intelligibles made possible by determinate things. The cardinal nodes of onto/meontoge-netic determination process are Godhead, God the Creator/Redeemer, Creation: from the symmetry of indeterminacy and nondeterminacy in Godhead, to the asymmetry (between Godhead and God) of determinate God, to the asymmetry (between God and creation) of determinate Creation. All roads to the theological mind start in these deliverances of soul. And there are consequences for theologically determinate intelligibles. For example, I emend the classical *nemo contra Deum nisi Deus ipse* (no one against God but God Godself) by *nemo contra Deum nisi Deitas* (no one against God but Godhead).

If the theological claims in this chapter serve to "out" me from the closet of heresy—or more exactly, heterodoxy—they are advanced on this occasion to make common cause formally with the grandest American heresiarch of the second half of the century just closed, namely, Thomas J. J. Altizer, as they are advanced materially to join him in the effort to rescue authentic Christianity from the sclerotic clutches of orthodox closure. The contest between orthodoxy and heresy of course is always a contestation of what is fixed and what is open. If heretics are they who hold out for openness in theology, Christianity may well be unique among the 'theistic' religions in that heresy is essential to it—is, that is, if its most fundamental claim is true, that God gives us our humanity and very God Godself in concert with historical time. Christian theology arose in part to think the delay of the parousia—as did the institutional church, but theology may not substitute its own *ousia* for parousia, as the church too often has. The only world-historical situation in which 'heresy' would be rendered nugatory (but no more so than 'orthodoxy') would be in actu-alized Apocalypse Now—whereupon theology itself would be without portfolio (as also 'the church'). The greatest merit of attending to those on the margins of the "certified" (the orthodox) is that they safekeep the questionable, the questionability of the gospel, the "good news," for without question, without questionability there is no news.

Because the key problematics of Altizer's oeuvre are intertwined they cannot be thought *seriatim*, only together. These problematics are God-head and God; genesis and apocalypse; the dialectical coincidence of op-posites; historical time as the exhaustive horizon of theology. While now one, now the other may have featured in a book title, Altizer has never presumed to do otherwise than to think all at once. Godhead and God have been at the center of Altizer's thought from the beginning; he does not cavil at describing himself as "God-obsessed" (and the cognoscenti will know that means Satan-obsessed as well). He is the contemporary American *theo*logian par excellence. That he should be so as the premier American voice of "the death of God" can be thought ironic or contradictory only by those wholly misunderstanding the theological intension and extension (and as I should claim, their inverse relationship) of the phrase "death of God."

Yes, it means the now banal cultural fact of the end of Christendom; but it does not mean (in the common but faulted construal of Nietzsche's remark) that "if God is dead, all things are possible." Indeed it means above all else not the possibility but the actuality of the self-sacrifice of God in the Crucifixion, the passion of Jesus, the scandal of the self-emptying of primordial transcendent Godhead, the self-alienation of God from Godhead fully into the world, itself alienated by reason of its own evil, and a full divine participation therein—an actualization all but immediately reversed and subverted by an emergent triumphalist Christendom. Thus arises Kierkegaard's problematic of "repetition," how not to 'remember' a past actualization (which could be but still at infinite remove, and in Hegelian terms a 'bad infinitizing' of a past actualization) but to be a contemporary of actualization. (Memory could only recur to a primordial past, an eternal return, but such a return is blocked by the self-sacrifice of primordial deity; and if on this point Altizer breaks with his old teacher Mircea Eliade, he is at one with him in Eliade's claim that the death of God is the one and only religious creation of the modern world.) Repetition—or in Nietzsche's terms "the eternal recurrence of the same"—provokes the problematic of genesis and apocalypse.[3]

Across the span of Altizer's texts the word recurring most frequently, apart from his favorite adverbs of extremity ("fully," "totally," "finally," "absolutely," etc.) is "apocalyptic," a recurrence reflecting his preoccupation with historical time (and by his lights fidelity to the Bible). From about midcareer on, *genesis* comes increasingly into theological play, and that because he is interested in no "ending" not prefigured in "beginning" nor any beginning whose transfigurations are not driven toward some ending actualization. One singular oddity marks his increasing concentration on genesis, that of his neglect or passing over of the rich history of the doctrine of creation—which if construed at all is by way of his favorite doctrine, that of predestination. (And this neglect is the more odd and unaccountable given the questionableness of the *nihil* in the classical *creatio ex nihilo* and his own equally and simultaneously increasing interest in nothingness.) The genesis that claims him is the genesis of God (although effected actually only by way of apocalyptic). Am I wrong in concluding that on his construal the primordial genesis of God is atemporal, is the functional Christian equivalent of Lurianic Kabbala, thus the transmogrification of En-Sof as G-d? If so, the constant conjunction of genesis and apocalypse is all the more curious if not problematic. If, as Altizer claims, the genesis of God is the disembodiment of an original and primordial totality, effectively its negation and subversion, 'where/what' is the 'space' of that disembodiment (does 'disembodiment' mean 'discarnate,' as it seems)? And if historical time (the exhaustive region of apocalypse) is nothing but the actuality of embodiment, must it not follow that the reversal or negation of disembodiment is atemporal, however effectively bespoken (in the "And God said . . .") in the breach of primordial discarnate silence (the biblical Genesis). In any case I too affirm the genesis of God but think that affirmation to require a theogony—whose parts are an elaborated distinction between Godhead and God, and between eternal and temporal creation.

As for the term "apocalypticism," Altizer's usage is so varied, perhaps even intrinsically ambiguous, as to submit to no controlling meaning, which may be inevitable in a word so central as to admit of no delimitation even by environing context. Even though the Greek word for it in the New Testament is usually translated "revelation," Altizer rarely gives it that connotation; indeed he rarely uses the word "revelation," and then commonly in connection with epic imaginative vision as the carrier of the biblical cognate. One New Testament denotation of 'apocalypse' is invariably retained and insisted upon, its reference to time and especially the "end-time." In a world-historical frame (not that, for Altizer, there is any other) the 'apocalyptic' refers to the end of an historical development/movement, particularly in connection with Gnosticism (but not an absolute end, since Gnosticism is a recurrent phenomenon and is the recurrent temptation of popular Christianity). In any case, apocalypticism is the end, negation, reversal of an (historically) established ground, the end of "old creation" and simultaneously the beginning of the "new creation." It would appear however that each "new creation" becomes "old," and in the sweep of historical time undergoes its own negation so that apocalypse is a ceaseless "forward moving repetition." Repetition of

what? Of apocalyptic God, of the absolute negation of primordial Creator "fallen" into the "old creation," and of the christological *kenosis* of
the Creator as Redeemer in the "new creation." (My way of putting it,
not Altizer's.) 'Apocalypticism' seems to be the crux, the term carrying
all Altizerian themes, for it appears to be the world-historical coincidence of opposites, the transformation/transfiguration of each of the opposites into the other. What remains undecided, or at least unaddressed,
is whether such an episodic end time obtains solely in a world-historical
frame. Is one's ownmost apocalypse, one's salvation, dependent on the
world-historical time in which one is born and lives one's limited days? No
doubt I will be told that the question bifurcates the opposites, the outward
and inward "times," world time and my time, while in authentic apocalypse they coincide. If that is so, rigorously so, is there nothing whatever I
can do about my own salvation if I live in the 'wrong' world-historical
time? Is that the net result of Altizer's "predestination"?

What is to be said of Altizer's "dialectic of the coincidence of opposites" and time as the sole horizon for their play is of course already an-
ticipated. If the contemporary theologian's philosophical choice for
framing this problematic is itself between two opposites, an ancient and a
modern, Altizer's choice is clear. The ancient (at least Platonic) option
was that reality is complex and diverse, and 'dialectic' comprises those
synthetic and analytic ('collecting' and 'dividing') acts of mind required
to be commensurate with that reality. The modern (at least Hegelian,
more generally 'identity-philosophy') option is that reality is fundamentally unitary, although only episodically so, comprising a restless identity
incessantly diversifying itself through self-alienation, a diversification that
proceeds through sublation in time; and on this view 'dialectic' marks not
so much acts of mind as the very enfolding/unfolding of 'Spirit' itself.
Between these stark opposites Altizer chooses the modern option. With
strong qualifications (which cannot be entered here other than as
sketched above), I think he is right, and I do not see how a contemporary Christian theologian can do otherwise. However nineteenth-
century German idealism may otherwise have gone wrong, its thinking
of "the determination process more ultimate than determinate intelligibles" was arguably the greatest achievement of modern philosophy and is
not to be gone back on. It is another matter whether the dialectic of the
coincidence of opposites can be the carrier of determinate intelligibles—
witness the fortunes of 'dialectic' to the right and to the left of Hegel.

Do we ever encounter *determinate* opposites (opposites in time)? Pure good, pure evil? The just-closed most horrendous century, the twentieth, with Stalin's gulags, Hitler's Holocaust, Mao's "cultural revolution," surely if ever there was pure evil, it was there? Yet if coincidences are at work in all determinate things there was a coincidence of 'outward' and 'inward' in such events; for the victims, of course a coincidence of both outward and inward evil. For the perpetrators, can one imagine that, however much they may have perceived some outward evil in their acts, they had absolutely no inward sense of *some* good? And even if they be judged as absolutely wrong in that inwardness (as they should be), can such a judgment be based on anything other than what transcends that (or any other) temporally determinate situation? One can agree with Blake (*The Marriage of Heaven and Hell*) that "without contraries is no progression," and with Altizer that *negation* is the carrier of the contraries and their relation, but across the range of contraries that claim Altizer's oeuvre (freedom and predestination, identity and difference, being and nothingness, God and Satan, heaven and hell, etc.), each set is troubled by the question whether each is the *opposite* of the other and whether the 'right' relation between them is that of "coincidence." The most difficult set of all (and no denying that Altizer has come to take "nothingness"— and modern nihilism—as the deepest theological problematic, in which he is surely right) is Being and Nothing(ness).

But Being is not the opposite of Nothing; 'something' is the opposite of 'no-thing.' Only if God is 'something,' albeit a supreme something, is Nothing the opposite of God, and Altizer would never affirm that God is 'something.' Omitting many steps, one may say that there is a fundamental problematic in each of the contraries and not alone in their 'opposition.' That says (as Hegel saw with unparalleled genius) that Being itself, no less than Nothingness, is a barren notion; in my terms, that both Being and Non-Being (or Nothingness) are not themselves determinate intelligibles and depend for such figural sense as can be made of them upon a determination process more ultimate than they—which further says, dependent upon the 'reserve' of Godhead, the atemporal sacred that groundlessly grounds God from whom both being and non-being are derivative. Human life consists not so much in the 'dialectic' of being and nonbeing as in inhabiting the *metaxy*, the 'between' of their force, between being-from the first 'not' of creation and being-toward the second 'not' of redemption. The two 'nots' are not the same, nor are they simply opposites; between them we cannot know their purity but trust them to the purview of God. That trust is empowered by the Kingdom of Eternal Life (precisely not 'eternity') announced and embodied in the crucified Jesus, the man from Godhead and toward God, the man who models *metaxy* for us men and our salvation (from creation toward redemption), above all the second 'not' of crucifixion—whose plenary Kingdom (parousia) awaits the 'kenary' emptying of the first into the second 'not' in a simultaneous realization of both inwardness and outwardness.

It is without question the American epic *Moby-Dick* that Altizer embodies theologically, and of that book's characters, it is a theology of the coincidence of Ahab and the great white whale (Moby Dick) that Altizer gives voice. To be sure, it is a Calvinistic-Hegelian Ahab brought to voice in Altizer, retaining the biblical but not the Shakespearean rhetoric, just as it is a Nietzschean Moby Dick, the white, voiceless, indifferent ("as indifferent as nature and her God") Satan-God figure, the whale ("the blank, all-color of atheism"), the nihilism then unknown in nineteenth-century America but encroaching Europe at its end, that finally gains its American explicitly theological voice in Altizer, but with a difference. There in the blacksmith's shop on the *Pequod*, when Perth is fashioning a harpoon tip from Ahab's razors (Ockham's razors?), Ahab asks of his pagan netherworld friends a drop of blood from each in which to dip the tip. In what is manifestly a black baptism, an antiritual, Ahab on plunging the harpoon into pagan blood says (in Latin only slightly better than mine): "I baptise you in the name not of God but of the Devil." To get Altizer's coincidence of Ahab and Moby Dick one requires a slight but crucial emendation: "I baptise you in the name of Satan, that is, of God." *In nomine Diaboli . . . sive Dei.* Such an emendation is crucial for a theological realization of Melville's imaginative vision. For that on Altizer's part, and for much more, let us give thanks and praise.

## NOTES

1. One of the "Proverbs of Hell" in *The Marriage of Heaven and Hell.* The stunning profundity of Blake's Proverbs by comparison with the Proverbs of

Solomon (Old Testament) could incite one to demand a reopening of the canon—but for the fact that Blake, in company with the great epic poets of the Christian West, *extends* and revivifies the scriptural canon (a steady theme, not incidentally, of Altizer's oeuvre).

2. I use the term "broken symbols" as developed by Robert C. Neville in *The Truth of Broken Symbols* (Albany: State University of New York Press, 1996). While his theory goes well beyond my work, it has been construed not without reference to my *Unfinished Man and the Imagination* (New York: Herder & Herder, 1968).

3. I observe that Altizer has remarkably insightful things to say about sacrifice in his recent work, *Godhead and the Nothing*, especially chapter 2, "Primordial Sacrifice." Virtually everything characteristic of the human person—individual self-consciousness, fall, repression, actualization—harkens back to the Primordial Sacrifice, celebrated in all archaic cultures. It is a commonplace of the history of religions that sacrifice is the central rite of religions, and nothing more offends the modern mind than the more extreme forms of it (above all human sacrifice, but that of animals as well), and nothing more distances modern religious rites from their ancestry than such pallid surrogates as "tithes and offerings." One thinks of social-scientific accounts of "gift exchange" and "appeasement of the gods." But sacrifice is not essentially appeasement, but loss, *ascesis*, of dispossessing; it is self-negation simultaneously of human/animal and of the Godhead itself, a double self-negation by which Godhead empties into the human person and the human person into Godhead, a deification of the person and an anthropomorphosis of God.

CHAPTER 5

Absolute Atonement

Brian Schroeder

> Nothing is more challenging to us than the very possibility of an ultimate call.
>
> —Altizer, *The New Gospel of Christian Atheism*

In traditional or orthodox Christian theology, the concept of 'atonement' refers to the sacrificial death of Christ that redeems a fallen humanity from the bondage of original sin. Yet while this atonement has already occurred for the believer in Christ as the realized *eschaton*, orthodox soteriology nevertheless holds that the final, complete actualization of this atonement lies with the establishment of the otherworldly Kingdom of God. Thus does the concept of atonement reveal a deep connection to a yet unrealized eschatological future, wherein the apocalyptic cosmic battle between absolute good and absolute evil is waged, with the outcome being the prophesied victory of God over Satan. In this scenario, heavenly transcendence reigns supreme, earthly immanence is vanquished, and the promised "world to come" is established. Those on the side of goodness are completely atoned with God, and those siding with evil are irrevocably separated from Him.

In the radical theology of Thomas Altizer one encounters a different conception of atonement. Rather than absolutely dirempted, good and evil are reconciled, atoned, as *coincidentia oppositorum*, a movement

occurring first within the Godhead to rectify the "fall"—the separation
of the transcendent from the immanent—within Godhead itself. Only
thereby is the subsequent atoning sacrifice of the Christ made possible as
an actual event, that is, as something realized by conscious thought. The
originary atonement of God with God thus inaugurates the genesis of
creation, setting into motion the *Heilsgeschichte*, or salvation history, first
apprehended by the prophetic revolution of Israel and absolutely realized
in Jesus' prophetic mission. The atonement of Godhead is not however
an ultimate annulment of the difference between the terms 'good' and
'evil,' one effecting either a fusion of meaning or a complete negation of
one term. Drawing on the Hegelian concept of *Aufhebung*, Altizer interprets this reconciliation in terms of apocalyptic totality, which makes
possible the epistemological standpoint of radical theology. Here the dialectical opposites of good and evil, transcendence and immanence,
sameness and difference, are grasped as necessarily dichotomous in their
abstraction yet simultaneously unified in their historical actualization.

The verb "to atone" derives from the adverbial phrase "at one" (from
the Middle English *at oon*), translated from the medieval Latin term
*adunamentum*, meaning to reconcile opposing parties or perspectives. The
difference between the radical and orthodox theological positions concerns the locus of this action. "Nothing is more revealing of [orthodox]
Christianity than its understanding of the atonement," writes Altizer, "an
atonement occurring in the crucifixion, yes, but there occurring only as
the sacrifice of the humanity and not the divinity of Christ. Here atonement is the annulment of the sin of humanity, and the annulment of that
eternal death that is the consequence of original sin, an annulment returning humanity to its pre-sinful, or original, or primordial condition"
(*NG* 105). Thus does orthodox or ecclesiastical theology reveal its connection to and complicity with a far more ancient religious myth, that of
the eternal return, but now one that is "a return to primordial Godhead,
and an absolutely primordial Godhead, one never previously manifest in
the West, and one only called forth by the full advent of Christianity"
(*NG* 21). Radical theology identifies the nothingness of this return as
"pathological," wherein self-consciousness is construed as an essentially
reactive consciousness, a "bad" or "guilty conscience." Nevertheless, as it
is the strength of one's enemies that makes oneself stronger, radical theology can understand this orthodox reversion as necessary in order to make
possible the future advance of new forms of historical consciousness and
thus new understandings of atonement and apocalypse.

"A Christian apocalypse is not a heavenly apocalypse, it is a historical apocalypse" (*GA* 86), writes Altizer, thereby precluding any association with a beyond in the sense of metaphysical transcendence, a primordial Godhead, or even a preoriginal past. "Only the final loss of an ancient Heaven and heavens can make possible this new interior and apocalyptic resolution, for only the final loss of an original paradise can free all life and energy from an attachment and bondage to the sacrality and ultimacy of the primordial and the past" (*HA* 173). And yet he declares, "ultimately apocalypse is the apocalypse of God" (*CJ* xxv). To the orthodox believer, these are seemingly contradictory remarks, but the radical Christian knows God now only as history, but only so through a knowledge of the prior *kenosis* of the Godhead. The death of God is not only the demise of the heavenly being; it is also the death of the historically incarnate embodiment of the transcendent Godhead, Jesus. This death is a dual event, each distinct yet inseparable and ultimately meaningless apart from the other: incarnation and crucifixion. In the incarnation, God is atoned with God through the kenotic self-emptying of the Godhead. In the crucifixion, God is atoned with the whole of creation by completely annihilating all vestiges of transcendence, eradicating the distinction between the sacred and the profane. In the divine self-sacrifice is enacted the reversal of genesis itself, but only in that reversal is genesis revealed as apocalypse and apocalypse as genesis. This point cannot be overstated as evidenced by Altizer's own emphasis on these words: "*apocalypse can finally have no meaning if it is divorced from genesis*" (*GA* 11).

Grounded in the free act of Godhead that is simultaneously the act of creation and predestination, resulting in a grace that is "the grace of absolute genesis, a genesis that is the sole source of our existence, and thus that existence is wholly and only good" (*GG* 49), atonement is now absolute.

> Christianity knows the eternal act of predestination as the eternal act of redemption, for not only is predestination the ultimate source of redemption, but thereby predestination is inseparable from incarnation and crucifixion, a crucifixion and incarnation which is an inevitable consequence of the absolute will of God. For that will is an absolutely free will, and therefore an absolutely responsible will, a responsibility which is enacted in redemption which is the incarnation and the crucifixion of God. . . . Now Godhead can be known as an absolutely free and

> therefore an absolutely responsible Godhead, a Godhead whose absolute will is an absolutely responsible will, and therefore a will that wills justification and judgment at once, or atonement and fall at once, or apocalypse and genesis at once. (GG 177–78)

Augustine first begins to realize this, thereby breaking with the worlds of ancient Christian and Neoplatonist gnosticism and providing theology with the first full account of the free will. But Augustine is unable to apprehend the radical free will in God that makes God responsible for evil and can only think of God as pure goodness itself. Still, Augustine identifies the will, even if that will is only grasped as the finite will, as the source of evil, as a turning away (*aversio*) from the immutable goodness of God toward changeable goods. The will is therefore only an "intermediate good," and though its proper use is an indispensable aid in coming to know the truth of God, by itself the will is unable to arrive at this truth. Only through the proper alignment of the will (*volitio*) with reason (*ratio*) and understanding (*intellectio*) does one attain knowledge of God, but this knowledge is nevertheless incomplete, and thus the radical significance the concept of atonement remains elusive to consciousness.

Atonement is not grasped by a pure knowing until the thinking of Hegel, who consequently only knows the eternal self-negation or self-emptying of the Godhead as finally an eternal self-affirmation. But here will is superseded by reason, and so does Hegel fail to comprehend the full measure of divine responsibility of the will in Godhead. This does not occur until the philosophy of Nietzsche. What Hegel conceptually grasps, Nietzsche realizes in an apprehension "more Augustinian than Augustine himself" (GG 90), namely, the primacy of the actuality and responsibility of the will. Following Nietzsche, Altizer understands atonement as an act of the will and not as an act of abstract conscious thought. However, this will is not our will alone but rather the will of God called forth in the kenotic event. Only therein is a genuine atonement possible since the alienating otherness of the Godhead is dissolved and disseminated in the totality of space-time as the actuality of historical spirit.

The early apocalypticism of Christianity, according to Altizer, broke with all previous conceptions of time and history, becoming even quickly estranged from its original historical ground of Judaism, especially after the Diaspora. Christian orthodoxy negated the initial apocalyptic orientation of the early faith, replacing it with a new variant of primordial thinking so that in time 'apocalypse' became an almost foreign and dangerously heterodox concept. The pervasiveness of the orthodox perspective is now such that its effect has clearly extended beyond theology, affecting even the secular world of postmodernity, denoted by this world's apparent incapacity to project and advance a genuinely new sense of beginning, if only because of its inability to recognize the actual dissolution of previous forms of consciousness and hence prior conceptions of history. And yet this is a deep contradiction with postmodernity itself, for no other age so completely embodies apocalypse and forms a totally new horizon, even if that horizon is nihilistic.

However, this nihilism is precisely apocalypse itself, and far from designating an ultimate collapse it is actually demarcates the fullness of historical continuity. "Apocalypse is clearly dichotomous, for it is simultaneously the total ending of an old world and the total beginning of a new world, each inseparable from the other, and yet each the very opposite of the other. Therefore apocalypse is a *coincidentia oppositorum*" (*CJ* xiv). Borrowing the term from the fifteenth-century thinker Nicolas Cusanus, but rendering it in a significantly different and novel way, Altizer's construal of *coincidentia oppositorum* is the glue that holds radical theology together, connecting it with the entire history of theological and philosophical ideas: "Nothing is more essential in a full and genuine apocalypticism than the *coincidentia oppositorum* which it realizes between an absolute No-saying and an absolute Yes-saying, one inseparable from the final advent of an absolute darkness and an absolute light."[1] *Coincidentia oppositorum* is practically synonymous with Altizer's concept of atonement, a concept that lies not only at the heart of his philosophical theology as divine self-sacrifice but at the center of most world religious expressions in the form of sacrificial action (cf. *NG* 104–05). "Yet that sacrifice is both a sacrifice of God by God and a sacrifice of God to God, a sacrifice which Christianity in its very beginnings knew as atonement, an atonement occurring through the sacrificial death of the Lamb of God, but only in a modernity launched by Luther and Milton and consummated in Nietzsche and Joyce, and thus a modernity that knows the death of Christ as the death of both the humanity and divinity of Christ" (*GA* 158). Arguably more than any other, the singular term 'atonement' best captures the embodiment of the ultimate sacrificial event that is the death of God and as "*coincidentia oppositorum* embodies absolute novum. This is the novum that is the crucified and resurrected Jesus, a novum that can be and has been envisioned as an absolutely new and apocalyptic Godhead" (*CJ* xxi). Moreover, "nothing is so unique in apocalypticism as is its enactment of a new totality, an absolute novum that is the polar opposite of a primordial totality, but a novum in full apocalypticism that is already dawning or near at hand, just as in Jesus' initial eschatological proclamation that the time is fulfilled and the Kingdom of God is at hand."[2] Though the concept of atonement is thoroughly grounded in the history of scriptural, theological, and philosophical writing, it is only with the advent of modern European thinking, specifically the trajectory of philosophical thought from Hègel to Nietzsche and the corresponding literary line between Milton and Blake, that its apocalyptic meaning is finally revealed, as well as disclosed.[3]

The great challenge, the "ultimate call," facing radical theology, especially in this time of world crisis, is calling forth an apocalyptic ethics equally as powerful as a primordial ethics, one that advances the historical fullness of apocalypticism without lapsing into an originary ground. Accepting "the challenge that a genuinely theological thinking must be an ethical thinking,"[4] at the conclusion of his most recent work Altizer identifies the dilemma as a "contemporary Either-Or, either the purely primordial or the purely apocalyptic," and asks whether perhaps we have now "transcended it by our radically new ability to hear nothing but a primordial call" (*NG* 146–47). Orthodox theology, he fears, has become so inclusive as to seemingly foreclose all options for a radical thinking that is not a return to a primordial standpoint, so much so that it has apparently effected a reversal of even the universal apocalypticism of modernity and postmodernity. Such a move can only be characterized as conservative and reactionary, he argues. But is the current situation truly an Either-Or dilemma? Heidegger and possibly Derrida, Altizer admits, conjoin the primordial and the apocalyptic, but in the case of Heidegger this is finally disclosed as *Gelassenheit*, as a neutrality or passivity that can allow for the most horrific abuse and manipulation, as witness his sanctioning of Nazism (*NG* 148–49). What other alternatives are possible that, to put it philosophically in line with dialectic thinking, are truly synthetic, or theologically stated, are absolutely reconciliatory? Does the openness to the future that apocalypticism necessarily entails render this possible?

Though contemporary apocalyptic theology affirms joy, love, responsibility, and freedom, what is the ground—admittedly a problematic term, and one made more so after the death of God—of ethics in this theology? This is a point that Altizer never fully develops, though there are certainly indications that an ethical sensibility is indeed present. But strangely, especially when considering that this theology is precisely the calling forth into "total presence" all previously construed mystery, thereby fulfilling the line of thinking from Cusanus through Spinoza to Hegel, the ethical ground in apocalypticism is conspicuously concealed. If nothing else, the modern realization of the death of God has as its deepest consequence the dissolution of this and all similar grounds. The challenge then is the determination of a new "ground," a veritable groundless ground, one that is not a *Grund* but an *Abgrund*, for the ethical. This chapter considers the possibility of such a revalued "ground," but only so through a realization of the death of God, and moreover through a realization of the radical movement of absolute atonement that occurs commensurate with that death.

What distinguishes radical theology from orthodox theology is that it takes seriously the question of nihilism. Nevertheless, "both the purely primordial and the purely apocalyptic can each be known as an absolute nothingness, and neither the purely primordial nor the purely apocalyptic can escape or transcend that horizon; each is manifest as a pathological fantasy in our common thinking and judgment, and yet their profound power in our history is undeniable" (*NG* 150). This is why an apocalyptic ethics also seems illusory, just as the infinite obligation of responsibility imposed on the self by the other in a primordial ethics appears equally unreal, or untenable at any rate, to many. Apocalyptic theology, however, does not seek solely to vanquish nihilism but to affirm its necessity as the groundless ground of freedom. An apocalyptic ethics is therefore an ethics that equally affirms necessity and chance, law and freedom, responsibility for others and self-overcoming. Unlike a purely primordial ethics, which denotes a hierarchical relationship between the absolutely other and the same, and thus between the other person and the self, apocalyptic ethics renders the ground of all such hierarchical ordering impossible to consciousness, only thereby allowing for a genuine revaluation of values, a revaluation that is a full affirmation of existence here and now: the great Yes but one dependent on the equally great No. This is in fact the very nihilistic point of apocalyptic thinking: the absence of an absolute ground that makes possible the proliferation of multiple grounds, the manifestation of creative imagination and willing itself, thereby enabling the negation and overcoming of nihilism as a purely negative ground.

Now the most innovative and important recent proposal for a primordial ethical "ground" is arguably found in the philosophy of Levinas, who exposes all previous philosophical and theological grounds of ethics as wholly abstract and devoid of any real significance and power. Levinas attempts to inculcate a sense of ethical meaning in the world through an appeal to a "pre-original," "an-archic" command by the wholly other, recognized by the subject via the trace of that absolute alterity in the face (*visage*) of the other person. This trace is present to consciousness as a disturbance or interruption, as a "psychism," wherein the idea of infinity is "revealed" and the radical separation between the other and the same is made manifest. Levinas characterizes the temporal realization of the ethical superiority of the other in the "face to face" relationship as a diachrony, a moment indicating the radical disjunction between time and eternity. This noncoincidental movement between the same and the other renders the possibility of a truly ethical peace as "eschatological," that is, outside of the framework of conventional interpretations of history. Here, however, the future possibility of ethics is not negated or left forever out of reach. Rather, this future is designated as surprise, as a moment whose realization exceeds the capacity of consciousness to rationally determine its historical advent.

In the thinking of Levinas, the notion of eschatology undergoes a radical transformation in meaning. While he invokes the notion of "prophetic eschatology,"[5] this is an idiosyncratic phrase, scarcely resembling anything that the prophetic tradition of Israel understood as eschatological. It must be remembered, however, that 'eschatology' is a concept that developed primarily as such during the Christian period, and any "Old" Testament conceptions of eschatology remain, for the most part, vague and highly debatable. Indeed, what common aspects of eschatology one finds in the Jewish prophetic tradition are generally linked to a nationalistic, not individualistic, conception of messianism. This fundamentally historical conception of eschatology is therefore properly understood as apocalyptic and is precisely what was recognized by early Christianity and reversed soon after by ecclesiastical orthodoxy. The apocalyptic significance of eschatology is refused by Levinas, though he does retain the crucial aspect of the messianic. But is Levinas truly opposed to any and all conceptions of historical eschatology? Or does he instead transform the notion of eschatology so as to permit a retention of a primordial memory of ethical meaning without regressing into the older preprophetic myth of the eternal return that captivated the ancient Hebrews along with the other Mesopotamian peoples of the time, a myth subsequently revived and given new impetus and expression by Christian orthodoxy? This raises the question of whether and, if so, to what extent, Levinas has been influenced by such orthodoxy. For example, while recognizing numerous differences, there are striking parallels between the philosophy of Levinas and that of Plotinus, who so heavily influenced orthodoxy, not to mention the more obvious and addressed connection with Plato. And certainly both Plato and Plotinus and the ensuing traditions of Platonism and Neoplatonism are bound to certain conceptions of eternal return. In this sense, eschatology, in Levinas's use of the term, is shaped more by the Greek world than it is by the Jewish world. With this all too brief genealogy in mind, Levinas's preoriginal ethics can also perhaps be characterized as an eschatological ethics, a nomenclature that serves to underscore not only the difference but also the subsequent continuity between eschatological and apocalyptic notions of ethics that are possible in a radical theological position predicated on the notion of absolute atonement.

"The dominant expressions of twentieth century theology have sought an ultimate dividing line between eschatology and apocalypticism, but it is now clear that such a division is finally impossible, so here we find yet another chasm between theology and New Testament scholarship" (*CJ* xi). While Altizer's use of the term "eschatology" is conventional, and therefore significantly different from Levinas's appropriation of it, this statement is nevertheless applicable to the division between a primordial and apocalyptic thinking, a division that is most pronounced theologically in the difference between preprophetic Hebraism and early Christianity. The divide between early Old Testament and New Testament thinking is obviously nothing new, but neither is it unbridgeable. In fact, central to Altizer's thinking is the conviction that prophecy is an ongoing phenomenon, its very continuation attesting to his thesis that history is apocalypse. His unwavering insistence on the foundational significance and continuation of the prophetic tradition, a line connecting not only preexilic to postexilic Israel but extending to the present era, has led him to expand the theological canon to include such heterodox voices as those of the philosophers Hegel and Nietzsche as well as the poets Milton, Blake, and Joyce. However, of far greater concern to Altizer is the relatively recent separation between theology and New Testament studies. Here Altizer falls on the side, not of theology, as might be expected, but of biblical scholarship. Despite the philosophical tone of his theology, the guiding insight is scriptural—the *kenosis* or self-emptying of the Godhead.[6] This thought remains obscure to Jewish thinking as a whole, as it does to the world of Greek philosophy, and its apprehension by early Christian theology testifies to the uniqueness of that witness. In *kenosis* occurs the movement of absolute atonement of God with God, which in turns allows for the atonement of God with humanity.

This is the heart of radical theology, its most heterodox position, and that which makes it possible to conceive a final reconciliation between primordial and apocalyptic conceptions of ethics.

Integral to a primordial or eschatological conception of ethics is the conviction that an absolute alterity cannot adequately be thought. This is the principal difference between apocalyptic and primordial modes of thinking, and so it would seem the ultimate obstacle toward reconciling these two approaches. It is at this very juncture that Altizer's theology speaks most forcefully, interpreting apocalypticism as ultimately an absolute negation of any primordial stance. But more than that, an apocalyptic ethics negates all previous theological ethics, as they are predicated on a transcendental ground in turn grounded on the existence of the transcendent Godhead. Altizer expresses this in numerous ways, but the language that he borrows from Nietzsche of the eternal recurrence as opposed to that of the archaic eternal return is perhaps most germane. However, while this language is apropos when applied to most variants of primordially based thinking, one wonders whether it is wholly adequate with regard to the unique interpretation of ethics proffered by Levinas. In any case, it is not the intention here to remain necessarily faithful to the philosophy of either Altizer or Levinas, but to move beyond, if indeed that is possible, both their respective positions in order to arrive at an apocalyptic eschatological conception of ethics that is attainable only by thinking through the death of God, and thinking through that death by way of absolute atonement.

To ask whether such a reconciliation is possible invariably calls forth the relationship between Judaism and Christianity. The present division between eschatology and apocalypticism is surely fostered in part by the enormous influence exercised by late Jewish thinking on theology, for example, that of Jabès, Kafka, Schoenberg, Buber, Rosenzweig, Levinas and Derrida.[7] For his part, Levinas refrains from employing the term "apocalyptic" in his writing; however, if Altizer is correct in assigning its use to denote Hegel and Nietzsche's philosophies, then it is surely apropos to assert that Levinas dismisses apocalypse as synonymous with the ontology of totality.[8] As the very title to one of Altizer's numerous books testifies, history is apocalypse, and it is precisely the "jurisdiction of history and the future" over beings that Levinas most resists.[9]

But is the judgment that Levinas associates with the end of history, with the "last judgment" of orthodox ecclesiastical theology, with Hegel's philosophy, the same as the apocalypse that Altizer names? Are we faced with truly polar positions here? Or is this perhaps better grasped as a clash between like prophets who are merely using different semantics? On the one hand, Altizer clearly construes theology as a prophetic movement toward a rational comprehension of the kenotic, apocalyptic presencing of the Godhead in and as history alone, actualized, which is to say conceptually realized, in the events of the incarnation and the crucifixion of Jesus. But because this is so, this "final" judgment is precisely a historical judgment and the judgment of history itself: simultaneously damnation and salvation, absolute mortality but also absolute freedom. On the other hand, for Levinas, history itself is judged prior to the commencement of history, and the command of infinite responsibility toward the other, of ethical meaning before the meaning rendered by historical consciousness, is imposed from beyond by the absolutely other, or God. Rather than being the arbiter and executioner of divine justice, history itself is weighed in the balances and found wanting, to invoke the prophet Daniel's imagery.[10]

Like the ethical command and the judgment of history, a purely eschatological peace is also "beyond" the totality, beyond "history," adumbrates Levinas. But what does this mean? Can it have any meaning at all for history and the beings that make it up? In short, radical theology's answer is a firm no. But then, is it truly possible, or even meaningful, to think the terms "eschatology" and "apocalypse," so long linked together, apart from each other? Does the radical theological interpretation of atonement occurring within Godhead itself instead reconcile these two apparently divergent positions? Does the impossibility of a primordial eschatological ethics, an ethics reversed in apocalypticism, but also taken up and its passive ethical power preserved, *aufgehoben*, make this possible so that the trace of the Infinite can now be interpreted as the advance or project of the future? Is the promise of messianic peace realized in the apocalyptic will to power, not as a quiescent but rather as dynamic peace, one that is genuinely able to respond to modern nihilism, not only as desire but as the affirmative willing of the totality, and also of a beyond but now in the sense of a reaching toward that power? But to ask this is also to ask, what is the "ground" of this "power"?

A significant aspect of the death of God is the seeming withdrawal of any determinate sense of ground. Altizer's theology represents a sustained attempt to revaluate, in the Nietzschean sense of the term, the concept of 'ground' in the wake of the groundlessness left by God's demise. Reading Nietzsche alongside Hegel, a surprising move for many, if not most, contemporary philosophers who only know Nietzsche as a voice opposed to dialectical thinking, Altizer repeatedly argues that Nietzsche's proclamation of the death of God would not be possible without Hegel's prior realization of it. In a remarkable and important passage, one that prefigures any possible move toward theologically understanding the "Self-Annihilation of God," a phrase borrowed from Blake, Altizer writes:

> Hegel alone conceptually knows the atonement as the atonement of God with God, as the atonement of the inactive and abstract God which is "in-itself" with the totally active and embodied God which is "for-itself." This occurs only through the death of that abstract God itself, a death which is crucifixion, yes, but which is also the resurrection of concrete totality into absolute freedom. Here, crucifixion is resurrection, an identity which is first proclaimed in Paul and the Fourth Gospel, and thus an identity which is the very center of an original Christianity, but an identity which was not fully realized theologically until Hegel. And it was realized by Hegel only by way of passage into the very depths of God, depths which are nothing less than the *kenosis* or self-emptying of the Godhead, and depths which release that Godhead into the "otherness" of Godhead itself. (GG 39–40)

In *kenosis* the ground of Godhead manifests itself as nothingness, a nothingness that Hegel knows as logically coexisting with being, but like being itself as an "empty concept," one wholly without power in its abstraction. However, it is precisely this abstract or empty nothingness that Hegel can recognize as "evil," according to Altizer, an evil that is present within Godhead "as a withdrawal into self-centeredness" and not exterior to it (cf. *NG* 137–40). That is to say, evil does not exist independently of God, as something that God permits despite his own goodness. Rather, evil becomes real or actual in the self-externalization of Godhead, the moment when Godhead is "only" God the Father and thus alienated from the total "body" of Godhead. The wholly transcendent God is evil itself, and only through dying the absolute and eternal death is that evil "in-itself" eradicated. In the *kenosis* of Godhead, both good and evil now become actualized in and as history, reconciled as Spirit, as the knowable ground of freedom itself, and hence the ground of all ethical and moral action. Only in God's atonement for God's own "evil" is Godhead forever united with creation and both creation and God redeemed.

This is the nothingness that Nietzsche later identifies as "the *will* to nothingness pronounced holy" (emphasis mine),[11] therein calling forth and enacting a nothingness fully and actually present, here and now. The difference between the two accounts lies in the fact that Hegel only comprehends the death of God on the purely conceptual level, ultimately returning the concept (*Begriff*) to itself, and thereby does not fully break with the orthodox theological conceptions of the transcendent Godhead. In Hegel, the death of God is continually enacted, whereas for Nietzsche, the death of God is final and irreversible. Here Nietzsche departs from Hegel, in that the negativity of this event is absolute and culminates in the complete negation of the conscious subject.

> Finally Hegel understood the death of God as the resurrection of God, a resurrection which is a return of the Godhead of God, and the return of the Godhead of God as the center and ground of self-consciousness and history. That is precisely the return which is ended in Nietzsche's vision of eternal recurrence, and it is ended by a new proclamation of the death of God, a death that is now, and for the first time in our history, a full and final death, and thus it can return only as that death, and never as a resurrection of the Godhead. (*GA* 140)

Hegel and Nietzsche thus form a dialectical union, a veritable *coincidentia oppositorum*. What Hegel knows through the power of negation, that is, the annulment of metaphysical transcendence, Nietzsche in turn affirms as the fullness of historical actuality, or what Altizer terms, to borrow from the title of yet another of his books, "total presence."

> Both a forward and a backward movement to eternity are present in Hegel's thinking, but in Nietzsche's thinking, or Nietzsche's mature or final thinking, there is only a forward movement to eternity, and this is a forward movement ever more finally reversing every backward movement to eternity. Hence eternal recurrence is an absolute reversal of eternal return, one shattering or dissolving every possible primordial totality, and ushering in an absolutely new totality which is the total embodiment of time and the world.[12]

Despite his own inability to completely negate the negation, that is, to fully realize the concrete historical actuality of Spirit, Hegel's thinking is in full continuity with the dialectical move that Nietzsche is able to effect, as it is the absolute conceptual negation of the negation that opens the way for Nietzsche's subsequent apocalyptic closure and overcoming of metaphysics. "Nietzsche's mature thinking and vision revolves around an apocalyptic *coincidentia oppositorum*, a final union of an absolute No and an absolute Yes, but can we understand that union as a reflection or embodiment of apocalyptic Godhead itself?"[13] This is the question for Altizer, and if one is to continue to follow him at this most critical juncture, one needs to recognize the implicit dialectical character of Nietzsche's own thinking. It is this move, perhaps more than any other, that confounds most readers of Nietzsche, who tend to interpret the death of God either along the lines of neopaganism, the affirmation of the divinity or sacrality of the earth, or as an espousal of the position that God has never existed.[14]

In Nietzsche's apocalyptic reversal of the primordial alterity of God, disclosed by Hegel as the evil of transcendence itself, the knowable ground (*Grund*) of God's kenotic death is also reversed. Now the ground becomes groundless as becoming alone (*Abgrund*) and all subsequent attempts to furnish knowable grounds fail. In the Hegelian realization of the death of God, the primordial otherness of divinity is nullified, transformed into the "total presence" of historical actuality. In the Nietzschean realization, however, this alterity is once again recovered, though now not in the sense of an eternal return to a primordial plenum or transcendence, but as the openness to futurity, as eternal recurrence. In effect, Hegel reverses his own dialectical reversal and therein remains closed to an actual future; hence his conception of social ethics remains ultimately conservative, that is, self-centered. This is precisely the thinking that Levinas critiques as the "imperialism of the same," the legacy of a purely "ontological" standpoint that privileges the freedom of the self-same above all else. Nietzsche, though, is truly open to the future and, like Levinas, understands that future as a fecund future, but not a future that is a ground for a jurisdiction over beings.

Indeed, it is with regard to orientation toward the future that the opening lies for a reconciliation between a primordial, or eschatological, in the sense rendered by Levinas, and an apocalyptic conception of ethics. In the atonement occurring within the Godhead, the movement of return is reversed and the forward movement of recurrence commences. But as Hegel definitively demonstrates, what is negated is also preserved and advanced as something altogether new and different. The originary ethical command—the prohibition against murder that sets into motion all other laws—is now, as Levinas argues, only present to consciousness as the trace of an absolute preoriginary alterity in the face of the Other (*l'Autrui*). This command, however, does not retain any sense of power in the sense of coercion; rather, it is absolute passivity itself. And while this passivity is exposed, vulnerable, to possible abuse, as Levinas knows, this can occur only in the wake of complete freedom. From the apocalyptic standpoint, such freedom is only actualized by the death of God. Without accepting this death, any conception of a realizable ethics remains historically impossible. Thus, even though his conception of an eschatological ethics is not contingent on a return to a primordial other, Levinas is unable to conceive of the possibility of an ethical historical future and consequently must think the possibility of messianic peace as beyond the totality that is history itself.

Radical theology, on the other hand, is fully historical or actual, though it is so only through its realization of the atonement of God with God. In this absolute atonement, which is absolute because it is both a final absolution and an absolution occurring within the Absolute itself, the future becomes actual in time and space by becoming present and not merely promised. Thus does the Godhead, having predestined the horizon of the future, also retain the element of newness, a *novum* that allows for the possibility of the unforeseen, of surprise, of what Levinas knows as the messianic and Nietzsche as the *Übermensch*.

Theologically interpreted, the *Übermensch* is the future "one" who overcomes the bad conscience of guilt and embodies the redemption from sin. But the *Übermensch* is not a singular, unique individual, a new or rather second-come Christ. Paralleling Levinas's reconception of the One as the social multiple, the *Übermensch* is the eschatological possibility for each and every individual ("Here Comes Everybody," as Joyce writes), but only for those who are capable of realizing the full grace of freedom and freedom of grace that permits this possibility. Thus, this "one" is the actualization of the absolutely free will who is able to be ethical as a consequence of willing the overcoming of the negative, reactive will of the bad conscience. This overcoming is therefore self-overcoming and possible only by affirming the death of God which alone allows for a complete release from such a conscience and thus from the psychological nihilism of guilt and *ressentiment*. In order to accomplish this an active sense of the will is needed. But this active willing can only be effected through an active negating of the reactive will. The affirmation of the death of God is also the affirmation of the death of the traditionally construed subject, a subject that is ultimately called forth in Hegel and made manifest as the transcendent Godhead. This is the God that finally dies in Nietzsche's thinking, making possible the dissipation of every previously known "will" or "self-centeredness." And while this is the nihilistic moment par excellence, this is now a nihilism that makes possible a fully actual nothingness, the groundless ground that is the fullness of redemptive liberation, the prophesied "promised land."

Far from construing guilt as mere paralysis of the will, in a move paralleling that of Dostoevsky, who Nietzsche writes is the only person who taught him anything about human psychology, Altizer interprets the guilt associated with the bad conscience as a calling forth of responsibility. Here Levinas and Altizer are in full accord. And even though Levinas explicitly declares that his conception of ethical responsibility neither assumes the form of orthodox Christian charity, or pity, nor resembles the guilt of original sin,[15] we are nevertheless "hostage" to it. Does this position, however, necessarily contradict the radical theological standpoint that revaluates the "original sin" as God's own sin for which God atones by dying the ultimate death but thereby also condemns us to death as its unavoidable dangerous consequence? From the perspective of a primordial ethics, one always falls short of one's infinite ethical obligation; the self is never able to do enough for the Other. "Peace then is under my responsibility. I am a hostage, for I am alone to wage it, running a fine risk, dangerously."[16] That is why Levinas claims, "of peace there can only be an eschatology."[17] But like Nietzsche and Altizer, Levinas too appeals to Dostoevsky in support of this position: "We are always guilty before the other and none more than I."[18] In the pivotal notion of responsibility eschatological ethics and apocalyptic ethics coincide. Is not the preoriginary sense of responsibility for the other perceived by Levinas as the ethical command revealed in and as the trace of the Infinite, or God, the same as the very command self-imposed by God on God to assume responsibility for the "evil" of a wholly alienating otherness? In God's self-sacrifice, the responsibility is completely assumed, taking the form of absolute *kenosis* out of an abiding compassion and concern for the world, and the sin of absolute sovereign transcendence fully atoned for. This is precisely the self-atonement of God, which makes possible the overcoming of such guilt and the reconciliation of the opposites good and evil.

God's atoning sacrifice, however, is not the release from ethical responsibility on our part. It is in fact the very opposite. Now responsibility is wholly ours alone, made both possible as apocalyptic ethics knows and impossible as eschatological ethics reveals. The issue is not the status of the totality, the domain of freedom, as both Altizer and Levinas would agree. The issue is rather the status of the "beyond." In absolute atonement, the beyond itself is transfigured. The archic becomes the telic, the past and the future merge as the present here and now. Hegel could know this dialectically and portray infinity, now comprehended as infinite time-space, as a circle, and moreover as a "circle of circles,"[19] but this is a solely conceptual move. Nietzsche's vision of eternal recurrence releases the teleological constraint of this purely conceptual movement of return and transfigures the circle as the concrete spiraling movement of eternal recurrence. Could the same be said regarding Levinas's identification of the "curvature of intersubjective space"?[20] No longer the primordial plenum, the transcendent God, could the beyond now be construed as the horizon of the future wherein all movement is forward and irreversible? Could the ethical command of the preoriginary past be retained as the trace of memory but now wholly present and actual as the project into the future? Eschatological ethics knows this projection as fecundity, as does apocalyptic ethics, and therefore as the source of both possibility and hope. The death of God alone makes this actual, and without its affirmation all ethics remain empty and illusory.

Like Jesus' proclamation that the "kingdom of God is at hand" for the "children of God," Nietzsche's vision of the *Übermenschen*, the "children of the future" (*Kinder der Zukunft*),[21] is both apocalyptic and eschatological. It is apocalyptic in the sense that this future is actual, here and now, not remote and beyond realization. It is eschatological in that its final form is necessarily undetermined, being the embodiment of a truly free will. In this sense it is "beyond good and evil," "beyond being." The element of undecidability in this conception of the beyond points toward a new absolute alterity, as it stands outside the ability of a knowing reason to grasp the moment of its realization. This realization is now the task of the truly affirmative will to power.

Is it now a matter of calling forth the will that can aspire to the heights of responsibility demanded in all ethical relationships, a responsiveness to the pleas of the other that is not contingent on a reciprocal response? The infinite obligation imposed on the subject by the other in eschatological ethics assumes the guise of ethical responsibility to the point of "substitution," of "one-for-the-other."[22] Is this the very same sense of obligation that Jesus invokes when he proclaims that no greater love has one for another than that one's life is given for another? Is this the very action of atonement that occurs in the incarnation and crucifixion and thus in the Godhead itself? Levinas writes in a statement that captures the essence of his ethical metaphysics, "The absolutely other is the other person."[23] This reveals a fundamentally apocalyptic insight, even if it is unrecognized as such by Levinas, but it also parallels in a remarkable way the principal ethical commandment of Jesus. In confronting the Pharisees, who, in seeking to trap him on some theological point, ask him what is the greatest of the commandments, Jesus replies that it is to love God above all else and to love your neighbor as yourself; in this all the laws and teachings of the prophets are contained.[24] In other words, the only access to the absolutely other is through ethical responsibility to the other person—the neighbor, and even more, to the stranger. Is this not the crux of the parable of the good Samaritan? Is this the same as what Altizer identifies as an expression of "apocalyptic morality," of service as the embodiment of strength?

> This is the praxis which Nietzsche could know as being called forth in the Sermon on the Mount, and while this is the purest of all slave moralities, it is simultaneously a noble morality, and the only noble morality which the mature Nietzsche could affirm. Yet this is a noble morality which is an apocalyptic morality, one inseparable from the immediate Kingdom of God, and if that kingdom is truly a self-emptying kingdom, embodying a Godhead which is the crucifixion or the sacrifice of God, it is that sacrifice which is "blessedness" itself, and a blessedness which is finally the only reality. Yes, Nietzsche could name this reality as Eternal Recurrence, or even name it as *the Will to Power, but that is a power which is the very opposite of what we commonly know as the will to power, and is so as a sacrificial or self-emptying power, and precisely thereby absolute power itself* [emphasis mine].[25]

Nietzsche philosophically shatters the I-ego of traditional conceptions of the will in the affirmation of the eternal recurrence by and as the will to power. This power belongs to the individual of truly affirmative will, who is both liberated and bound, redeemed and damned, gifted and cursed equally by life and death, precisely through the knowledge of the death of God, which alone makes possible a renewed, revalued interpretation of existence. The nihilism that both belies and issues forth from the death of God is addressed ethically by the will that joyfully affirms life as eternal recurrence.

Only the noble individual is capable of such joyful willing and of the "active forgetting"[26] requisite to rise above and beyond *ressentiment*. Here is precisely where Nietzsche advances the ethics of Jesus, the ethics almost immediately reversed by the so-called apostle Paul, who could not forget the manner in which Jesus died, so he turned, says Nietzsche, what was a necessary death into the cosmological resurrection, but now a resurrection for only the "elect," the chosen few. For the majority, however, this new salvation scenario is the ultimate cosmological nightmare, resulting in the supreme form of *ressentiment*—the "last judgment."[27] And how could such a judgment occur if there were not something to damn for all eternity? So it is that the notion of the immortal soul, that "little more," the cornerstone of orthodox theology, is arguably the most dangerous and subtle attempt to eradicate the possibility of a noble humanity, those who realize that the "kingdom of God is at hand."

The eternal recurrence points toward a new language distinct from the historical language of both philosophy and theology. Instead of saying No to time and the world, the eternal recurrence invites the great Yes, and in such a saying absolves humanity from the paralyzing reactive will of the guilty conscience and *ressentiment*. This is the eschatological apocalyptic ground of Jesus' ethics. "In the whole psychology of the 'evangel' the concept of guilt and punishment is lacking: also the concept of reward," writes Nietzsche. "'Sin'—any distance separating God and man—is abolished: *precisely this is the 'glad tidings.'* Blessedness is not promised, it is not tied to conditions: it is the only reality—the rest is a sign with which to speak of it."[28] The state of "blessedness" is the truly affirmative will, which alone is capable of active forgetting over and beyond mere forgiveness, the strength and ability not to carry the injustices of the past into the present-future as a feeling of *ressentiment*. To do this, however, it is necessary to affirm the eternal recurrence as the outcome of the death of God. Nietzsche writes that "the will cannot will backwards,"[29] but the will's liberation, its very redemption, lies precisely in its ability to look back into the past and to affirm time and its passage, and to look forward and into itself and to affirm itself as willing that passage. The fallen, enslaved, reactive will of orthodoxy cannot will backwards, but the purely active apocalyptic will can. This is what Zarathustra prophetically calls upon the individuals of the future to do. Only because God is dead is the will now so empowered. With regard to praxis, the question now is, "How shall this be brought about? Who could teach [one] also to will backwards?"[30]

The concept of atonement is integral toward realizing and articulating this "new" ethical "ground." According to Altizer, this ground is the will to power and is synonymous with Christianity's naming of the absolute will of God (*GG* 120). Could this conception of will to power be the concrete expression of absolute atonement, at once apocalyptic and eschatological, primordial and futural, predestined and free, object and subject, other and self—in other words, "absolute power"? Could it be that only from the standpoint of this "new unity" is consciousness finally able to articulate the absolute coincidence of the ethics of freedom and the freedom of ethics? Here the will to power is now the will to ethics. Is this ethics an actual apocalyptic eschatological ethics, then, an ethics of self-overcoming, an ethics wherein power and passivity are reversed, and through this reversal are joined together, atoned, as *coincidentia oppositorum*?

The death of God as the promise of eschatology fulfilled apocalyptically: Only through a realization of the originary instance of atonement, without which all other examples of atonement remain but relative expressions, and which, from the standpoint of radical theology, alone is absolute because it is the atonement that occurs within Godhead itself, is this possible. Herein lies the basis for any revalued notion of "ground" for a theologically articulated conception of ethics in the wake of the death of God.

## NOTES

1. Thomas J. J. Altizer, "Apocalypticism and Modern Thinking," *Journal for Christian Theological Research* 2:2 (1997): http://apu.edu/~CTRF/articles/1997_articles/altizer.html, §26.

2. Ibid., §5.

3. While not the same by definition, revelation and disclosedness (in the Heideggerian sense of *Unverborgenheit*) are both present in radical theology. Insofar as radical theology is scripturally grounded, the aspect of prophetic revelation is in full play. However, the continuance of revelatory significance is predicated on the actualized embodiment of the truth content of revelation.

This embodiment is history itself, in which truth is fully dynamic and in process (again, similar to the Heideggerian interpretation of the Greek term alêtheia as the endless movement of revealing and concealing, later construed as Ereignis, the appropriating event of being). The dual significance of unveiling is possible only with the death of God. From a traditional theological perspective, which retains the classic thesis of the metaphysical transcendence of God the Father, revelation remains the operative mode of the deity's self-expression and manifestation. Modern philosophy, basing itself solely on the evidences of reason, has for the most part necessarily eschewed the devices and claims of prophetic revelation, thereby looking to truth from the vantage of disclosedness, thinking it to be fully present. This is the very notion of presence criticized by Heidegger and others as a cornerstone of ontotheological metaphysics, the same metaphysics rejected by radical theology.

4. Excerpt of a personal correspondence from Thomas Altizer to Brian Schroeder dated May 1, 2000.

5. Emmanuel Levinas, *Totality and Infinity*, trans. Alphonso Lingis (Pittsburgh: Duquesne University Press, 1969), 22 f.

6. Altizer writes of *kenosis* that "while as a noun this word is not found in the New Testament, its correlative verb occurs in Philippians 2:7, 'emptied himself,' in which Paul says that Christ 'though he was in the form of God, did not count equality with God as a thing to be grasped, but emptied himself, taking the form of a servant, being born in the likeness of men'" (NA 67).

7. Altizer stands at the forefront of contemporary theological discourse in addressing this relationship, inquiring twenty years ago now: "Is it possible that a uniquely twentieth-century Jewish witness will bring the whole tradition of modern Christianity to an end, and thereby make possible a new Christian beginning?" (Thomas J. J. Altizer, "History as Apocalypse," in *Deconstruction and Theology*, ed. Carl Raschke [New York: Crossroad Publishing, 1982)], 151). Considering the influence of Hegel and Nietzsche on recent Jewish thought, Altizer locates the Lurianic Kabbalistic undertones of deconstruction and determines that, while eschewing the death of God, much contemporary Jewish thinking nevertheless affirms the nihilistic impulse and actuality of late modern or postmodern thought.

8. For a fuller development of this point, see Brian Schroeder, *Altared Ground: Levinas, History, and Violence* (New York & London: Routledge, 1995), 141–144.

9. "The eschatological, as the 'beyond' of history, draws beings out of the jurisdiction of history and the future; it arouses them in and calls them forth to their full responsibility. Submitting history as a whole to judgment, exterior to

the very wars that mark its end, it restores to each instant its full signification in that very instant: all the causes are ready to be heard. It is not the last judgment that is decisive, but the judgment of all the instants in time, when the living are judged. The eschatological notion of judgment (contrary to the judgment of history in which Hegel wrongly saw its rationalization) implies that beings have an identity 'before' eternity, before the accomplishment of history, before the fullness of time, while there is still time; implies that beings exist in relationship, to be sure, but on the basis of themselves and not on the basis of the totality. . . . The first 'vision' of eschatology (hereby distinguished from the revealed opinions of positive religions) reveals the very possibility of eschatology, that is, the breach of the totality, the possibility of a *signification without a context*" (Levinas, *Totality and Infinity*, 23).

10. See Daniel 5:27.

11. Friedrich Nietzsche, *The Antichrist*, in *The Portable Nietzsche*, trans. and ed. Walter Kaufmann (New York: Random House, 1954), §18.

12. Thomas J. J. Altizer, "Nietzsche and Apocalypse," *New Nietzsche Studies* 4, 3–4 (2000–2001): 10.

13. Ibid.

14. On the difference between a radical theological and neopagan reading of the death of God in Nietzsche, see Brian Schroeder, "Blood and Stone: A Response to Altizer and Lingis," *New Nietzsche Studies* 4, 3–4 (2000–2001): 29–41.

15. Emmanuel Levinas, *Otherwise than Being or Beyond Essence*, trans. Alphonso Lingis (The Hague: Martinus Nijhoff, 1978), 121.

16. Ibid., 166.

17. Levinas, *Totality and Infinity*, 24.

18. See Emmanuel Levinas, *Time and the Other*, trans. Richard A. Cohen (Pittsburgh: Duquesne University Press, 1987), 108; "Transcendence and Evil," in *Collected Philosophical Papers*, trans. and ed. Alphonso Lingis (Dordrecht: Martinus Nijhoff, 1987), 168; *Ethics and Infinity*, trans. Richard A. Cohen (Pittsburgh: Duquesne University Press, 1985), 98, 101.

19. G. W. F. Hegel, *Science of Logic*, trans. A. V. Miller (New York: Humanities Press, 1969), 842; also, *Phenomenology of Spirit*, trans. A. V. Miller (Oxford: Oxford University Press, 1977), §18.

20. "This surplus of truth over being and over its idea, which we suggest by the metaphor of the 'curvature of intersubjective space,' signifies the divine intention of all truth. This 'curvature of space' is, perhaps, the very presence of God" (Levinas, *Totality and Infinity*, 293).

21. Friedrich Nietzsche, *The Gay Science*, trans. Walter Kaufmann (New York: Vintage, 1974), 338.

22. Cf. Levinas, *Otherwise than Being*, 99–103.

23. Levinas, *Totality and Infinity*, 39.

24. Matthew 22:37–39; Mark 12:29–31; Luke 10:27.

25. Altizer, "Nietzsche and Apocalypse," 10.

26. Friedrich Nietzsche, *On the Genealogy of Morals*, trans. Walter Kaufmann and R. J. Hollingdale (New York: Vintage Books, 1967), §1.

27. "The Redeemer type, the doctrine, the practice, the death, the meaning of the death, even what came after the death—nothing remained untouched, nothing remained even similar to the reality. Paul simply transposed the center of gravity of that whole existence—in the *lie* of the 'resurrected' Jesus. At bottom, he had no use at all for the life of the Redeemer—he needed the death on the cross *and* a little more" (Nietzsche, *The Antichrist*, §42).

28. Ibid., §33.

29. Friedrich Nietzsche, *Thus Spoke Zarathustra*, in *The Portable Nietzsche*, "On Redemption" II, §20.

30. Ibid.

❧❧

# CHAPTER 6

# Crucifixion and Alterity

## Pathways to Glory in the Thought of Altizer and Levinas

### EDITH WYSCHOGROD

I s it possible to wend one's way errantly from the christological apocalyptic theology of Altizer to the ethical metaphysics of Emmanuel
Levinas's rabbinically inspired thought? Does Levinas not routinely
dissociate himself from death of God theologies? And who can approach
the texts of Altizer without terror, a terror that is the *Stimmung* through
which an ineliminable nothingness that infiltrates the I AM of God's biblical self-assertion must be read? But is there not also a terror before the
demand that Levinas sees as placed upon the passive self by the Other,
who simply by virtue of her alterity always already commands me to de-
sist from violence. And might there not be a certain violence in proscription itself? I shall envisage their responses as texts in transit from one
to another.

Consider first the theological nothingness of Altizer, an apocalyptic
nothingness of the biblical I AM, not a sempiternal nothingness that is
ultimately overcome, but an ineliminable NOT embedded in transcendence itself. Pierced by it, wounded in its ownness, I AM is always already infiltrated by the nothingness that is its obverse. An ontological
sublation of this nothingness in a Plotinian or Damascian plenum is
ruled out if there is to be more than an undifferentiated and static
whole. Similarly, the historical overcoming of negation through its sublation in a Hegelian Absolute *kommt nicht zur Frage* in that, as Altizer

contends, historical thinking for Hegel becomes pure thinking, thus subordinating the historicality of existence.

What then is one to make of Altizer's pure apocalypticism, of a theology that proclaims: "But I AM is simultaneously I AM NOT, a simultaneity which is the source of absolute otherness, and the source of absolute otherness at the very center of itself, an otherness which is an essential and intrinsic otherness, and therefore an otherness which is not and cannot be either open to or an embodiment of a polar harmony or coinherence" (*GA* 108).

Consider next Altizer's claim that fall and apocalypse are the realization of a *felix culpa*: without the fall there would be no incarnation (*GA* 110), a route already mapped by Paul Tillich in his assertion that fully developed creatureliness is fallen creatureliness, that creation and fall coincide.[1] Are we then to envision Altizer's view as the theological adumbration of an astrophysical black hole, in which what had been world collapses into emptiness? To reply affirmatively is to forget that Altizer is a profoundly christological thinker whose most recent elaborations of the contemporary envisagements of Jesus show the relation between apocalypse and Crucifixion: the death of Jesus is an apocalyptic death (*CJ* xiv). The advent of Jesus inaugurates an unprecedented aeon, a new time that is a "full coming together of . . . total ending and total beginning, and the opposites of a totally old world or aeon and a totally new aeon or world" (*CJ* xiv). The dawning of the new age initiates a split between the "apocalyptic totality" and the "old world," one that is presaged by an expectancy that challenges all assurance. Such a contemporary Jesus is a renewal of the "original" Jesus who is, in Altizer's view, revived in the epic and poetic traditions of Western literature from Dante to Milton, from Blake to Joyce. In the manner of Kierkegaard, Altizer resists Christendom's repeated rejections of these incursions, which it fails to recognize.

It is negation read as the apocalyptic dimension of the crucifixion that leads Altizer to his appreciative reading of an early and crucial challenge to Christianity and one of the most persistent, Arianism, the rejection of the full divinity of Christ.

The actuality of the crucified one, the one who is the subject of pain and suffering, wends its way errantly in the history of doctrine and is attested in its reemergence in this 1999 letter circulated by a group of German Christians, the Evangelisher Stadtkirchenverband Koeln:

*Wir geben zu bedenken ob man die ueberlieferte und gewoehnlich gebrauchte trinitararische doxologie Formel der Liturgie "Ehre sei dem Vater und dem Sohn un dem Heilegen Geist" nicht folgendermassen abwandeln koennte: "Ehre sei dem Vater durch den Sohn im Heilegen Geist."*

We offer for thought whether the traditional and customary trinitarian doxological formula of the liturgy, "Glory be to the Father, the Son and the Holy Spirit" could not be modified as follows, "Glory be to the Father through the Son in the Holy Spirit" [translation mine][2]

On this interpretation, the Son is the passageway to the Father but not identical with him.

Although the principal thesis of the doctrine is commended, Arianism is insufficiently radical in that the crucified Jesus cannot, in Altizer's view, be thought apart from the total *kenosis* of the Godhead. It is precisely in this Patripassian gesture, in this total self-emptying of the Godhead, that Altizer envisages an immanence through which the Godhead becomes more deeply itself. It is worth attending closely to the implications of this claim: For Altizer, the version of early medieval Christianity that apprehends Christ as an epiphany of heavenly glory nullifies the pain and pathos of incarnation itself. Thus, absolute glory in the medieval sense is a reversal of incarnation, which in our time undergoes another reversal, one "releasing that glory in the actuality of the world" (*GA* 116). But, despite a certain sympathetic reading of the Arian position—perhaps a response to the pain and wounding of human flesh—Altizer must ultimately accept the drama of the death of God contained only in the Chalcedonian formula: "Christ is truly God and truly man." Without this claim the meaning of the cross is divested of its power.

## SUFFERING FOR THE OTHER

It is precisely the invocation of a death that is actual and the reworking of the concept of 'glory' so that it is attributable to the suffering Christ that brings together the christological apocalyptic of Altizer and the rabbinism of Emmanuel Levinas's account of God and the suffering Other. In a paper, "A Man-God," delivered during the week of Catholic Intellectuals in 1968, which constitutes a rare and respectful foray into christological speculation, Levinas adumbrates the meaning of the suffering Christ. Levinas reflects on the "idea of a self-inflicted humiliation on the part of the Supreme Being, of a descent of the Creator to the level of the Creature" and on "the idea of expiation for others, that is of a substitution."[3] In a remarkable essay on this theme, "Substitution," Levinas declares that one always already stands accused by the sheer existence of the other prior to any decision or activity. The self thus described is not that of consciousness, which always reassumes itself in acts of self-reflection, but an absolutely passive interiority, anarchic and self-accusatory. This self is free of "the postulates of ontological thinking, where eternal being assumes what it undergoes" and is instead obsessed with responsibilities.[4] This claim can only be stated in terms of a nonbeing that is lived as "the burden of bearing the misery and failure of the other," a nonbeing that is not sheer nothingness but is rather a divestiture of self to the point of becoming hostage for the Other.

In a gloss on Milton's *Paradise Lost*, Altizer describes the lineaments of one of Jesus' many personae, the Protestant Jesus, and arrives at a complex figural rendering, a text to which, it might be said, Levinas's account of the transcendental conditions of ethics is in transit. Altizer sees the death of God as God's self-sacrifice, "a kenotic emptying that is the embodiment of total compassion, the love that is finally the deepest depths of actuality itself" (*CJ* 137). Jesus as a man-for-other-men can be seen as a figure of Levinasian substitution, for is not sacrificial love that is fully and totally lived as *caritas* what is meant by substitution?

But here one must be circumspect. For Altizer the compassion that constitutes the depths of actuality in its apocalyptic embodiment is an embodiment that is also a realization of a union of Christ with Satan. It could be argued that the ethical stance of Levinas is anomic, a self-emptying prior to law, whereas Altizer's merger with Satan has profound antinomian implications. While caution is required in positing affinities, one must also first inquire, "Who is Altizer's Satan?" to which Altizer's reply is, "*Satan* is the Christian name of an absolutely alien power—the deepest depth of a 'Selfhood' that is the alien and fallen Creator" (*CJ* 137). If it is Selfhood in the divine life that is Satan, the Godhead itself is subject to the demand of self-divestiture. Depicted as an intradivine drama, the death of God is an immolation of self, the emptying of a divine and transcendent self and a death that is actualized in the death of Jesus as a sacrifice of absolute compassion. Is not the sacrifice of the divine, of the Creator God, the very principle of active creation in Altizer's account, replicated in Levinas's deontologizing of the subject and in his refusal to identify the primordial conditions of an Ethics of ethics with human spontaniety, cognition, or production?

The difficulty of a too easy conflation of Levinasian and Altizerian selflessness lies in Levinas's acute suspicion of a self-divestiture that is also an appropriation. For Altizer, Satan is intrinsic to the divine life and must rearise in what, for Levinas, would appear to be a perpetual reemergence of the Dionysian, a glorying in rather than a lamenting of the antinomian in the world of history and polity. For Levinas, transcendence enters the human world only as a trace or track of a divine life that has, in his terms, always already passed by and thus can never be apprehended but is inscribed in the human other.

It could be argued that if for Altizer the nothingness fissuring the divine life is a redemptive nothingness, Apocalypse is transmuted into Messianism, Messianism into Apocalypse. All this comes about in and through a cruciform brokenness that attests both a human and a cosmological Christ. In one of the most powerful passages of post–Barthian Protestant theology, Altizer writes: "This cosmos is the resurrected Christ, but a resurrected Christ who is inseparable and indistinguishable from the crucified Christ, for now the Christ of glory *is* the Christ of passion. So it is that the body of Christ can only be a dark and broken body, but it is a body that is present in all the immediacy of an unformed and primordial matter, as a totally fallen body now realizes itself in the pure immediacy of world" (*HA* 254).

For Altizer, identifying primordial matter with the Christ of the passion is bound up with his assertion of the identity of genesis and apocalypse. It would seem that nothing could be further removed from Levinas's analysis of ipseity and substitution. In describing the way in which the ego is in itself, Levinas denies that it is in itself as matter insofar as matter is wedded to form, but, he goes on to say, the ego is in itself like "matter weighing on itself . . . conceal[ing] a materiality more material than all matter."[5] If Altizer and Levinas can yet again be imagined as texts in transit, as engaged in reciprocal acts of reading, could we not discern in the ipseity of Levinas, Altizer's vision of matter prior to creation, the nothingness of genesis that is not nothing? For Altizer, matter before creation is linked to the undoing of corporeality in the brokenness of the crucifixion, whereas for Levinas preoriginary matter is bound up with the self's passivity and subjection to the Other.

In Altizer's view, the shattered body of the crucifixion reveals itself in the immediacy of the word, whereas for Levinas the one who is for the Other is attested in the preoriginary vocation of language, the immediacy of a primordial Saying that is prior to propositional language. I cannot enter into the complex relation of an apophatic Saying to propositional language, to the said, but am merely claiming that the immediacy of the word of Altizer's Protestant Christ can be reread as a word that is not yet logos but is manifested in the brokenness of the body as an apophatic word.

## THE ANONYMOUS SUBJECT

It is just this apophasis beyond propositional truth that characterizes what Levinas calls "persecuted truth," a truth that he finds in the thought of Kierkegaard. Wary at first of the invocation of Kierkegaardian subjectivity as a perennial response to German idealism, Levinas considers Kierkegaard's legacy as one of "exhibitionistic, immodest subjectivity." Critical also of Kierkegaard's treatment of God as the God above ethics in the narrative of Abraham's sacrifice of Isaac, he argues that, for Kierkegaard, the universal traduces subjectivity, the I's secret. Kierkegaard's mistake is his identification of the ethical with the universal rather than with the Other who places an inescapable responsibility upon the self that resists generality. Yet Levinas perceives that what is signficant in Kierkegaard is not only that, as for Descartes, doubt goes all the way down but that doubt cannot be overcome in that it is intrinsic to truth. Doubt and truth are not related to one another as certainty to uncertainty but rather as "truth triumphant and truth persecuted."[6] On this interpretation of Kierkegaardian skepticism, Levinas can question the possibility of revelation itself in that it purports to deliver transcendental truth. Because such truth can show itself only in and as persecuted truth, he adds a point that is of considerable consequence for a reading of Altizer: "One may wonder whether the *incognito* should not be the very mode of revelation and the truth which has been said should not also appear as something about which nothing has been said."[7]

Altizer sees in the provocation of Kierkegaard a radical transformation of subjectivity, the disintegration of the subject as a center of self-consciousness in which radical alterity has been sublated and recognized as belonging to the subject. In our own time, he proclaims, this sublation of consciousness has opened the way for an unprecedented anonymity. In conformity with the descriptions of this new world as a culture of the spectacle according to Guy Debord, or as a world of simulacra in the language of Jean Baudrillard, Altizer maintains: "A new 'electronic' humanity is now manifest as postmodernity, a humanity whose depth is indistinguishable from its surface or mask, . . . anonymous . . . because it is a nameless humanity" (*CJ* 187).

That the world is undergoing an unprecedented change in the conception of being and truth as they have come to be understood by the information culture and as reflected in the language of biological research is by now a truism. This new conception can be condensed in the Pythagorean formula: the world is made of number. The body is quintessentially its coded genetic structure; knowledge is transportable information currently encoded as 1 and 0. If the real itself has been "virtualized," does it then follow that the phenomenality of the suffering body can be manifested only as a virtual body? And if there is nothing other than virtuality, this could not be known in that our ontological categories would have been transformed.

In sum, can the corporeal brokenness of the crucified one provide what Altizer might call a "post-Christian" response to this neo-Pythagorean volatilization of the body? What is crucial for Altizer are the implications of the ending of self-consciousness for a new christology, one that heralds an anonymous Jesus and of the relation of Jesus to a new anonymous humanity. It is Kierkegaard who, on Altizer's reading, saw the reciprocal coinherence in a single event of the dissolution of a unique and singular self-consciousness and the death of God, a complex of conditions that can only be described as the advent of a pure and total anonymity.

It might be thought that there is little to connect Levinasian ipseity, the nonsubject of persecuted truth, with Altizer's anonymous humanity, that in fact one might more fruitfully compare this emergent apocalyptic totality with Levinas's account of totality, understood as the organization of history, economy, and polity, each manifesting its own mode of being and unified into a cognizable aggregate. Often seen as derived from Franz Rosenzweig's view of the sociopolitical whole, Levinas's depiction of totality can also be linked to descriptions of the dislocations of mass society by Marcel, Heidegger, and others. But Altizer is too subtle a thinker simply to equate postmodern anonymity with the homogeneity ascribed to mass society by midcentury existential philosophers. To be sure, for Altizer totality denotes the dissolution of interiority and of the natural and sacred worlds (*CJ* 203), but the abyssal anonymity thus generated is precisely a *divine* abyss, the abyss of crucifixion itself.

Could one not envisage a Levinasian reading of Altizer's account of anonymity as depicting an ipseity divested of own-being, that is no longer an egoity but has become an anonymous self? Does not Levinas contend that, shorn of distinction, the identity of ipseity is "not due to any kind of distinguishing characteristic . . . like fingerprints, and which as a principle of individuation would win for this identity a proper noun and a place in speech?"[8] Is Altizer's anonymity then not a simulacrum of the Levinasian incognito through which persecuted truth disguises itself, and conversely, is Altizer's anonymous humanity not a mask of this persecuted truth? Thus Altizer writes that an apocalyptic Christ is "the ending of any possible Christ who is Christ and only Christ, . . . the ending of a Christ who is nameable as Christ" (*GA* 181). Both Levinas and Altizer insist that concealment does not mean a turning away from the world but rather, for Levinas, a deeper engagment with the Other who is not part of the world and, for Altizer, a disappearance of otherness insofar as the otherness of modernity is an otherness of and within the self.

We have seen that when the notion of the real itself is under attack, putting into question the phenomenality of the suffering body, the phenomenality of the suffering body can be manifested only as virtual, and, if there is anything beyond virtuality, it would transcend our ontological categories. Yet from the standpoint of Levinasian alterity, does not a certain prescriptiveness still attach to the Other's body because it is the body that feels pain? Must the Other not be her or his body as the "owner" of her or his pain? For Levinas, the body of the Other is flesh and blood but, at the same time, proscriptive and prescriptive discourse, the prohibition against violence and the prescription of responsibility for another.[9] For Altizer, the crucified body enters the specular stream, the stream of images to speak the language of pain without speaking.

## THE TROUBLE WITH IMAGES

We have seen that Altizer's account of the anonymous Jesus as the Jesus of a truly universal body is an envisioning of this body in terms of a new electronic virtuality, a culture of images. For Levinas there lurks a deepseated suspicion of images grounded both in Judaism's aniconic tradition and in his critique of knowledge as based upon the model of vision, in that seeing dominates what it sees and cannot provide a model for ethics. To grasp the difference between older accounts of the image and the radically new virtualization of phenomena as spectacle, a brief historical excursus into the meaning of images is warranted.

Consider first Maimonides's description of the fear of images in relation to the unity and incorporeality of the divine nature, elements of
which persist in Levinas's thought.[10] So important are these attributes of
God for Maimonides that his *Guide for the Perplexed* opens with a proclamation and defense of this idea. Struck by the biblical claim that God
makes man in his image (Hebrew: *zelem* [Gen. 1:26]), Maimonides is
driven to reinterpret the term *zelem*, the form or shape of a thing, so as
to preclude its applying to anything material. If the form of God and
man are homologous and the term "form" entails corporeality as is generally assumed, then it might be concluded that denying God form and
shape entails denying his existence. But, says Maimonides, the Hebrew
term *toar* is used for form in its ordinary acceptation, whereas *zelem* signifies essence. Thus "the specific form, [is] that which constitutes the
essence of a thing, whereby the thing is what it is; the reality of a thing in
so far as it is that particular being."[11] Thus interpreted, the biblical depiction of a theophanic event is made to conform to Aristotle's account of
human form and that of his Mu'tazilite interpreters: what constitutes the
essence of human beings, their form, is intellectual perception. Although
there is virtually no vestige of Maimonidean rationalism in Levinas's
thought, Maimonides's aniconicity persists.

For Maimonides then, the most serious theological error consists in
the imputation of corporeality to God, an error that undergirds idolatry,
the attribution of mediating agency to a particular form that is thought
to represent God to his creatures.[12] These errors are precipitated by the
unfettering of a figural imagination required by ordinary mortals in order
to render theological truths accessible but which disfigure this truth
through figuration itself. But figuration does not leave the proscenium
quietly, in that Maimonides concedes that prophecy requires the imaginative as well as the logical faculty, even if the rational faculty predominates.

Levinas allows himself to speak of the Other as "an epiphany," given
"in expression, the sensible, still graspable, [that] turns into total resistance to the grasp."[13] The face that for Levinas is a central figure of his
thought is to be read as proscribing a violence that expresses itself within
sensibility but does so as a powerlessness that fissures the sensible. Thus
Levinas: "The presence [of the other] consists in *divesting* himself of the
form which nevertheless manifests him. His manifestation is a surplus beyond the inevitable paralysis of manifestation. It is that which expresses
the formula: the face speaks. . . . To speak is before all else this manner of
coming from behind his appearance, from behind his form, an opening

in the opening" (translation mine).[14] For Levinas, the face disconnected from iconicity is in the track or trace of transcendence. Neither an image nor an intraworldly discursive sign, the trace disturbs the order of the world, means without meaning to mean. "It intervenes in a way so subtle that it already withdraws unless we retain it."[15] Far from yielding an essence of the human or a universal moral law as a distillate of faciality, the face transcends images, remains exterior to them. The form both reveals and conceals, but the proscriptive power of the face is not lodged in the form.

The insistence upon divine incorporeality is continued in medieval Christian descriptions of divine perfection. Of importance in the present context is Aquinas's contention that bodies cannot be noble and that God as the most noble of beings cannot be corporeal. Like Maimonides, Aquinas maintains that the biblical claim that humans are made in God's image refers not to corporeal but to intellectual likeness.[16] Because for Aquinas knowledge is a kind of seeing, the suspicion of images requires explanation. Rather than appealing to voice or audition as does Maimonides, Aquinas turns to the mind's eye. For Aquinas, both sensible and intellectual vision require a certain inwardization, "the power of sight and the union of the thing seen with the sight."[17]

The effort to adjudicate these incommensurables, what is seen and the faculty that apprehends it, raises the related question of outside and inside. In the case of physical objects, only the image of the object can be in the seer and not the object *in concreto*. Intellectual insight grasps intellectual objects in their own-being. But how can intellectual insight comprehend the essence of God, which, in the case of God, is his very existence? The superior cannot be comprehended by the inferior. Aquinas concludes: "To see the essence of God there is required some likeness in the visual power, namely the light of glory strengthening the intellect to see God. . . . The essence of God, however, cannot be seen by any created likeness representing the divine essence as it is in itself."[18]

Unlike Maimonides, who appeals to metonymic expansion, Aquinas offers something like a phenomenology of double perception, for we shall see God as we see the life of another as that "which is at once not known by sense, but at once together with sense, by some other cognitive power."[19] Thus divine presence is known by intellect "on the sight of and through corporeal things," as a result of both "the perspicacity of intellect" and "the divine glory" that will affect the body after its final renewal. This doubleness and its sublation enter into Levinas's account of the face not in terms of an opposition between sense and intellect but rather as aniconic shape, figuration that erases itself as it is apprehended, and as "expression" that commands one ethically.

## REREADING GLORY: INCARNATION AND THE INFINITE

How is the divine glory through which Aquinas proclaims one can know God to be conceived? Are we to assume that for Aquinas the Christ of glory can be identified with the figures of glory depicted in the exalted images of the resurrected Christ, and the same can be excoriated by Altizer for their remoteness from the brokenness of the crucified one? Altizer attributes the traducing of the crucifixion, its transformation into a glory that is eternal life, an absolute glory that evades the here and now, to a Christian Gnosticism that is reversed in Aquinas's theology (*GA* 78–79). Despite its stress upon intellectual vision, Altizer argues, Aquinas's philosophy inaugurates a profound shift from Neoplatonic to Aristotelian categories through which glory can be freshly conceived. The image of a distant divine gives way to a present glory that enters into the fabric of the world. Thus, for Altizer, Thomistic ontology is an entering wedge into the ultimate *kenosis* of the Godhead, its full and total immanentization and, as it were, its self-emptying, an emptying that defines the trajectory of his christology. The world of Aquinas, no longer the eternal world of ancient Greek thought, is designated by Altizer as *novitas mundi*,[20] in that Aquinas now can assert what was impossible for Aristotle: "God is the pure Act-of-Being, and this 'act-of-being' is the actuality of being as being," a being that is not the being of thought but of actuality (*HA* 104). Altizer insists that, with Aquinas, existence can finally be celebrated as God's creation, a new glory discovered in the world itself and the body of Christ pictured as a human body that is at the same time the body of God. Altizer concludes that for gnosticized Christianity the divine–human relation was depicted as requiring a derealized corporeality, and this is reversed in the theology of Aquinas. Recall that, for Aquinas, divine presence is known by intellect "on the sight of and through corporeal things," as a result of both "the perspicacity of intellect" and "the divine glory" that will affect the body after its final renewal.

In a surprising move, Levinas too adopts the language of glory, a language that seems bound to sensible intuition, in order to describe not the majesty of God in the apprehension of divine presence but rather the suspension of the conatus to know or do, to become pure receptivity or passivity. Glory depicts a subject who places her or himself at the disposal of the Other and "is but the other face of the passivity of the subject," he insists.[21] Yet far from embodying an intellectual vision in the Thomistic sense, the subject is "a seed of folly, already a psychosis."[22] Open to the point of total defenselessness, the subject who is one for another is described as wholly and unreservedly sincere. Unlike the philosophy of Jean-Paul Sartre, in which sincerity is in bad faith because it imagines that it can, *per impossibile*, be in good faith, Levinas sees sincerity as incapable of dissimulation, scandalizing in its assumption of limitless responsibility. Levinas depicts glory as disrupting the cognitive subject, transcending its intraworldly imbrication in facts and states of affairs, and as opening subjectivity to an excess of Goodness that exceeds intellectual comprehension.

But does not the passive subject run the risk of pride in its very passivity so that passivity reverses itself and becomes active? Thus the subject must remain vigilant, redouble its passivity so that no act could arise from it. Subjectivity must give itself as Saying, by which, it may be recalled, Levinas means discourse prior to predicative language or to essence, the precondition that makes possible the subsequent thematization of language in what is termed "the said." Saying points to the glory of the infinite, an infinite that is always in excess of the thought that attempts to think it, that renders thought moot and resists capture in phenomenality. The glory of the infinite leaves the subject of ethics no place to hide. Responsibility described by midcentury existential philosophy and elaborated in the context of economy and polity requires for Levinas an infinite that is refractory to thought as its precondition. Thus, it could be said that God is encountered in glory, the glory of the infinite that traumatizes egoity, expels the subject from itself as self-presence and that, conversely, glory is the outcome of that trauma, the willingness of the subject to substitute him- or herself for another. "The an-archic identity of the subject," says Levinas, "is flushed out without being able to slip away."[23] The one who in self-giving says to another, "Here I am," placing her or himself at the Other's disposal, bears witness to the infinite. By intertwining transcendence and immanence Levinas is able to assert: "The Infinite does not appear to him that bears witness to it. On the contrary, the witness belongs to the glory of the Infinite." Yet, he goes on to say, "It is by the voice of the witness that the glory of the Infinite is glorified."[24]

In a movement of reversal, in which outside becomes inside, Levinas claims that the exteriority of the infinite is interiorized, a move that would appear to endorse the inwardization roundly condemned elsewhere as mystification. But Levinas sees no contradiction: the infinite is an outside that maintains its exteriority when inwardized, in that glory persists in the internalized infinite as disrupting thematization and "giving sign" to the Other. In a visual metaphor rare in Levinas's accounts of transcendence, the glory of the infinite is described as dazzling and arousing adoration.[25] One might ask whether the glory of the infinite is not a mere pleonasm, in that glory adds nothing to the infinite to which nothing *could* be added. But if glory is Saying, substituting oneself for another, taking responsibility for the Other, proclaiming peace or proscribing violence, and if infinition *is* this process as Levinas thinks, then glory is the dynamism of the infinite. The infinite as epiphany astounds by virtue of the commanding presence of the Other seen as always already at a height. It cannot be the other's destitution that dazzles but rather the imperative force of her or his presence.

## GLORIOUS TIMES

For Levinas, the glory of alterity can be "read" as freeing or absolving one from the time scheme of everyday life and as quotidian time's giving way to a new time of requirement and obligation, an absolutely archaic time of the absolutely transcendent. Yet if the time of transcendence is a past that cannot become present, it can be argued that for Levinas eschatological time does not differ from the archaic past: when past and future are nondifferent, Genesis and Messianism come together.

Is the crucifixion not for Altizer a profoundly Christian account of this self-emptying, the descent into the world of an infinite compassion and a reversal of the lofty images of an etiolated resurrection body uncontaminated by pain? Yet transcendence persists as an absence, a specter that haunts the virtual, as the permeability of beginning and ending to one another. What Altizer writes of this view of time is reminiscent of Levinas's account: "Their respective and contrary identities now appear to be passing into one another, thereby dissolving and erasing the integral and individual identities of both beginning and end" (*HA* 9). Time cannot be comprehended in any linear, previously understood historical sense, but rather as the time of a staging of images, of the volatilization of corporeality, of a world in which the inversion of transcendence has itself suffered an inversion, one whose consequences cannot yet be envisaged.

# NOTES

1. Paul Tillich, *Systematic Theology*, vol. 1 (Chicago: University of Chicago Press, 1951), 255–56.

2. The group that drafted this letter (dated April 1999) is led by German theologian Hans-Georg Link.

3. Emmanuel Levinas, *Entre Nous: On Thinking of the Other*, trans. Michael B. Smith and Barbara Harshav (New York: Columbia University Press, 1998), 53–54.

4. Emmanuel Levinas, *Basic Philosophical Writings*, ed. Adriaan T. Peperzak, Simon Critchley, and Robert Bernasconi (Bloomington: Indiana University Press, 1996), 89.

5. Levinas, *Basic Philosophical Writings*, 86.

6. Emmanuel Levinas, *Proper Names*, trans. Michael B. Smith (London: Athlone, 1996), 77.

7. Ibid., 78.

8. Levinas, *Basic Philosophical Writings*, 84.

9. Robert Gibbs, *Correlations in Rosenzweig and Levinas* (Princeton: Princeton University Press, 1992), 213–16, speaks of the absolute accusative of alterity as a gnawing away at one's own body.

10. An earlier version of several of the following paragraphs on Maimonides's view of images was read at the Enrico Castelli conference, 1998. Held biannually at the University of Rome and organized by Professor Marco Olivetti, these conferences consider issues in the philosophy of religion.

11. Moses Maimonides, *The Guide for the Perplexed*, trans. M. Friedlander (New York: Dover, 1956), 13; reprinted from the second edition, Routledge and Kegan Paul, 1904.

12. Maimonides, *The Guide for the Perplexed*, 51–52.

13. Emmanuel Levinas, *Totality and Infinity*, trans. Alphonso Lingis (Pittsburgh: Duquesne University Press, 1969), 197.

14. Emmanuel Levinas, *En decouvrant l'existence avec Husserl et Heidegger* (Paris: J. Vrin, 1967), 194.

15. Ibid., 208.

16. Thomas Aquinas, *Summa Theologica* I, q. 3, a. 1. Quoted from *Basic Writings of Saint Thomas Aquinas*, ed. Anton Pegis (New York: Random House, 1945).

17. Ibid., I, q. 12, a. 2.

18. Ibid., q. 12, a. 2.

19. Ibid., q. 12, a. 3, reply obj. 2.

20. D. G. Leahy's account of the history of being uses this phrase as the title of a complex tracking of the history of being. See his *Novitas Mundi: Perception of the History of Being* (New York: New York University Press, 1980).

21. Emmanuel Levinas, *Otherwise than Being or Beyond Essence*, trans. Alphonso Lingis (The Hague: Martinus Nijhoff, 1978), 144.

22. Ibid., 142.

23. Ibid., 144.

24. Ibid., 146.

25. Levinas, "Transcendence and Intelligibility," 157.

❦

# CHAPTER 7

# The Diachrony of the Infinite in Altizer and Levinas

*Vanishing without a Trace and the Trace without Vanishing*

### D. G. LEAHY

Nietzsche proclaims the death of God, the absolute fatality of existence. God's fate is the great liberation from all responsibility and from all purpose: radically fragmented totality, a chaotic cosmos, the whole al(l-)together without unity: totality al(l-)together caught up in God's fate. This absolutely radical fatality of being itself begins a new day of being, begins in every now purposeless freedom from responsibility.[1] The divine fatality is nothing but God's infinite nothingness: nothing but the nothingness of God's infinity: nothing but the nothingness of God's very divinity. The death of God is nothing but the abyss. The fatality of being itself—this nothingness—this death of God, which is nothing but nothingness—*this* nothingness of the death of God *is life*—this fatality that is the totality in which each one is—together with all that is past and all that is future—is the radical simultaneity in which all things recur eternally in every new beginning. The truth of the will to power eternally recurring is expressed in Nietzsche's revision of the Cartesian *cogito*, to wit, *vivo ergo cogito*.[2] This derivation of the finite self-consciousness of the *cogito*—the derivation part and parcel of having killed God[3]—indispensable to having murdered the infinite self-consciousness precisely this derivation requires that any subsequent denial of the "no-outside-of-itself" of the exhaustively finite self-consciousness, if it is to be anything more than Nietzsche's "foolery" of speech and "falsehood" of music, must be (impossibly!) not the eternal recurrence of all things, but the *end of the eternal recurrence of all things,* indeed, the absolute inversion of the (Nietzschean) abyss: God's affirmation of death as his very own! Indeed, so it is, not in Nietzsche, but in Altizer! He will have the wisdom of Zarathustra's "buffoons and barrel-organs" beyond the eternally insatiable Nietzschean yearning. Altizer wants the "ecstatic vision" of Zarathustra's talking animals minus the wise old fool's post-Hegelian Kantianism, minus the trace in Nietzsche of Kant's dualism, minus Nietzsche's ultimate refusal of the unity of the totality, minus Zarathustra's own animals' testimony that he, in the end, resigns himself to being enmeshed qua prophet in a "complex of [in effect, inefficient and purposeless] causes."[4] If it is impossible for Zarathustra to give himself uncritically to the deceptions of phenomenal and insubstantial connections, however desirable their reality might be, Altizer insists upon "a breakthrough and a joy which is *clearly* present when we *fully* listen to music" and "*no less* present in the presence of another, but only when that other has *no point of contact* with our own within." Reconstructing Nietzsche's text, Altizer will have those talking animals "celebrate that unity" in which "now *all* identities and *all* events *flow into* one another," and "do so precisely by way of their most immediate actualization: 'Being begins in every Now.'" For Altizer "that actualization is a total actualization, an actualization in which everything whatsoever is totally present, and is present by way of the total release and embodiment of consciousness" (*TP* 79).

For Nietzsche what had occurred was the end of the *other* world: the *other* world ended in the form of the eternal recurrence of all things. In fact, for Nietzsche what had occurred was the end of *all* other worlds. For Altizer, beginning where Nietzsche leaves off, what has occurred is the end of *this* world, indeed, of just this very world: this is the actual apocalyptic nothingness: *this* world ending, in effect, in the *end* of the eternal recurrence of all things. Nietzsche proclaims the end of the life-denying spirit, the end of an alien interiority, the end of reason apart from reality, the end of reason abstracted from concrete life. He writes, in praise of Thucydides and Machiavelli, "Thucydides, and perhaps the *Principe* of Machiavelli, are related to me closely by their unconditional will not to deceive themselves and to see reason in *reality* [*die Vernunft in der Realität*]—not in 'reason,' still less in 'morality.'"[5] But Altizer considers Nietzsche to have "resurrected a chaos of meaninglessness lying deeply buried within the psyche of Western man" (*GCA* 148). The theologian Altizer takes Zarathustra's "vision of Eternal Recurrence" to reflect "a totality of perpetual and meaningless flux" (*GCA* 149). Far beyond Nietzsche, Altizer proclaims the end of the "reason *in* reality," the end of life's very own reason: the end of this world, the demise of the life-affirming spirit: the very death of the eternal self. Utter meaninglessness and spiritual chaos. God's death is God's own doing: God's death is the very form of God's own and absolute affirmation of life! For Altizer, God *is* Jesus, God *is* the Redeemer: the death of God is *self*-sacrifice. And this absolute *self*-sacrifice is the absolute beginning of the apocalypse: absolutely apocalyptic beginning: the absolute triumph of the Kingdom of God (*GG* 182 ff). The death of God is the self-embodiment of God, the end of *all* transcendence: the end of *all* we have known as individual and interior identity. Zarathustra had said: "For me—how could there be an outside-of-me? There is no outside!" For the prophet of the Overman "words and music" are "rainbows and seeming bridges between things eternally separated." For Zarathustra, Altizer's "voice and gesture of another" and his "music" are "foolery" and "falsehood" contrary to the fact that the all-recurrence is *pieces*, indeed, a fatality in which the prophetic yearning for the future uniting of the fragments—through the creative will to power, which would redeem man from all pastness by means of the intoxication of words and song— is itself *finally* but a piece entangled in the "great year" of eternal recurrence. It is precisely at this point that it can be clearly seen that Nietzsche's denial of unity to the totality is, in Peircean terms, the denial of the Second, of the End, indeed, of the Other: the denial of reactive singularity or determinate individuality. In Nietzsche human being is the *particular* that is the *totality*—is *man* (the indefinite 'someone'). Nietzsche explicitly denies unity as the singular, the individual (*der Einzelne, das "Individuum"*).[6] The so-called individual is not a singular, not actually an in-dividual, but rather represents one or the other of the two lines of "man." This partial and representative "individuality" precisely articulates Nietzsche's deep unswerving allegiance to an irreducibly indefinite reality. This vagueness or indefiniteness, from which determinate existence is a sheer abstraction, as are, therefore, responsibility and purpose, is, for Nietzsche, the very logic of reality, the reason *in* reality: the universal and the particular without singularity: wholeness and regularity eternally *without synthesis: absolute indeterminate ordering.*

Nietzsche joins in the dance of life, but explicitly as foolery.[7] This is so because when, in Nietzsche, the Infinite vanishes, it does so not without a trace. That trace is the trace in Nietzsche of Kant's dualism: the ineradicable refusal of unity to the totality of parts. But when the Infinite vanishes without a trace in Altizer, when he actually *reverses* Nietzsche's *reflective* grasp of the death of God, returning, after Nietzsche, to Hegel, he sees, as through a looking glass, the Nietzschean refusal of *unity* as (if it were) the refusal of *particularity* (*TP* 98 f). In Nietzsche the chaotic cosmos was not immediately present to the self-enclosedness of the particular consciousness, was not its own, and the presence of others was a happy fiction to be joyously affirmed. In Nietzsche the identification of the particular with the totality *sans* unity was the form of (his! alas!) resistance to *utter* nothingness or chaos. This real contradiction between the utter unreality of God and the shadows of God cast across the prophet's mind, this contradiction between the vanishing of the Infinite and its traces in his thinking, excruciated Nietzsche.[8] But Altizer discovers the unity of totality sans particularity: perfect regularity sans content: total presence: not Nietzsche's perfectly indeterminate ordering, but perfectly empty ordering, indeed, cosmic chaos immediately present: not the indeterminate absolute order of Nietzsche, but the form of a new universal consciousness radically eliminating the self-enclosedness of the particular consciousness, so that what now can be said is that *our own* consciousness is no more: total presence is the presence of all the others in which all individual and unique interiority has vanished without a trace (*GA* 183). The resistance to utter chaos in Nietzsche has altogether given way in Altizer.

How is this reversal of Nietzsche's fragmentary totality, his fatality of pieces, to the absolutely empty order of the macrocosm, to pure chaos, to be understood? The operative reality is Altizer's post-Nietzschean return to Hegel, the nature of which manifests itself in this historical analogy: as the "*cogito, sum*" of the Meditations is to the "*cogito ergo sum*" of Descartes's *Replies*, as the immediately clear, distinct, undeniable self-certainty of consciousness is to its appearance in the reflective consciousness, as Hegel's *speculative* is to Kant's *reflective* philosophy, so is Altizer to Nietzsche when he, in effect, first removes the *ergo* from Nietzsche's *vivo ergo cogito* in order to restore the original apocalyptic immediacy (the apocalyptic immediacy of the origin) otherwise incompletely, that is, ideally, recovered by Nietzsche. For Altizer the immediacy of the apocalyptic origin cannot be *vivo, cogito*: for Altizer there is nothing but the sheer *immediacy* of the consciousness which *is*! Therefore, Altizer inverts (the particularity of) Nietzsche's *vivo* to (the singularity of) the Cartesian *sum*, at once restoring and updating the latter: the *sum* now in the first place: *sum, cogito*. Just here, just so far, *sum, cogito*, can be seen the formal coincidence of thought in Altizer and Heidegger.[9] But, whereas the priority of *sum* to *cogito* in Heidegger signifies, in the first instance, "I-am-in-a-world,"[10] and, ultimately, Being beyond essence, Being other than being, the ontological difference, in Altizer, to the contrary, the priority of *sum* to *cogito* signifies in the negative, in the first instance, *non sum*, *I-am-not-in-a-world*, and ultimately, Nothing beyond essence, Nothing other than being, the ontological difference reduced to Nothing: the abyss of difference, the *actual* nothingness of existence. *Non sum, cogito*: the immediacy of the totality prior to "all individual and interior presence." Altizer's inversion of the relation of unity and particularity in Nietzsche's thought, his substitution of the denied singularity, qua denied, for the latter's particularity—false as it is to Nietzsche's text—nevertheless achieves what Nietzsche—precisely because he was, excruciatedly, the *desiring* of it—never did achieve, to wit, the *vanishing* of the trace of the Infinite: the vanishing of the trace of Kant's dualism, which last had remained in Nietzsche (and, mutatis mutandis, in Heidegger) as the irreducibly discrete moments of exigency (*Noth*) and play (*Spiel*). The removal *post factum* of the *ergo* from Nietzsche's reflective proclamation of God's death, at once the immediacy of the death of God in the form of the substitution of *non sum* for *vivo*, is the actual restoration of a new immediacy, the release of a "new silence" and a "new solitude."

This new silence and solitude—absolute solitude and totality of immediacy—is the total presence that manifests itself in a new music, in the music of the new world. In Altizer music is not a "rainbow," nor, therefore, a "seeming bridge between things eternally separated." Indeed, for Altizer, "perhaps nowhere is the immediacy of a total presence more manifestly present than in the fullest moments of American jazz"—that most concrete of musics (*TP* 107 f). The power embodied in American jazz finally shatters all individual and interior identity. The power of American jazz shatters the identity that was impervious to the charms of European music. In the power of this music of the new world "the solitude of the 'I'" vanishes. This new world music's "pure rhythm"—completely displacing and replacing the *ergo*—is manifest in and as Altizer's reversal of Nietzsche's thought: the immediate and radical reversal of the priority of interiority[11] (form and matter) to exteriority (efficiency and finality), which is Nietzsche's reversal of Hegel's reversal of Kant's reversal of the Cartesian order, is manifest in and as Altizer's fourth power reversal which in no way is a simple retreat to the starting point of the series, but which rather is in fact and at once the shattering of the simultaneity of time, the reversal of the Nietzschean will to power (*vivo*) to the realization of the apocalyptic beginning which is the *absolute will* (*non sum*) or *I-am-not-in-a world* of God (*GG* 181). This "actuality of will," which "is an *is* that is wholly other than the *was*, yet an *is* that now is that which that *was* once was," is the end of the eternal recurrence of all things: the immediate and radical reversal of the will to power: the absolute annihilation of the path of return and recurrence (*GA* 179). This is the radical updating of the point of departure: the point of departure departing from itself in an utterly forward motion in which *it is now* what it *was*: the absolutely unconditioned origin of freedom and responsibility: the same a present never past: the absolutely apocalyptic beginning.

Altizer's speculative retrieval of Hegel's comprehension of the death of God,[12] this vanishing, after Nietzsche, of the Infinite without a trace, is not and cannot be, however, without a trace of the trace of the vanished Infinite in Nietzsche, is not and cannot be without a trace of the trace of Kant's dualism, without the trace of the "foolery" and "falsehood" of consciousness. This trace of the trace now manifests itself as the strict insincerity of the absolute self-negation of consciousness, the latter embodied in an absolute otherness *at once its very own*.[13] At the furthest extremity of modern consciousness this is the radical perpetuation of its absolute self-restriction, constituted in its beginning with its own conception of divinity. So much is this so that in the depths of its atheism modernity cannot get beyond itself or can get beyond itself in the form only of this radical and strict insincerity. Thus Altizer speaks of the beginning that is the "beginning of pure difference" at once "the once and for all irreversible beginning" which is the absolute act of creation (cf. *GA* 109; *SEG* 63ff). The Infinite vanishing without a trace is the absolute act of creation in the form of the "self-negation or self-laceration" of the transcendent God. The unresolved and excruciating contradiction in which liberation from God was not without the trace of God (Nietzsche) is finally resolved in Altizer in the self-crucifixion of God, which is at once the resurrection of the apocalyptic body of God or totality itself (*GG* 111 ff). Here Altizer actually unites—in the absolute *coincidentia oppositorum* of the beginning—in the person of God the Creator—the resentful one (*der Grollende*) and the fool (*der Narr*)—God himself damns himself and, in that act of self-laceration, liberates himself (*GA* 142–43 f; *GG* 119 ff). This radical and strict insincerity in the manner of the death of God is the very form of the dialectical power, which is the absolute coincidence of genesis and apocalypse, responsibility and freedom (*GA* 178–79 f). The realization of one's (God's) (cf. *DH* 160) intrinsic otherness as one's (his) own is the absolute freedom and responsibility which is the absolute disintegration of one's (his) parts (absolute self-frag-mentation) and, at once, the absolute loss of the facts constituting one's (his) very form (the absolute loss of self-definition). The absolute end that is the absolute act of creation is the total disappearance of God qua matter and form.

The Infinite Self-Consciousness vanishes without a trace—in its (his) *very own* otherness! in the very abyss of owning: in *owning not owning*. The form of this abyss of owning is "the *is* that is wholly other than the *was*, yet an *is* that now is that which that *was* once was." In Peircean terms, the absolute Second (apocalypse) identical with the absolute First (genesis) in the event of the reduction to Nothing of the Third (every measurable point of time):[14] a second without a first yet a second that now is what the first was: a second without a bridge back to the beginning, that is, with-out the simultaneity of time, a second now the absolute beginning: the second/the other/the last the absolute future: the singularity which is ab-solute future sans the vagueness attaching to particularity, that is, without the indefinite number of individuals: unity and totality sans particularity: God the Creator identically God fully revealed: now every single individ-ual without exception is immediately the point of the absolute generality or absolute orience. This is the absolute identification of the creation with the absolutely determinately existing world: the macrocosm dis-placing all that was formerly interiority: the nothingness of the particu-lar: absolute determinate universality of consciousness its own absolute otherness: the immeasurable/unmeasurable point of time (the absolute singularity) which everyone actually is: the absolute universality of ab-solute singularity: at the expense of being someone, as if being someone [in particular] should now make any difference. Indeed, the universal anonymity—absolute solitude—now comes to embody itself in every single existing individual (*DH* 157 ff). Every naked temporal-spatial self or point is, in pragmatistic terms, one of a set of seconds with no past— no longer seconds to a set of firsts, no longer seconds to the original "mind of God."[15] The *simultaneity* of time is transformed into the *actual-ity* of time. The "kind of existence" of the firsts constituting the Ameri-can pragmatic "mind of God" is transformed into the *actual* existence of the seconds constituting the apocalyptic (dead) body of God. I-AM-NOT-IN-THE-WORLD: the Infinite vanished without a trace, each member of the unenclosed and unconfined set of seconds is now what each of the firsts was: general or universal (anonymous) singulars embodying—beyond all indefiniteness and particularity—beyond essence, beyond will to power—*absolute* essence, that is, absolute will, or, actual nothingness (GG 139 ff). The conatus of being that took shape in Nietzsche as will to power and desire to create the future—now (dis)appears in the universality of the self-surpassing consciousness of the chaos which is the radical updating of the point of origin. The eternal recurrence of all things ends in the form of the absolute will or absolute act of God the Creator emptying itself out into the very form of the macrocosm: perfectly empty ordering: pure chaos or total presence whose other is the absolute future.

At the antipodes of Altizer's theology is the thought of Emmanuel Levinas. In Altizer the Infinite vanishes without a trace (the present now totally without a past) but not without *a trace of the trace* of Kant's dualism in Nietzsche, not without a trace of the notion that the overcoming of the separation and isolation of the self is "foolery and falsehood," therefore, not without the necessity that this *absolute* foolery and falsehood is *self*-betrayed in and as the fact that God, if he is to be fully and finally dead, must have sacrificed himself. But in the thought of Levinas there is, in the opposite direction, the trace of the Infinite without vanishing (a past without ever having been present), but not without the *vanishing of the vanishing* of Kant's dualism in Nietzsche, not without the vanishing of the notion that the vehicle for the "great overcoming" and "going down" is the Zarathustrian or Dionysian role, not without the vanishing of the notion that the vehicle for the great redemption is words and music! Altizer fulfills, impossibly, Nietzsche's aspiration to be able to take seriously the notion of the beyond of self-consciousness, to be able to take foolishness with complete seriousness.[16] He discovers the liberating power of a music and rhythm actually shattering all interiority—a rapture profounder and wider than anything imaginable to Nietzsche. But in Levinas the very notion that the relation with others—the beyond of self-consciousness—is a role to be taken on, assumed—no matter whether relatively or absolutely, whether by Nietzsche's Man-ascending or Altizer's God-descending—whether in the form of will *to* power or *absolute* will—whether in the mode of Nietzsche's self-conscious foolery or Altizer's absolute foolery—the very notion of *will*, the very notion of the *assumption*—indeterminate and ideal in Nietzsche, determinate and actual in Altizer—of the *role* of absolute self-forgetfulness—this intrinsic and strict insincerity of *kenotic will*—is radically rejected. In the first place, Levinas distinguishes the prosaic nature of discourse from all poetry and mysticism, from all incantation and ritual.[17] Levinas starts with the difference between discourse and incantation. But for Levinas even this distinction between sublimated and pure sincerity, incantation and ethics, poetry and prose, is just a foreshadowing of his conception of a metaphysical ethics, an ethics beyond, on the hither side of, form and matter, an ethics that is a matter of efficiency and finality infinitely prior to interiority, a matter of the infinite responsibility and immemorial election of the self, altogether a matter of the preoriginal and immemorial straightforwardness of Self to Other, at once the disintegration of the parts of the self and the deconstruction of its constitutive factuality.[18] Not in Nietzsche's abusive *language*, but in his *laughter*—which *refuses* language—*flashes* the subjectivity breaking with essence.[19] This subjectivity is before consciousness. What flashes in laughter is the positivity before positivity *and* negativity, before seriousness *and* play, before love *and* rejection.

Levinas means to uncover this dark flashing as the Other in the Same.[20] If phenomenology "intends to study the essence of pure consciousness,"[21] to think "what it was to be" consciousness,[22] then Levinas thinks the essence of phenomenology, thinks "what it was to be" phenomenology. But, then, Levinas must think "what it was to be" phenomenology without returning to consciousness, therefore, *beyond* consciousness. But, then, thinking the essence of phenomenology, thinking after phenomenology but beyond consciousness, thinking the essence of reflection upon the essence of consciousness, must be found before consciousness. Thinking "what it was to be" phenomenology is necessarily the inversion of consciousness: the absolute reversal of the nothingness of consciousness (the absolute reversal of the abyss in Nietzsche) to subjectivity before being *and* nothing, to subjectivity before nothing *and* consciousness. This is the absolute inversion (not of the abyss, as in Altizer, but) of consciousness sans nothingness: the trace of the Infinite without a vanishing. In Altizer the absolute inversion of the abyss is the absolute inversion of the nothingness of consciousness (Nietzsche) to the actual nothingness of the macrocosm: the vanishing of the Infinite without a trace. But, for Levinas, to think the essence of phenomenology is to think the phenomenology of the idea of the Infinite: to think the reflection on what it was to be consciousness of the idea of the Infinite: to think what it was to be the thought of the essence of consciousness: to think the Infinite before consciousness. If phenomenology is reflection on the essence of (prereflective) consciousness, then reflection on the essence of reflection on the essence of (prereflective) consciousness, reflection on the essence of thinking beyond consciousness, reflection on the transcendence of (prereflective) consciousness, reflection on beyond consciousness (reflection on the essence of the idea of the Infinite) is reflection on *what it was to be* beyond, that is, *before* consciousness. Phenomenology of the idea of the Infinite is reflection on the preessential beyond of consciousness: reflection on what it was to be preconsciousness transcendence: prereflective thought on what it was to be pure prephenomenological sensibility: reflection on the preessential, preconsciousness, prephenomenological sensibility that contains the uncontainable.[23] The thought of the Infinite older than the thought of the finite—older than the thought of consciousness—this essence of phenomenology *conceived* essentially—thinking what it was to be preconsciousness infinite transcendence—is the transcendence of *life.* This pure transcendence of life is not thought in the formal phenomenology of Husserl but is attested to, inversely, by the necessity of the phenomenological reduction.[24] Descartes, repressing the Augustinian *vivo,* understood the *cogito, sum* to mean that to think was, undeniably, to be.[25] Altizer, beyond Nietzsche, inverts Nietzsche's retrieved *vivo* to Nietzsche's *non sum.* Altizer, suppressing *vivo,* posits the priority of *non sum* to *cogito,* the absolute immanence of life identically the self-sacrificial death of the transcendent God, posits, as indubitable, I-AM-NOT-IN-THE-WORLD, the totality empty altogether of any trace of divinity. This is the clear, distinct, and undeniable *novum* wherein the absolutely determinate *cogito* (the *non sum, cogito* where the ontological difference is Nothing) recognizes the idea of the death of God as the form of its own intrinsic otherness. In this *novum* beyond the *cogito* the idea of the Infinite ends in the *end* of any idea of the Infinite (including the Nietzschean eternal recurrence of all things) apart from the infinity of time and space. This is the furthest possible *extension* of the essence of modern consciousness: the *cogito* gone to the *thither* side of itself in the form of a *novum* younger and emptier than the *cogito,* in the form of absolute otherness, absolute future: the absolute self-embodiment of God whose other is the absolute future: the actual nothingness of existence: the same and the other after all appearing and vanishing: *coincidentia oppositorum* in the form of the absolutely new nothing. *Non sum, cogito* is the new state of affairs where being *is* nothing: the actual nothingness of immediate sensible reality, the Nothing that is the essence of thought, the Nothing otherwise than being, the Nothing beyond essence.[26] But for Levinas beyond essence is neither being nor nothing, not *thither*, but *hither* the *cogito*. As Kant's "Copernican revolution" denied self-evident reality to the substance of the *sum* of Descartes' *cogito*, so Levinas denies the self-evident ground of the purely phenomenal *cogito* of Nietzsche's *vivo*. Further, just as in Kant the Cartesian *cogito* transcends its *sum* in such a way that the latter's substantiality is understood to be purely phenomenal, so in Levinas Nietzsche's *vivo* transcends its *cogito* in such a way that the latter's reality is necessarily grounded in pure prephenomenal sensibility. Just as pure phenomenology of consciousness transcends substantiality, so the pure prephenomenal sensibility of the *vivo* transcends the pure phenomenology of the *cogito*, and, in doing so, transcends very *vivo*. While Altizer knows indubitably *non sum, cogito*, Levinas thinks, beyond all doubt and certainty, *vivo, non cogito*: the radical priority of sensibility to consciousness: the transcendence of life to the *cogito*, to the unity of transcendental apperception. In Altizer the Infinite vanishes without a trace when life is inverted to nothing prior to thought, the *non sum* prior to the *cogito*, when life is inverted to being in the beginning thinking nothing: the absolute immanence of life: life inverted, in effect, to being the mind of God for which Nothing *is* thinkable.[27] But, in Levinas, the Infinite, without vanishing, without ever having been present, without having been, for the pure prephenomenal sensibility which grounds essence, an essence, nevertheless, is the trace: the trace in the self of what immemorially overflows the self: the Other in the Same, the uncontainable contained.

Altizer completely reverses Nietzsche's absolute priority of interiority to exteriority. This reversal is at once the absolute inversion of the abyss, which is the absolute inversion of the will to power which remained *enclosed and confined* as *matter and form* in Nietzsche—enclosed and confined in time's simultaneity to a "Thus I willed it!"—enclosed in an interiority of which there was no outside and confined to overcoming the past by the brave song that the past always had been present—the absolute inversion of will to power to absolute exteriority, to absolute freedom and responsibility. In Altizer the self-same point of origin of the *cogito* empties itself out absolutely into the unmeasurable and immeasurable points of a nonsimultaneous temporality and space, the absolute exile of self-consciousness from itself, at once the radical updating of the beginning of consciousness (of the *cogito*), empties itself out into the form of a *convex without a concave*, a *total and immediate presence beyond every possible interior*, a convex without a center, into the form of absolute will, the will to power "unenclosed and unconfined." But in Levinas occurs the complete inversion of Nietzsche's absolute posteriority of exteriority. This inversion is at once the absolute reversal of the abyss in Nietzsche, the complete reversal of the antithesis of will to power which remained *unenclosed and unconfined* as *efficiency and finality* in Nietzsche—unenclosed and unconfined in the priority of interiority to "There is no outside of me!"—unenclosed as nothing outside the totality and unconfined to a past that had always been present—this inversion is the reversal of the antithesis of will to power—the reversal of purposeless finality (fatality) and inefficient responsibility (irresponsible action) to absolute interiority, to absolute passivity and guilt. But, then, this is an absolute interiority at the very heart of which is, *irremovably* and *inexplicably*, and *not incidentally*, the Nietzschean exteriority! In Levinas responsibility is for what one is not, and cannot be, responsible: the past never having been present: an efficiency absolutely before any question of initiative. Freedom is freedom to suffer what one has not chosen: passivity more passive than any passivity. Finality is absolutely before any question of the mind's purposing: preontological finality: the return of the self to a point behind, hither, its point of origin. If Altizer's theology is the reversal of all interiority to exteriority, the "eternal outwardizing of the within,"[28] the convexity of an unenclosed and unconfined center, absolute convexity, the convex without a concave, then Levinas is the inversion of all exteriority to interiority, the enclosed and confined concavity of the center, absolute concavity: *the concave without a convex,*[29] the *eternal inwardizing of the exterior*, the eternal inwardizing of the without. If for Nietzsche contact with the others was finally a fine dream, it was because, in the end, there was nothing outside of himself. But for Levinas the other is inside of the self, contact with the other is a fact beyond all possibility or impossibility. When Altizer inverts the relation of interiority and exteriority in Nietzsche, the absolute priority of exteriority to interiority leaves the latter behind essentially, but not absolutely, since the negative reference to the past, the present never past, is the surviving integral part and constitutive fact of subjectivity (the Infinite vanishing without a trace but not without a trace of the trace of the Kantian dualism) in the form of the self-embodiment of God. Likewise, in the opposite direction, in Levinas exteriority is infinitely prior to interiority in the way of being there before any thought of the latter's commencement, but, as in Altizer, essentially, not absolutely, since the negative reference to the present, the past never present, is the surviving integral part and constitutive fact of subjectivity (the trace of the infinite without vanishing, but not without the vanishing of the vanishing of the Kantian dualism) in the form of the immemorial election and responsibility for the other.[30] This vanishing of the vanishing of the Kantian dualism is the very form of the election to the other, of the immemorial contact, of the ineluctable proximity that is the strict sincerity of the-self-for-the-other.[31] In thinking a prose not merely in opposition to poetry, but a prose before discourse, before rupture and commencement, a prose without poetry, a rupture without rapture and without initiative, univocity without possibility of equivocation, sincerity without possibility of sublimation, a prose this side of prose *and* poetry, Levinas stands clear-eyed in opposition to Nietzsche's infinite-resignation-followed-by-self-abandonment-to-foolery-and-falsehood. He stands directly opposite the absolute coincidence of history and ritual that is Altizer's self-sacrificial death of God (*HA* 209 ff). Altizer inverts the moment of infinite human resignation and renunciation in Nietzsche's text[32] into the moment of apocalyptic divine self-laceration, transforming the Nietzschean moment of human foolery into absolute foolery/foolery of the Absolute, the moment of possible presence into total presence, the moment of possible fulfillment into total fulfillment, the Nietzschean aspiration into realization, and, indeed, overcoming "all that interior distance separating men from men and self from self" (*DH* 169) in the form of the absolute equivocation of a self beyond consciousness *its own absolute otherness*, the absolute equivocation that is the absolute *novum* of the beginning: *nothing beyond essence*. But Levinas thinks the absolute univocity of a self before consciousness whose otherness is absolutely not its own, the notion of being beyond self-consciousness that is neither the relative (Nietzsche) nor absolute (Altizer) coincidence of *gravitas* and *levitas*, which is neither form of the coincidence of the seriousness of prose and the playfulness of poetry (cf. *DH* 125 ff; *HA* 211). Indeed, Levinas thinks the absolutely prosaic address of the self to the other beyond contrariety and contradiction: beyond contrariety and the *coincidentia oppositorum*. *Vivo, non cogito*: the life of the Infinite, hither the idea of the Infinite, hence hither the death of God, whether ideal (Nietzschean) or actual (Altizer). The God who is not a value cannot be either transvalued or the end of all value and meaning.[33] This is life at the preoriginal point where life is without death, where life is "'being able to die' subject to sacrifice," absolutely without the possibility either of murder or of self-sacrifice. The transcendence of life: absolutely *subject to sacrifice*: victim and hostage to the Other.

The universal determinateness or absolutely empty ordering in Altizer is the absolute quality of the (Nietzschean) abyss. Altizer transcends
the relative quality of the (Nietzschean) abyss. Nietzsche was resigned to
the impossibility of the synthesis for which he yearned: there was no singularity, but there was totality and particularity (the latter the opening for
an eternally recurring desire). In Altizer there is totality and singularity
absolutely coincident, but without particularity: the absolute realization
of the creative will: the absolute quality of the abyss/the abyss of absolute
quality: absolute quality not absolute quality: the middle excluded, the
absolute quality of the singular: the absolute otherness of the absolute
self: beyond essence, beyond particularity, the totality of singularity: sheer
beginning of the universe of others: the vanishing of infinity without a
trace but not without a trace of the trace of Kant's dualism: otherness absolutely the self's own otherness: the other absolutely the self's own. But
in Levinas is uncovered the absolute *quantity* of the abyss: the singular,
not merely without logical particularity, as in Altizer, but also without,
that is, outside of, hither, totality. In Levinas is the absolute quantity of
the abyss/the abyss of absolute quantity: absolute quantity not absolute
quantity: the beginning and the (logical) middle excluded: the singular:
the absolute quantity of the singular: the absolute fission of self stuffed
with the other: beyond essence: beyond (logical) particularity and totality, sheer singularity, the trace of infinity without vanishing but not without the vanishing of the vanishing of Kant's dualism: *the other* (absolutely
not the self's own) *within the self from time immemorial.* For Levinas the notion of being beyond essence (the logical middle excluded) is neither
nothing nor something: it is the excluded middle between something
and nothing (the beginning excluded): beyond essence: otherwise than
being: the unmeasurable/immeasurable point of time excluding not only
logical particularity (the logical middle) but beyond (hither) the beginning of logic itself, the singular beyond (hither) the logic of genus and
species: the unmeasurable/immeasurable point of time before the beginning of the being of totality: the excluded middle the second not only
without a first, but without the very notion of a first, not only without a
beginning other than itself, but without the notion of a beginning: the
last absolutely without the first, therefore the second for which the infinity of time is *infinitely* excluded. In Altizer the infinity of time is not
infinitely excluded. Indeed, the infinity of time in Altizer is excluded qua
not-infinity, excluded qua vanishing of the Infinite without a trace. The
Infinite becomes the finite, *non sum, cogito.* In Levinas the infinity of time

is infinitely excluded, not excluded qua not-infinity, but excluded qua infinity, that is, the infinite exclusion of the infinity of time in Levinas takes form precisely as the trace of the Infinite without vanishing. There is the trace of the Infinite without a vanishing: the trace of the Infinite never having been present. This trace of the Infinite without a vanishing is not the infinity of time (and space, in which the Infinite vanishes without a trace, the Infinite become the finite); rather it is the finition of time, very finition of the finite: the diachronous time absolutely prior to the instant of "rupture and commencement": absolute prose: absolute straightforwardness to the other. *Vivo, non cogito.* This is a prose not caught up in the alternatives of prose *and* poetry: absolute *gravitas*. This finition of the finite is at once the infinition of the Infinite, the glory of the Infinite, the Infinite transcendence of the finite.[34] This is the transcendence of life, the Infinite transcendence of the finite, which is inconvertible into forms, that is, inconvertible into the forms of being and nothingness, inconvertible into a "present of appearing" so that the excluded middle that is the preoriginal "me" (the excluded beginning of "me") escapes the reduction to pure nothingness, in the form of the "infinitesimal difference" that is irreducibly the "seed of folly" disrupting the otherwise absolute self-consciousness.[35] For Levinas, it is not, as it is in Altizer, a matter of a totality of singulars sans particularity, the transcendental apperception of Nothing; rather it is a matter of the singular sans (logical) particularity *and* totality, a unity beyond transcendental apperception, otherwise than (hither) the transcendental apperception of Unity *and* Nothing: beyond the unity of the one and the many, the unity of self-containing-the-other constrained by Goodness:[36] beyond ontology the diachronous nonindifference, in immemorial contact, of the one to the other.[37] The Infinite transcending the finite, the trace without a vanishing, but not without the vanishing of the vanishing of Kant's dualism, the extraordinary responsibility for the other, floats over "the waters of ontology" as the divine wind, hither the divine word, swept over the waters, hither the first day.[38]

When Altizer transforms the Nietzschean will to power into absolute will, he transforms the *moment of infinite resignation*, together with its abandonment to "foolery and falsehood," into the absolute foolery of a *totality of infinite designation*. This totality of infinite designation is the actual nothingness (actual falsehood) of an intentionality become altogether the *cogitatum* in the form of the *novum*, which is the "absolute future," the strict insincerity of the self emptying itself out into its own intrinsic otherness. But when Levinas thinks, hither the Nietzschean moment of infinite resignation, together with its abandonment to "foolery and falsehood," hither intentionality and will, he thinks the opposite of Altizer's *novum*. Levinas thinks the *veternum*, the unity of self before all simultaneity, "I" immemorially in the accusative case, "me" under *assignation*, the very "*seed of folly.*" Altizer thinks the falsehood of an intentionality actually beyond itself. But Levinas thinks the truth of a pneuma (the spirit over the waters) radically prior to intentionality.[39] Beyond "fine words or songs," that is, hither all "foolery and falsehood," at the opposite pole from Altizer's absolute freedom and responsibility, at the opposite pole from the absolute foolery of the kenotic speech of an absolute selfhood self-emptying itself into a state of actual nothingness, the actual falsehood of an intentionality (*cogito*) become the *novum*, Levinas thinks the actual truth of life, the veracity of a responsibility altogether before the notion of freedom, indeed, an "alienation that does not empty the same of its identity, but constrains it to it, with an 'unimpeachable assignation,' constrains it to it as no one else, where no one could replace it," where, therefore, it cannot replace itself with "its own intrinsic otherness."[40] This "unimpeachable assignation" of the self *is* the approach of the self to the other, indeed, the saying before the said, the signifyingness of signification, a signifyingness which *is* sincerity, *is* veracity.[41] Insofar as the American death of God theology is the realization of the actual end of this world, the actual death of God, the realization of an actual nothingness, absolute solitude, absolute silence, just so far it is, qua absolute foolery, qua absolutely impossible *conatus essendi*, qua absolute impossibility of the attempt, the absolute embodiment of the saying in the said (*SEG* 81–96), the absolute dissimulation of saying itself.[42] Just here can be clearly seen the historicological relation wherein Nietzsche's thought is the mean proportional between the extremes that are Levinas's *veternum* and Altizer's *novum*, to wit, "seed of folly" (Levinas) : "foolery" (Nietzsche) :: "foolery" (Nietzsche) : absolute foolery/absolute dissimulation of saying itself (Altizer), or, infinite assignation (Levinas) : infinite resignation (Nietzsche) :: infinite resignation (Nietzsche) : infinite designation (Altizer); or, strict sincerity and veracity (Levinas) : fatality and "foolery and falsehood" (Nietzsche) :: fatality and "foolery and falsehood" (Nietzsche) : strict insincerity and falsehood (Altizer). Thus in different perfectly complementary directions do Altizer and Levinas perpetuate the historically exhausted dialectic of *self* and *other*. The immanence of life in Altizer and the transcendence of life in Levinas, taken together, constitute, exhaustively, the perfect voiding of the Nietzschean fatality of life. On the one hand, in Levinas, beyond Nietzsche's "beyond good and evil," inverting the Nietzschean fatality of life, the veracity of the spirit of creation, the "original goodness of creation."[43] On the other hand, in Altizer, likewise beyond Nietzsche's "beyond good and evil," the ego invested in its imperialism, glorying in eternal darkness—reversing the fatality of life in Nietzsche—absolutely insistent on its autonomy, binding itself to the necessity of the original evil of creation, unconditionally affirms—beyond the radical particularity of Nietzsche's text—the unity of good and evil. Indeed, Altizer inverts Nietzsche's "anti-Gnosticism," inverts and reverses Gnosticism itself, affirming absolutely the Christian Creator's radically evil will as the conditio sine qua non of autonomous human freedom (GG 134, 114 ff). The actualization of "our freedom" is "our eternal act, and our only eternal act." But true freedom "can be neither an eternal act nor an eternal state, it can only be a realized freedom" (GG 178 f). Therefore there is nothing for it but that the actualization of freedom is the inversion of (Nietzsche's) not an eternal act (the eternal recurrence of all things) to an eternal act (the end of the eternal recurrence of all things): the abysmal inversion of eternal act to the beginning of an actual nothingness. Nietzsche's "full green *vivere*"[44] becomes in Altizer "our freedom," which is "our only glory," damned living, the life of damnation (GG 134)!

Although both Altizer and Levinas are clearly beyond "beyond good and evil," nevertheless, neither the "glory of damnation" in Altizer, the vanishing of the Infinite without a trace, nor the "glory of the infinite" in Levinas, the trace of the Infinite without vanishing—neither the one nor the other—is beyond a *reminiscence* of "beyond good and evil." Neither is Altizer beyond a trace of a trace of the good (the "eternal act of God"), nor is Levinas beyond the vanishing of the vanishing of evil (the "self involved in the *gnawing away at oneself*"). This is to say that neither is beyond a reminiscence of *beyond the law*, whether in the way of immanence (the life of damnation) or in the way of transcendence (the life of the Infinite), whether in the way of liberation from transcendent moral imperatives or in the way of subtending societal imperatives with preoriginal nonreciprocal responsibility for the other. Altizer articulates the furthest possible *extension* of the modern essence (*conatus essendi*), the furthest possible extension of the point of departure thither itself to the point of the *novum*, to the point of activity more active than activity, form more formal than form, to the point of the "absolute future," absolute actuality sans actuality, to the point of the absolute will to evil, to the point of the falsehood of an intentionality actually beyond itself (absolute *conatus essendi*, sans being—the metaphysical Nothing, Nothing beyond being and nothing, Nothing otherwise than being, Nothing beyond essence, Nothing beyond *the attempt to be*). In Levinas is articulated the furthest possible *contraction* of the modern essence (*conatus essendi*), the furthest possible contraction of the point of departure hither itself to the point of the *veternum*, to the point of passivity more passive than passivity, matter more material than matter, to the point of the absolute past, absolute potentiality sans potentiality, to the point of the pre-original recurrence to oneself, to the point of the pneumatic veracity of a prephenomenal sensibility (sans *conatus essendi*, sans being—the metaphysical Good, Good beyond being and nothing, Good otherwise than being, Good beyond essence, Good beyond *the attempt to be*). But neither Altizer nor Levinas perfectly voids the fatality of life in Nietzsche, nor do they, taken separately or together, think essentially beyond the category of other and self, *essentially* beyond the category of evil and good. Thus the terms of the polarity remain: sincerity/insincerity, veracity/falsehood, transcendence/immanence. Neither the infinite preoriginal substitution of the same for the other in Levinas, life without death, the "constraint to corporeality" which is the transcendence of life, nor the absolute postoriginal substitution of the other for the same in Altizer, life actually death, the liberation of corporeality which is the immanence of life, neither the one nor the other, *essentially* transcends the dialectic of the exhausted self.

## NOTES

1. Friedrich Nietzsche, *Twilight of the Idols* and *The Anti-Christ*, trans. R. J. Hollingdale (London: Penguin, 1990), 64.

2. Friedrich Nietzsche, *The Use and Abuse of History*, trans. A. Collins (New Jersey: Prentice Hall, 1997), 68–69 f.

3. Friedrich Nietzsche, *The Gay Science*, trans. W. Kaufmann (New York: Vintage, 1974), §125.

4. Friedrich Nietzsche, *Thus Spoke Zarathustra*, trans. R. J. Hollingdale (New York: Penguin, 1978), 237–38 f.

5. Nietzsche, *Twilight of the Idols*, 116–17 f.

6. Ibid., 95–96 f.

7. Nietzsche, *The Gay Science*, §357.

8. Ibid., §109.

9. Martin Heidegger, *Being and Time*, trans. J. Stambaugh (Albany: State University of New York Press, 1996), 195.

10. Ibid.

11. See D. G. Leahy, *Foundation: Matter the Body Itself* (Albany: State University of New York Press, 1996), II.4, 221 ff.

12. See ibid., esp. 209, 221–22 f.

13. See ibid., 231 ff.

14. See ibid., II.4, III.5, IV.1–2, V.1, V.3.

15. Charles S. Peirce, *Collected Papers*, ed. C. Hartshorne and P. Weiss (Cambridge, MA: Harvard University Press, 1933), vol. 6, 199.

16. Nietzsche, *The Gay Science*, §382. Also, cf. Emmanuel Levinas, *Collected Philosophical Papers*, trans. A. Lingis (Dordrecht: Martinus Nijhoff, 1987), 127 ff.

17. Emmanuel Levinas, *Totality and Infinity: An Essay on Exteriority*, trans. A. Lingis (Pittsburgh: Duquesne University Press, 1969), 202–03 f. Also, cf. Nietzsche, *The Gay Science*, §84.

18. Emmanuel Levinas, *Otherwise than Being or Beyond Essence*, trans. A. Lingis (Dordrecht: Martinus Nijhoff, 1991), 8–9 f.

19. Nietzsche, *The Gay Science*, §92.

20. Emmanuel Levinas, *Outside the Subject*, trans. M. B. Smith (Stanford: Stanford University Press, 1994), 83.

21. Emmanuel Levinas, *Discovering Existence with Husserl*, trans. R. A. Cohen and M. B. Smith (Evanston: Northwestern University Press, 1998), 17.

22. Levinas recalls (*Discovering Existence*, 22) Husserl's originality *vis-à-vis* Descartes. Cf. the treatment of the Aristotelian essence in D. G. Leahy, *Novitas Mundi: Perception of the History of Being* (Albany: State University of New York Press, 1994), 35 ff.

23. Emmanuel Levinas, *Time and the Other*, trans. R. A. Cohen (Pittsburgh: Duquesne University Press, 1987), 135 ff.

24. See Levinas, *Discovering Existence with Husserl*, "Philosophy and Awakening," 178–79 f.

25. Augustine, *The Trinity*, trans. S. McKenna (Washington, DC: Catholic University Press of America, 1963), X, 10.

26. See Leahy, *Foundation*, 201 ff.

27. See Peirce, *Collected Papers*, vol. 6, 490.

28. Leahy, *Foundation*, II.4.

29. Levinas, *Otherwise than Being*, 49.

30. See Leahy, *Foundation*, V.3; also cf. Leahy, *Novitas Mundi*, "Prolegomena in Comprehension of the History of Being."

31. Levinas, *Otherwise than Being*, 142–43.

32. Nietzsche, *The Gay Science*, §§27, 285.

33. Levinas, *Otherwise than Being*, 128.

34. Ibid., 90.

35. Ibid., 91.

36. Ibid., 118.

37. Ibid., 141.

38. Genesis 1:2.

39. Levinas, *Otherwise than Being*, 141 ff.

40. Ibid., 11.

41. Ibid., 143, 151–52.

42. See Leahy, *Foundation*, 473 ff.

43. Levinas, *Otherwise than Being*, 121.

44. Nietzsche, *The Use and Abuse of History*, 68–69.

# CHAPTER 8

# Abyssal Absences

## Body and Place in Altizer's Atheology

### Edward S. Casey

Embodiment is presence.

—Altizer, *The Self-Embodiment of God*

The body itself is the totality of life for the first time.

—D. G. Leahy, *Foundation: Matter the Body Itself*

T otal Presence"! "Original identity"! "Original immediacy"! A "totally actual present"! "Immediate and total presence"!¹ How dare one talk in these outlandish, not to say outmoded, metaphysical ways these days? In these days, a time of deconstruction when the metaphysics of presence has been put to grief—chased off the philosophical playing field, exorcized from the establishment, cleansed of its barbarism. In this circumstance, how can one continue to utter words such as "presence," "identity," "actual," "immediate," "total"? To speak this language is to speak the language of Western metaphysics. It is to speak the unspeakable.

To encounter the language of rank metaphysics in a text that nonetheless *speaks*—and speaks *to us*, speaks *now*—is to raise the question: How,

with what words, can one speak? How can one speak, not just in theology
or philosophy, but how can one speak at all? How can one begin to speak?
How can one begin?

But speak one must, even if it is only to begin speaking again, to take
up familiar refrains, otherwise and with a difference this time, which is
what Thomas J. J. Altizer just barely manages to do. He plays the dangerous game of Western metaphysics in his own devilish way, falling into
abysses where angels might fear to tread, and yet from these very abyssal
depths (those of metaphysical thought itself) he emerges into a quite
nonmetaphysical light; or rather, he creates this light itself from within
the darkness of his own speech.

My concern is quite focused and reflects my own preoccupations.
Where are body and (to a lesser extent) place as these figure in Altizer's
processional exit from the metaphysical? What form do they take in his
thought? These are the questions I shall address here. But first I need to
consider the perplexing matter of Altizerian language.

It is only fitting that we can discern a distinctly Hegelian schema at play
in this unfolding drama. The traditional language of metaphysics—
largely Greek and German language—is reversed in Derrida's dazzling
deconstruction of it; this deconstruction is in turn reversed in Altizer's
equally dazzling middle works, on which I shall here focus: *The Self-Embodiment of God* and *Total Presence*. This reversal of reversal does not attain
synthesis in any Hegelian sense, but it does reach beyond the moment of
negation as skepsis where Derrida leaves things in his early deconstructive writings (which are those with the most influence on Altizer). The
result is not exactly deconstruction, or perhaps we could say that it is a
unique form of àpres-deconstruction, deconstruction on Altizer's al-
tered/altared terms. Neither aporetic deconstruction nor dialectical synthesis, Altizer's theology makes its own way between these uneasy
epicenters of modern and postmodern thought. This is a way in which
body and place receive less explicit recognition than they deserve, but in
which, nevertheless, a certain space has been cleared for them.

A. Thesis. This is the moment of the Western metaphysical tradition.
In this tradition, Being gives itself as determinate presence—*Anwesenheit*
in Heidegger's locution.[2] Not only is Being made conceptually determinate, but it is considered permanent (not subject to temporal dissolution

and displacement), arranged in hierarchies (ontotheology: in which God, or Being itself, comes out on top), and totalized (part of a system that legitimates every item within its realm of operation). All of which is to say that Being lends itself to static analysis—so static that Becoming itself is conceived as determinate presence. Hence the predictable proclivity for thinking of Being in terms of actuality or form or identity.

B. Antithesis. Derrida's deconstruction—undertaken in the wake of Heidegger's *Destruktion* of the history of ontology—aims to question and reverse the hegemony of the terms that together compose the circle of presence. Their unquestioned priority is to be reversed before the subsequent step of dissemination is pursued.[3] The reversal is effected not just by pointing to manifest contradictions—this would be to limit deconstruction to dismantling from without, to "dismemberment" in Altizer's term[4]—but by detecting fatal flaws *within* a given concept or system, flaws that undermine the concept or system on its own terms. In short, it is a matter of "auto-deconstruction," self-dismantling or self-dismemberment.

C. Synthesis. This is the Altizerian moment, even if not intended to be such (much less named as such) by the author himself. I here posit it as a way of understanding a primary paradox in reading Altizer, especially in his middle period (that is, 1977 to 1985). Writings in this period are insistently metaphysical, seemingly unremittingly so. The reader is continually confronted with statements that seem to carry forward the metaphysics of presence, if not outright ontotheology, without apology or qualification. This happens not only with regard to major concepts—as is evident in the phrases cited at the beginning of this chapter—but even with respect to the situation of speech: "Whether in interior monologue or in exterior confrontation and response, speech is our primal mode of realizing identity and meaning, and neither meaning nor identity can be actual and real apart from speech" (*SEG* 1). Or take this sentence: "The act of speech is just that, an act or utterance, and as act it is actual, it is present, and present alone, in its own embodiment" (*SEG* 10). This would seem to leave little space for absence, whether as otherness or as difference. When writing in this vein, Altizer seems to permit absence only as a function of presence: "Presence becomes manifest in the very act of speech, and the manifestation of presence makes absence audible" (*SEG* 9–10). Indeed, even an ostensible absence such as silence can enter into relation with speech only as a presence: "When silence is present in speech, it is not a mere emptiness, just as it is not a simple absence, it is far rather a presence, and a presence which is present in the presence of speech" (*SEG* 9). Instead of being merely "an absence of speech" (*SEG* 8), silence realizes presence thrice over! Altizer here appears to endorse the very logomachia so greatly feared by the Derridean deconstructionist and thus to abide by this regressive thought: nothing counts unless it is a form of presence. And the regression is only exacerbated by its insistent phonocentrism: nothing counts unless it reaches speech. But to promote speech is to court perdition. If Derrida is right, it is in the purity of speech, wherein breath directly animates meaning, that all genuine otherness vanishes and that all difference dissolves in the proximity of self-presence. If Altizer brings us to the brink of unredeemable presence by his unrelenting insistence on full speech, he also and simultaneously bursts the bonds of such presence in an act of auto-deconstruction. Altizer's text takes itself apart. In the usual act of deconstruction, an other—someone other than the author, who is duped by his own text—is required to dismantle the text, or at least to demonstrate how it dismantles itself. In Altizerian deconstruction, the author dismantles himself; no other is required, or let us say that the other inhabits the text, a text for which the author and the other are one and the same.

If this is synthesis, it is of a diabolical sort. It is a synthesis that knows no unity and that undermines every lasting identity. Presence is affirmed but only as paired with absolute absence; sameness is asserted but only as otherness; proximity is supported but only as distance; totality is averred but only in the form of singular actuality. Synthesis occurs, yet only in a radically nondialectical manner whereby opposites do not conjoin in time and history but are *always already together*. This is an ontology riven from the start, a self-upbraided form of thought that deconstructs itself at every turn: an infernal self-dismantling machine. This makes for difficult reading, but reading that ends somewhere specific and not in the limbo where Derrida so often leaves us. Where is this?

Let me here indicate several of the most prominent ways in which this demonic self-undoing proceeds. Having *named* with apparent insouciance a series of metaphysical titulars such as "presence," "totality," "silence," "actuality," "identity," and so on, Altizer proceeds to subvert these very terms. He takes them to the cleaners; he searches for the limits of their own otherness. Silence, for example, cannot exist for itself but only as subverted into speech. There is no such thing as simple silence: once the naming of

God is taken into account, "then silence is impossible, or impossible as a silence which is only itself" (*SEG* 32). Not to be reduced to mere stillness,
silence is already speech: "when silence is meaningful it is so only insofar
as it is related to speech" (*SEG* 9). Conversely, speech is not the mere overcoming of silence but is its very realization: "speech as speech can be present only through the presence of silence" (*SEG* 10). What would seem
to be a mere contrast between absence of speech and presence of silence
gives way to a situation in which there is presence of speech *and* absence of
silence: something quite different. Both speech and silence are present all
the way through—double presence. But there is double absence as well:
absent in silence is the said and the voice, absent in speech is the unsaid and
the still. Or we can say that the unsaid is the other of speech, that which
"becomes 'other' than itself in being spoken. And thereby it truly becomes
its own 'other'; it negates itself in speech, and only by negating itself does
it become embodied or present" (*SEG* 11).

Absence and otherness are there from the start, in the coeval themes
of silence and speech with which "Genesis" opens in *The Self-Embodiment of God*. Speech, the act and medium of genesis, far from being a
mode of untroubled self-presence, shows itself to be "self-division" (*SEG*
11). For Altizer, absence belongs to the unsaid and the unsayable, the
others of speech and their own others as well. Although starting from silence, Altizer sees self-scission at work. No sooner is speech "self-embodied," that is, once it has happened as an act or actuality, than it is
immediately self-divided: "Accordingly, the self-embodiment of speech
is a self-doubling, a doubling wherein the sayable and the unsayable become the intrinsic others of each other" (*SEG* 11).

It is crucial to note that the doubling and redoubling here at stake do
not happen in some simple succession. Timewise, we are not dealing with
diachrony but with a synchrony whereby the mutation of presence (here in
the form of speech) occurs right away, in a literally *split second*, a second that
splits into the self and its double. To this momentous moment we could
ironically apply the very phrase that Husserl had used to describe the grasp
of expressive meaning: "in the same instant" (*im selben Augenblick*).

Nothing stirs until the violence of speech arises. There is not even
presence, not even nothing, but once it does happen instead of having
*something* on hand, a form of simple presence, an entity, a created being,
there is instantly self-division. Whatever comes to be *is*, but only to be
other than any determinate presence, any *Anwesendes*. The *is* is not—is not
simply itself, is already other than itself, the negation of itself: "Whatever is

present in speech derives only from itself, from its own act or embodiment. And that act, precisely because it is only its own, is an act of self-negation" (*SEG* 11). Altizer's thought, albeit immensely influenced by Hegel, is non-dialectical. Here we see just how this is so. Instead of thesis/antithesis/synthesis, the claim just cited has instead the form Act/Antiact. But the antiact, the self-negation occurs as self-doubling and redoubling. So we must rather write: Act/Antiact/Self-Doubling of the Act. What is in the third position, the supposed moment of synthesis, is instead the self-scinding of the act of speech, its synchronic disjunction, its undoing by *dédoublement*. This is where Altizer takes us: into the semantic void wherein the third moment undoes itself timelessly.

We observe much the same logic, or antilogic, at play in regard to other major concepts in the theology of God's self-disembodiment. Each is an avatar of what we could call the Altizerian Axiom: "Now presence is another, it is otherness itself, and presence can be present only by being different from itself" (*SEG* 32). In other words, there *is* presence, but that very presence subverts itself, not because of some otherness that is other than presence itself (as the indicative, and more generally the spatial, is simply other than the expressive in Husserlian semiology) but because of an otherness that belongs to presence—or better, is/is not presence itself, is and is not constitutive of its very being. To be (at all) is to be other than/different from the presence by means of which one *is*. Thus, the act of speech is "actually present, only through the absence of a total presence or totality" (*SEG* 10). This totality, far from being a metaphysical posit or "world-whole" as Kant calls it, is detotalized in the actuality of speech that is a singular act. But as an absence that is spun off as the double of presence it haunts this presence as its absent other, giving the depth or ground that only such an absent-present doppelgänger can provide. Without such absence, speech "would have no ground upon which to stand, no ground whereby it could be present and manifest as speech" (*SEG* 11). This shows that self-doubling is no empty or formal exercise; it is part and parcel of presence itself.

Although total presence may haunt actual presence *as if it had been lost*—as a nostalgic metaphysical ideal—it is in fact flung off from actual presence in the very heat of the latter's own intense life. The same obtains for God's eternal identity. Regarding the latter, Altizer comes as close to nostalgia as he ever permits himself: "God is the name of the source or the origin of our estrangement from the silence of eternal presence" (*SEG* 31). But by saying "God," we not merely overcome such silence, we "embody in our voice an *original* negation of that silence" (*SEG* 31; my italics). I emphasize "original" to indicate that the silent and eternal presence of God does not simply precede theological speech, only to be negated subsequently; but that saying "God" instead posits such pure existence only to negate it at the time of saying itself. This is only fitting, given that God does not possess himself but is in perpetual exile from himself.[5]

A second axiom of Altizerian thought is close at hand: "[O]nly otherness can be manifest, just as only difference can be named" (*SEG* 32). Both otherness and difference appear in and through speech. Even if it is the case that "otherness is world, the world of actuality," this world arises for us only "in the horizon of speech" (*SEG* 32).[6] As for difference, it is bound to speech directly: "Difference becomes actual with the advent of speech. . . . Speech is difference, it is actually different, and it is actually different from the same" (*SEG* 19–20). What Derrida says expressly of writing, Altizer here says of speech. In the end (or more exactly, in the beginning it never fails to effect), speech is the locus of difference and otherness alike: "In speech difference is embodied in itself, and embodied in itself as itself, for speech is the actual immediacy of a difference which is ever other than itself" (*SEG* 23). Otherness is more encompassing than difference in Altizer's assessment, and the two are not to be confounded as happens in Plato's *Sophist*. Difference is constitutive of speech, whereas otherness extends beyond language to world and to God; yet these latter still come to appearance only in the horizon of speech, which has its own otherness: the field of speech is "a continuum which is other than itself, and other than itself precisely because it is itself" (*SEG* 21).[7]

From here it is but a short step to the deconstruction of three great symptomatic expressions of the metaphysics of presence: origin, actuality, and identity. Derrida's critique of the myth of the simple origin—an origin that shows itself on closer inspection to be always riven or split—is here carried forward in a characteristic Altizerian gesture:

> In speech beginning perishes as an eternal beginning [that is, as a timelessly simple origin], it comes to an end as a beginning which is only a beginning, and becomes actual as an origin which is becoming other than itself. . . . When origin becomes manifest, it becomes manifest as being beyond itself, as being other than itself. . . . When the beginning of speech is manifest, otherness is at hand, and at hand in the voice of speech itself. (*SEG* 24)

Origin is not merely other than that to which it gives rise—for example, the articulated voice—but, what is more important, "other than itself." It incorporates otherness into itself; as self-othering it cannot be simple. What would seem to be the epitome of the immediate—for do we not always *begin* with what is immediate?—shows itself to be, like sense certainty in Hegel, to be already overtaken by the nonimmediate: by deictic universals of the Here and Now in the case of sense certainty, by sheer existence in Altizer's parallel account: "immediacy is not a simple immediacy, not an immediacy that simply exists, it rather ex-ists, it stands out from itself in its presence. Hence an actual immediacy embodies an actual otherness" (*SEG* 25).

This means that actuality itself is other to itself. To stand *out* is to become other in relation to what is self-enclosed. But this is not a contingent development—as if some actualities stand out and others do not. To be actual at all is to stand out; still further, to be fully actual is to have attained the othering which standing out entails. This is why we must proclaim, "The presence of actuality, or its actual and immediate presence, impels a recognition of that otherness [belonging to it as fully realized actuality], for *the actual is actual only in its otherness*, only in its otherness from that identity which is simply and only itself" (*SEG* 25; my italics). The actual, we might say, is the acting out of otherness, its ex-pression, its being-there here-and-now.

Identity is the invariant core of actuality and as such is resistant to otherness. In its sheer resistance to change, such identity is "an original and undifferentiated identity which is eternally the same" (*SEG* 34). *This* identity must be left behind if the actuality of speech is to occur. For example, God's "eternal presence" is suspended in the very word that names him: "It is just because the naming of God makes manifest the finality of actuality that God can be named only when an original identity disappears. When that identity disappears, then the name of God is spoken" (*SEG* 34). The identity whose fate is to disappear is not only that of God's eternal presence; it is any simple identity—any identity thought apart from otherness. Just as any simple origin has to be surpassed, so any such identity has to be transcended if actuality is to begin: "actuality can only be itself by being other than itself, by being other than an identity which is simply itself, and simply itself whenever and wherever it is present" (*SEG* 30). But this leaves open the possibility of another, decidedly nonsimple identity, one that inheres in actuality itself and that is termed "self-identity" (cf. *SEG* 83 ff). Such identity is compounded of otherness through and through. In the end, "every identity is other, and other in its actuality, other when it is spoken" (*SEG* 34). Some identities are other qua external to actuality (such is God's ever-the-same identity), while other identities are other in their very internality to actuality—*other from within*. And these identities, that is, self-identities, are self-othering by their very nature. Even in "the speech of total speech"—in which any strict sense of self-identity (for example, as personal identity) is annulled—we witness "an ultimate self-transcendence in which the difference of self-identity becomes wholly other than itself" (*SEG* 83).

This does not mean that self-identity vanishes in the manner of simple or eternal identity; it means that self-identity manifests its own otherness. If this signifies that it "becomes wholly other than itself," it is still other in relation to that self and thus to its self-identity. At this apocalyptic moment, then, in which "the silence, or the otherness, of self-identity comes to an end" (*SEG* 83), the otherness of self-identity is retained as an ever-present avatar of speech. Only that identity that is a matter of undifferentiated (thus simple) plenitude is overcome by speech, indeed as itself a condition of speech: "Only the negation of such a . . . plenitude can establish the possibility of a real and actual act" (*SEG* 19). The demise of simple identity does not just lay down the possibility of speech; this demise *is* the advent of the actuality of speech: "[S]uch a negation does not simply establish the possibility of act, it rather embodies it, and embodies it as act itself" (*SEG* 19).

None of this is to deny that Altizer continues to speak in an unreconstructed metaphysical way. Toward the end of *The Self-Embodiment of God* he says unrepentantly, "A fully self-actualized presence can only be a total presence, and a presence in which speech and silence are one" (*SEG* 91). Here there is no shadow of otherness, of difference, of absence. Even with regard to speaking—which we have seen to be perforated with the porosities of difference and nonpresence—it is still said that the "speech of total speech can only be the speech of total presence" (*SEG* 81). How can we square this claim with what is said only a page later when, commenting on the Old Testament apothegm, "Before Abraham was, I am," Altizer says: "Speech now speaks in difference, and as difference as well, a difference which actually speaks" (*SEG* 82)? But this is not a matter of mere contradiction, of an exclusionary either/or. Just as there are two kinds of identity to be recognized—simple and eternal self-identity—so two kinds of difference are at stake; one of these is indeed excluded, while the other is incorporated into a detotalized total presence itself (requiring one to admit precisely that "Speech now speaks in difference"). The first kind of difference is "difference which is only difference" (*SEG* 82), that is to say, purely formal difference, a difference *between* things. The other kind of difference is internal to words; it is incorporated into them, embodied there, part of their infrastructure. Hence we can say at once, "Total speech can only be the disembodiment, the actual negation, of difference [that is, difference in the first, purely oppositional sense]" *and*, "that disembodiment from difference is also the full actualization of difference [that is, in the second, purely differential sense]" (*SEG* 82). Once the first kind of difference—"difference which is other and apart" (*SEG* 82)—has been excluded from meaningful speech, then the difference that remains can become fully actual, which is to say, it can become *embodied*.

It is time to talk of *body*, or rather, to acknowledge that we have been speaking of it all along. First of all, as the actualization of speech from silence. Silence is not simply stopped by speech but embodied in it. Then, as the sequel to the disembodiment just discussed, whereby disembodiment from oppositional difference, the difference that is external, that is, "other and apart," clears the way for the embodiment of speech in voice: "When speech is fully embodied in pure voice, it is disembodied from . . . all difference which is only [external or formal] difference" (*SEG* 82). Then again, as the concretization of otherness: "All actual otherness is now an embodied otherness, and an immediately embodied otherness, an otherness which is both immediately and totally present" (*SEG* 82). And still again, as the actuality of speech in the negation of complete or simple identity: embodiment is "an actual absence, the real absence of a simple or total identity" (*SEG* 19).

But what is embodiment? "Embodiment is presence" (*SEG* 19). Once again we must resist the temptation to regard this as an outright metaphysical statement—as a merely unreflective commitment to presence as plenitude or origin or end. The challenge is to think body as a unique form of presence in which otherness is constitutive and immanent. Rather than a body that is materially homogeneous and transparent—for example, the medical body and, in many respects, the lived body—we need to think a body that has otherness inscribed in its very being.

Altizer's model for such a body is speech as the embodiment of voice: "Voice speaks. And when it speaks, and as it speaks, it embodies itself. Speech is the embodiment of voice, and that embodiment is the act of voice itself" (*SEG* 63). Precisely in becoming speech, voice attains its own otherness: "[A]s speech, voice is other than itself, and is other than itself precisely because it speaks" (*SEG* 63). Voice becomes other than itself not just because speech is a different level of realization but because voice articulates itself as speech—in an expression that is tantamount to embodiment: "Voice enacts its otherness from itself, and embodies that otherness in its own speech" (*SEG* 63). In producing the speaking word, the speaker's intention is to say something that is actively embodied in the word that is articulated. Plenitude of meaning, the fully expressed sense, is most completely realized in the speaking word, when the word is lifted from the collective resources of language and animated by enunciation and pronunciation.

In *The Self-Embodiment of God*, Altizer acknowledges body to be sure, yet body only in the single register of speech. Speech is a richly ramified actualization of voice. Yet this promising direction puts Altizer into an eminently deconstructable position, a vulnerable position that, however, proves itself to be more wily and resourceful than appears at first glance. What presents itself as unmitigated phonocentrism ends by being something much more complex and interesting. The phonocentrism is evident and rampant: let no one attempt to deny this. Body expresses itself primarily in speech, and this corporeal speech is inseparable from that very voice that is the crux of Derrida's critique of phonocentrism: such speech presumes the animation of meaning by breath, an animation that is directly deconstructable because of its unanalyzed ties to interiority, life, and fully present sense. Yet even as he falls prey to this critique (albeit differently from Husserl), Altizer outflanks it in several shrewd sidesteps.

First of all, Altizer thinks body otherwise. He does so not in the expressly theological writings upon which I have mainly drawn but in the book that closes the decade on which I have been concentrating: *History as Apocalypse*. In this remarkable text, Altizer recognizes another avatar of bodily existence, that of the visual body—the body that sees and is seen. True, this book highlights such a body primarily as it arises in the period of archaic Greek sculpture (secondarily, though still importantly, in high Gothic sculpture of the human figure); but since this early period is seminal for the entire history of Western self-consciousness, the centrality of vision is of paramount significance for all that follows, including Altizer's own work as the hinge between late modernity and the postmodern.[8]

According to Altizer, the newfound visual body is a flight from any stable center. With reference to the scene of Athena's birth on the Parthenon pediment, he writes: "No centers at all are present here and cannot be present if only because all traces of center or ground disappear with the full release of bodily presence, a disappearance which is now incarnate before us" (*HA* 24). Such a decentered tableau, lost in the sensuous folds of the garments of the gods surrounding the sacred birth, cannot be captured in the net of deconstruction. The body unleashes itself in the very action of genesis whereby one body separates from another, its aboriginal center.

Second, this flight from the center, if not "from the center into X" (Nietzsche), is nonetheless into a *world*, that is to say, into a larger detotalized totality of which body itself, even in its greatest synaesthetic amplitude, is only a part. Put in terms of the seeing body, "it is not only an individual figure who is present here, but a *world or cosmos of dawning light*, a light enveloping the figure before us but also a light which is all encompassing, a light embodying a new world" (*HA* 20–21; my italics).[9] Still more radically, Altizer suggests that the Greek sense of body is not merely surrounded by world but *is itself world*—that is to say, it is already dispersed into the world of which it is not just a part but a part so integral that it embodies the world itself. At the same time, such a world-body is equally consciousness, the very same consciousness that the Greeks introduced to world history (cf. *HA* 25).

This is a radical thought, much more so than appears at first glance. Not only is the body more than a speaking body—and even more than a seeing body, and more even than a touching body—but the fully expanded body is at one with its world, being that very world: "[W]orld is here present as body" (*HA* 20). And conversely, *body is present as world*. A body brings a world with it, and not just consciousness and thought, speaking and seeing, touching and being touched.

If body is first and finally incarnate, it is so only as body-all. Such a momentous body as this, answering to an equally momentous world, is nothing other than the "primordial body" of which Altizer sometimes speaks as equivalent to the "apocalyptic body."[10] This expanded body is all the body in all the world; not just *in* but *as*: it is the body altogether as al-together the world. The primordial/apocalyptic body is the body as the world of which it is at once the beginning and the end. It incarnates not just itself but the world of which it is both progenitor and witness. Indeed, to attain total presence demands the whole body as its incarnate carrier as well as the whole world with which that body is indissolubly bound up.

When Altizer declares that "self-identity can be totally present only by embodying a total presence" (*SEG* 79), we would expect that such em-bodiment would be of the entire body as it bears its world. But it is reveal-ing that this axiomatic utterance is shortly afterward curtailed in its scope: "[E]nactment is self-enactment [that is, an enactment of self-identity], a self-enactment of pure act, and a self-enactment fully embodying the voice and hearing of pure act" (*SEG* 79).[11] Just as we thought we were beyond the phonocentric strain in Altizer, we find ourselves thrust back to speech from world and the full body that is finally identical with world, stopping short of an absolute identity that is deeper than any self-identity.[12]

In what we can now recognize as an act of self-retrieval, Altizer him-self admits that total presence "does not name itself in speech alone, and cannot do so, if only because all such naming detaches speech from act" (*SEG* 78). This is to acknowledge the delimitation of articulate speech, and it would seem to call for the subsequent acknowledgement of the whole body that encompasses and exceeds, even as it supports, such speech. No such expansive acknowledgment is to be found in *The Self-Embodiment of God*; it occurs only by deferment: namely, eight years later in *History as Apocalypse* and then only as characterizing the early Greek era.

A parallel case of the tension between full body and partial body is found in Altizer's talk of the Kingdom of God as "at hand" (*SEG* 72). For the Kingdom of God to be at hand—that is to say, for a divine world to be present—is to be present in and for one's whole bodily existence. But just at the brink of this important admission Altizer draws back once again: "Speech is spoken or said only insofar as it is enacted and at hand. For it is enacted by being at hand, and by being at hand in pure presence, *a presence in which speech itself is totally present*" (*SEG* 76; my italics). But does not pure or total presence, and all the more so the Kingdom of God as the world in its full glory, call for being actual in the complete body and not just in part of it, no matter how crucial this part may be in the context of a theology of the Word? Is the Kingdom of God truly "at hand [only] in the actuality of hearing . . . a hearing whose own immediate ac-tuality is the self-realization or self-embodiment of speech" (*TP* 12)? Is this kingdom not present if present at all in world as world, in body as body, and in body-as-world? Speech again threatens to undercut the full range, the all-in-all, of body and world.

In Altizer's theology of self-embodiment, the body is not quite all there, nor is the world wholly present, and we must accordingly ask of him: Where is *the rest of the body* and *the full presence of the world* once voice and speech have been accounted for? Where have body-all and world-all gone after their primal recognition by the Greeks? Has not Altizer's theology, here running athwart his own more ample vision, disembodied and disenworlded the speaking subject of that same theology?

What one mainly misses in Altizerian thought is just this: the body as all there, there in its own incarnate totality, and not just as voice artic-ulated as speech—however powerful and indispensable such speech is for human beings. To affirm the body's being-all-there is not to exclude oth-erness, only to describe it otherwise. Altizer's nondialectical theology eliminates any significant sense of becoming and replaces it with a con-tinually self-upbraided being, the immediate transition from voice to speech, simple to actual identity, absence to presence (and the reverse), primordial to apocalyptic, and other forms of instantaneous transition. There *is* enactive body for Altizer, but the enactment is not so much lived through as immediately realized. And there is world too, but this is a world already lost to the body that is its integral part. No wonder: if the whole lived body were to be taken into account along with the whole lived world, no such breathless transmutation would be possible; instead, we would have what we in fact experience: the prolongation, the *longue durée*, of discontinuous presence.

"Incarnation" as it is treated in *The Self-Embodiment of God* in the chap-ter with this very word as its title ends by being a strangely abstract af-fair. It is as if Altizer had found voice but lost the whole body, which is alone curative for loss of voice itself! This anomalous circumstance points to an important lesson: incarnation is an occurrence of the com-plete body. It is all or nothing. Partial incarnation is not just oxy-moronic; it is a contradiction in terms. Can I be incarnated in my nose and not in my foot, in my brain but not my heart, in my voice but not my hand? Incarnation is truly "all in all" to use Altizer's own favorite phrase.

It ensues that if Jesus is an incarnate being, he is certainly incarnated *throughout* his body: "a totally incarnate Jesus is a totally descended Jesus" (*CJ* 198). And in his dying Jesus doubtless suffered with his whole body: "crucifixion is all in all" (*CJ* 199). How could it be otherwise?

Later writings of Altizer begin to lift the veil of (an impossible) partial incarnation. In *The Contemporary Jesus*, for example, there is talk— inspired by Blake's idea of a "Universal Humanity"—of "a universal body that is present in every human face and voice, and above all present in our deepest pain and joy" (*CJ* 193). If face is here recognized in addition to voice—recognized again, two and a half millennia after Athens—why not other body parts? These other parts are at least implied in the claim that Christianity posits a Spirit that "is not only actualized through body and flesh, but is the consequence of the epiphany or realization of Spirit itself in the deepest depths of matter and body" (*CJ* 192). Flesh envelops the whole body and not just part of it; and if body is matter, it is matter through and through; indeed, it is earth.[13] Jesus' "incarnate 'I'" is said to be "present in the depths of body or matter itself" (*CJ* 194). Certainly these depths would seem to call for the entire body to be their fit vehicle, and all the more so if these depths are "deeply divided . . . beween a new interior or within and a new body that is the body of these depths themselves" (*CJ* 194). Only a whole concrete body could hold such a riven self together; only a fully earthly body could be what Husserl calls a "basis body" for the new body that is utimately the resurrected body. In short: only a primordial body can be an apocalyptic body.[14]

The mention of self—or for that matter, spirit—entails the important point, nowhere thematized by Altizer but implicit in his notion of self-embodiment, that the very nature of self is such that only a complete embodiment can be its material expression. However it is characterized, the self or spirit resists dissolution into independent parts (even if it does possess dependent *moments*: aspects dependent precisely on the whole which they qualify). And if this is so, then the embodiment on which Altizer everywhere insists, however disparately, must itself be equally holistic. This is as true of God's self-embodiment as it is for that of any mortal being. Self-embodiment cannot be confined to a single part such as voice, no matter how emblematic or privileged this part may be. For voice cannot be all in all for a being who, by its very nature, is indissolubly all in all—and all in all not just in the present but also in the future, in "an apocalyptic anonymity now becoming all in all" (*CJ* 196). Once more: only a *full* primordial body can be an effective apocalyptic body. As Husserl would say it, only a basis-body can be a world-body.

It follows as well that even the *dis*embodiment of the self—so distressingly present in Altizer's writing even as he flees its specter—is also all in all. If the loss of "original or primal identity" (*SEG* 76) entails the disembodiment of that prior self before it can be reembodied in the new self of self-identity, then the old body is disembodied as a whole; otherwise, room would not be cleared for the advent of the new body that is its actualized successor. What Altizer calls more generally "kenotic actualization" (*CJ* 201) has an ineluctably corporeal dimension, as Altizer, more than any other contemporary theologian except for D. G. Leahy, would insist. But he does not insist enough on the fact that the self-emptying and self-negation that lead to the actualization itself are all-body phenomena, or they will not work their full transformative effects.

Toward the end of *The Self-Embodiment of God* there occurs a development that would delight a deconstructionist. The text, from having been auto-deconstructive in numerous ways—only some of which I have here hinted at: the pervasive role of otherness and difference, the complication of origin and identity—suddenly reverts to an apparently outright metaphysics of presence that begs for an equally outright deconstruction. We read of a pure presence such that "once presence is present, and is totally present, absence disappears, and disappears in the totality of presence" (*SEG* 78). We hear of a self-identity without relation to any other identity, not even simple or eternal identity: "self-identity can be totally present only by embodying a total presence, and in that presence self-identity becomes identical with identity itself. Therefore no identity can stand outside of this identity" (*SEG* 79). In short, the immediacy of presence is affirmed, without the prospect of any significant mediation. From such immediate presence all otherness vanishes: "Then all self-identity, insofar as it is present and actual, is called to its own realization as the self-identity of a pure act. For the call of a pure and final actuality ends every present and actual identity which is other than itself. And it ends it by calling it to itself, by calling it to its own self-actualization" (*SEG* 79–80). This even begins to look like transcendental solipsism. With no otherness remaining, there can be nothing but self-actualization in the guise of self-identity. A curious kind of plenitude—plenitude of the self—is all that is left.

It does not matter whether this belongs to God or to human beings. Either way, there is nothing beyond self-presence, nothing but speech: "Before Abraham was, I am" (John 8:58).

Yet there is a way out of this closed "circuit of selfness" (in Sartre's apposite term). It is through the total body. The only way to make sense of Altizer's final pronouncements in *The Self-Embodiment of God*—as vulnerable to deconstruction as are the various particular phrases from this text with which I began—is to think of them as statements about the full body. This is the way out through incarnation as organic materiality. For we can say of the whole body that it is self-actualizing and self-present, that it "immediately actualizes all presence" (*SEG* 79). It is certainly a form of self-identity, as we know from its unique characterological or physiognomic style. And we can even say that it excludes every identity that is distinctly "other than itself" in the sense that when functioning as a (more or less) hale organic body it runs (more or less) on its own.

But the material body is not altogether without otherness, not just in that it depends for nutrition on the environment, and for emotional support on other human bodies. It incorporates such otherness into itself, thereby becoming "a self-identity in which difference embodies its otherness in the immediacy of a real and actual presence" (*SEG* 81), not just in the presence of voice, but in the simultaneous presence of all its parts, indeed their compresence in a circumambient world. This compresence of integral parts of a single whole body in a single whole world, of a body-all in a world-all, is as true of an incarnate God as it is for human beings: then the body is truly an incarnation of God and the world is the Kingdom of God.

If this reading of Altizer's ending statements in *The Self-Embodiment of God* is accepted, their apparently easy deconstructibility can be parried in two ways. First, if these statements can be seen to refer to the whole body (as later texts such as *History as Apocalypse* indicate may well be the case), then the charge of phonocentrism falls fallow, and with it the logocentrism with which it is invariably associated in Western thought. Second, this same body being material beckons to a spatial dimension that cannot be subsumed into the temporocentrism that is the third partner of the unholy alliance upon which the metaphysics of presence is built. For to be a material body is to be in space, and to be in space is to be outside the self-enclosure of presence within which meaning is intended and grasped *im selben Augenblick*, that is to say, simultaneously and without the mediation of space, including the indicative signs that ineluctably implicate that space.

Or more exactly: not that space, but that *place*. I will end with a few remarks concerning what may be even more conspicuously missing than
the full body from Altizer's most theoretically engaging theological work.
Yet it is the other way out of self-enclosed, disincarnate (or only partially
disincarnate) self-presence. The plenary body is the first way, place is the
second, and the two are closely connected. In fact, wherever there is a
whole body there is place, and the reverse is true as well.

If body incorporates otherness in its sheer materiality, it also engages
otherness by way of place. By being a body in place, a person *stands out*
in that place: *ex-ists* there in the locution that is common to Altizer and
Heidegger. But where ex-isting qua ecstatico-horizonal movement is a
feature of temporality for Heidegger, ex-isting is spatio-temporal for Altizer. For it is actuality that ex-ists, and it is spatial and temporal at once:

> If the actual was simply and only itself then it could not be actual,
> for then it could stand out from nothing whatsoever, and hence
> it could not stand, it could not become manifest. But the actual
> as actual is the manifest, it does stand out, it exists, and it exists in
> its pure immediacy. Nevertheless, that immediacy is not a simple
> immediacy, not an immediacy that simply exists, it rather *ex-ists,
> it stands out from itself in its presence.* (*SEG* 25; my italics)

I would suggest that any such standing out from itself is at the very least
a spatial trait and that it is more specifically a matter of place. For the
body that is the basis of any actuality is always a particular body, just *my*
body or *yours*, and thus the world in which it is located is equally particular. To paraphrase Archytas of Tarentum: *to be (a body) is to be in place.*

After the death of God, writes Altizer, we have to do with "a new
infinite space whose center is everywhere and whose circumference is
nowhere, a space both macroscopic and microscopic, and a new ubiquity of space inseparable from a new simultaneity of time" (*CJ* 196). It is
not that he advocates such space or time, much less its own omni-cen-
teredness. Indeed, he finds it as unacceptable as it is inevitable, intimat-
ing that we need to think out an alternative to it. His own effort to do
just this is found in his early assertion that the Kingdom of God, though
not spatial, is nevertheless here and now (*TP* 10, 12) and in these
suggestive later remarks:

Unlike a primordial simultaneity, or a mystical simultaneity, this [present, global, abstract simultaneity, modeled on infinite space] is a simultaneity in which time itself is a wholly abstract or simulated time [that is, as in television and video], and most abstract to the extent that it is simultaneous. So likewise are we being overwhelmed by a new ubiquity of space, a space that is omnidirectional, without any actual direction or perspective. Thereby center as center has truly disappeared, just as circumference as circumference has disappeared. . . . That time and space can only be wholly abstract and wholly simulated for us, unless at bottom we truly are a new radical anonymity, and an apocalyptic anonymity now becoming all in all. (*CJ* 196)

Altizer despairs of modern—and now postmodern—space (though finding a small window of hope in the acenteredness of apocalyptic anonymity), but he fails to turn to the only genuine alternative to abstractive universal space: namely, place in its sheer particularity and singularity.

Here Altizer ignores his own promising but unfulfilled move toward place in his endorsement of ex-isting as standing out. He also fails to own up to the consequences of his affirmation of a resurrected body, which is "the body of Satan only now being fully born" (*CJ* 197). Such a body—which is identical with the resurrected body of Christ and which thereby realizes the sameness of primordial and apocalyptic body—is altogether concrete and particular. This stands starkly in contrast with the Gnostic view, for which "resurrection is ascension, and not the ascension of an earthly body, but only the ascension of a glorified and heavenly body" (*CJ* 197). Once we take up this spiritualizing view, both body and space become ethereal. The affinity between nonmaterial resurrected body and empty infinite space—an affinity I have treated elsewhere[15]—is not altogether surprising. For *body as material calls for place as particular.* And this is all the more the case for the full body, which we have found to be lacking in Altizer's atheology: the fuller the body, the more complete the experience of place.

If the full body is the ground of speech, and world its horizon, place is the scene of this horizoned grounding. To be embodied, and all the more so self-embodied, is to be in place and not in space.

Just as "all speech embodies otherness" (*SEG* 31), the full body has its own otherness. This body, like its world, is not a determinate simple plenitude that cries out for direct deconstruction, as does voice. So place is other too: other to space as its antithetical other, other to body as standing *out* in it, and other to itself: for place harbors the abyss of nonplace hanging within it, the *unheimlich* coiled within the *heimlich*, the way that being lost is found in being found. Indeed, "embodiment is presence" (*SEG* 19), but this embodiment brings with it absence and difference and otherness, all of which characterize the circumstance in which body arises to become event in its occurrence in place. The true *coincidentia oppositorum*, the event in which the primordial becomes the apocalyptic, is found in the here and now of the full body that is once and for all, and finally, in place.

## NOTES

1. "Total Presence" is taken from *Total Presence: The Language of Jesus and the Language of Today*, as are "original identity" (5), "original immediacy" (4), "totally actual present" (7), "immediate and total presence" (12).

2. On determinate presence (*Anwesenheit*), see Martin Heidegger, *Being and Time*, trans. J. Macquarrie and E. Robinson (New York: Harper & Row, 1962), 47; in ancient Greek ontology (and still today) "entities are grasped in their Being as 'presence.'"

3. Concerning the "double reversal" of reversal and dissemination, see Jacques Derrida, *Positions*, trans. A. Bass (Chicago: University of Chicago Press, 1981), 41–43.

4. On deconstruction as dismemberment, see *TP* 5.

5. "When God is named as God, God is named as the God who is in exile, the God who is in exile from himself. The God who is named, the God who is spoken, is, and immediately is, only insofar as He is other than Himself" (*SEG* 32). Notice here again the antilogic of instantaneous negation whereby the "other" is the immediate double of the self.

6. The more complete statement is that the world appears only "in the horizon of speech, and in the horizon of the world embodied in speech" (*SEG* 32). For Altizer, as for Derrida and the later Heidegger, there is no world except through speech.

7. The same holds for voice: "an actual immediacy embodies an actual otherness, an otherness which is embodied in voice, and embodied in the actual and immediate otherness of voice" (*SEG* 25). Concerning the otherness of speech and voice, see also *SEG* 9, 22, 26, and esp. 31: "All speech embodies otherness, makes otherness actually present."

8. "If the naming of ultimate origin is the most primal ground of mythical language, an origin which by necessity is primordial and prehistoric, then a consciousness of concrete or actual beginning might be said to be a primal ground of historical language and consciousness" (*HA* 7).

9. Thanks to this light, we have "a new vision which is a cosmic vision and which is realizing and releasing a new world" (*HA* 21). Altizer adds that this is "a light releasing a vision in which the seer is the center of its world" (*HA* 21). Here the centeredness of pure vision in a seer such as Apollo is to be contrasted with the decenteredness of the scene of Athena's birth, in which the female figures who witness the miracle are dispersed by the epiphany of their vision.

10. In a conversation at Buck Hills Falls, Pennsylvania, on November 14, 1999, Altizer stated that "the primordial body is the apocalyptic body."

11. I am here ignoring an entire thematics of hearing that accompanies, and literally underlies, that of speaking: for instance, in the claim that "pure hearing is the total embodiment of voice, an embodiment wherein voice is the otherness of itself" (*SEG* 70–71).

12. The term "absolute identity" is that of D. G. Leahy in the same conversation noted above; Leahy used it to characterize the relationship between object and thinking that obtains in Leahy's notion of "the thinking now occurring." I here extend its meaning to include the intimate relationship between body-all and world-all.

13. This is in contrast with the Gnostic body, which achieves resurrection "only insofar as it ceases to be body or earth" (*CJ* 196).

14. On Husserl's idea of "basis body" (*Bodenkörper*), see Husserl's late essay, "Foundational Investigations of the Phenomenological Origin of the Spatiality of Nature," trans. F. Kersten in *Husserl: Shorter Works*, ed. F. Elliston and P. Mc-Cormick (South Bend: University of Notre Dame Press, 1981), 222–23, 227. See also the related idea of the "world-body" (*Weltkörper*) in Husserl, 224, 230. Concerning the resurrected body, Altizer says: "This is the new body that is the resurrected body, an apocalyptic resurrection occurring not in heaven but in a new aeon or new world" (*CJ* 194).

15. See Edward S. Casey, *The Fate of Place: A Philosophical History* (Berkeley: University of California Press, 1997), chapters 4, 5, and 10.

CHAPTER 9

Compassion at the Millennium

*A Buddhist Salvo for the Ethics of the Apocalypse*

JANET GYATSO

Perhaps the attempt to speak an alien language will restore to us the power of speech.

—Altizer, "The Buddhist Ground
of the Whiteheadian God"

H ere one reads, again, of the other. Buddhism is "that horizon
which is most innocent of God."[1] Buddhist consciousness "is
the very opposite" of the self-alienated consciousness of the
West.[2] Buddhism is that in which "there is no negation whatsoever" (*CJ*
164). Its timeless "original state of perfection" is "the essential and integral opposite of what Western Christianity has known as Christ . . . a
once-and-for-all event."[3] Have we encountered in Altizer's theology yet
another token of what is by now our classic Western orientalism: the
oversimplified portrait of an absolutely other?

Such a portrait has often been painted either to discredit its object so
that we could colonize it, or alternately, to idealize it so as to have a fantasy paradise to which to escape. Our postorientalist critics have in-
structed us well on how those two motives operate in tandem. Most
important, disdain and worship equally deny the object's own reality. In

147

both cases we still end up seeing only ourselves, either as the reverse of our opposite, which serves to reinforce by contrast our own self-definition, or simply as a shadow phantom of our fondest dream. Either way, the mirroring of ourselves is so precise that our view of the other is anything but faithful to the complexities and vicissitudes that properly belong to the actual historical object itself.

One cannot fail to be impressed nonetheless with the utter seriousness and centrality of Buddhism's place in Altizer's theology, a project whose goal is no less than to address the very core of the postmodern predicament: its vacuity, nihilism, ever-growing sense of purposelessness. Altizer would accomplish this by assimilating that very vacuous nihilism into a biblical eschatology in order to demonstrate that the apocalyptic moment *has* to be constituted in nothingness. And the invocation of Buddhism in this argument plays a key function. Altizer finds in Buddhism an important precedent wherein nothingness can be the source of wisdom and enlightenment. For just this reason, Buddhism for Altizer can instruct the contemporary Christian how to recuperate Christianity at the moment of the most serious challenge it has ever faced: the spiritual vacuity visited upon the West in the wake of the death of God. The font of insight that Buddhism represents even provokes Altizer to enthuse that "we are coming to understand that the ethics of Jesus is far closer to Buddhist ethics than to any established form of Western ethics"[4] and that the Buddhist community knows Jesus more deeply than does the Christian Church (*CJ* 164); at one point he even asks suggestively, "[C]ould Christ be a Christian name of the Buddha?"[5] And yet these effusions also implicate the double bind already foreshadowed above. How can it be that the very tradition named as our exact opposite might also promise to be a truer version of ourselves?

Let us first note that, whether as our other or our twin—or even, as Altizer would have it, some dialectical resolution of both—the name of Buddhism is legion throughout Altizer's oeuvre. He is especially enthusiastic about Buddhism when he reflects upon the thought of twentieth-century Japanese philosophers Keiji Nishitani and Masao Abe, and he has also been moved to discover a Buddhist thread in the thought of Alfred North Whitehead.[6] Altizer first became interested in Buddhist doctrine during his graduate years in the late 1950s at the Divinity School of the University of Chicago; he continued to study on his own the translations and overviews by Warren, Conze, Stcherbatsky, E. J. Thomas, Murti, and others in the succeeding decade. Later he gained another view of

Buddhist thought in a series of conversations with Nishitani and other Kyoto School philosophers in Japan. Still, the imprint of Eliade and Wach is clearly to be discerned in his presentation of Buddhism throughout his career. And one can say here that despite his limitation to secondary sources, it is impressive that Altizer knows that his exclusive focus upon Buddhist philosophy at the expense of everything relating to practice and historical institutions is a distortion (albeit a distortion fitting for a theologian who certainly constrains his own Christian tradition in much the same way).[7] Altizer also stands out among appropriators of Buddhism for his recurrent hestitancy to proclaim, as many others have done, that Buddhism offers itself as our most rational, or scientific, or modern, or even postmodern-seeming-but-actually-premodern non-Western counterpart. Resisting such glib pronouncement, Altizer is clear about certain very fundamental features that for him differentiate Buddhist views from Christian ones, and he is to be commended for being able to admit, even in the midst of his admiration, to his wariness at the too easy elision of such differences by the likes of Abe or Nishitani.[8]

But Altizer's work is uncautious for positing a unified and singular "Buddhism" with essential and eternal features that are metonymic of the tradition as a whole. This move is what enables Altizer to juxtapose such hallmark features with their equally essentialized Christian correlates— the Buddhist view of time, for example, as compared with the Christian one. The problem of course is that those generalizations do not adequately represent the very complex and vastly differentiated Buddhist tradition throughout its long history and multiple cultural appropriations; indeed, Buddhologists today are beginning to avoid the term "Buddhism" in the singular altogether. But Altizer shifts seamlessly between his sources, often presuming, for example, a pan-Buddhist conception of nirvana as total nothingness (*DH* 193–96) or as the absolute negation of conditioned existence (*CJ* 176), while in fact these represent only one particular kind of description of nirvana, contravened by other descriptions of a positive, even world-affirming nirvana, in many strands of Buddhism, both early and later.[9]

Not only do the demands of Altizer's argument often lead him to gloss over the historical fact that Buddhist tradition produced radically different schools of thought, so different that his—nay, *any*—generalization about Buddhist metaphysics in total cannot fail to be a distortion. His elision of history also prevents him from drawing on precisely those moments in Buddhist thought that could serve his argument well. For instance, totally missing from his invocation of Buddhism are the many tantric Buddhist traditions which actually thematize the power of the *co-incidentia oppositorum*—the famous tantric bliss and emptiness, for example, or wrath and enlightenment. Most promising of all for Altizer would have been the Kālācakra Tantra, which developed an overtly apocalyptic narrative.[10] Altizer also makes frequent reference to a primordial ground in Buddhism, apparently ignorant of the fact that the scriptures that developed such a notion in Buddhist history speak of a primordial presence, not the primordial nothingness that he attributes to Buddhism, and most of all that this Buddhist primordiality was roundly rejected by most other Buddhist thinkers as contradicting what they maintained is the authentic Buddhist view. Such debates in Buddhist history would not have to disqualify a Western theologian's appropriation of a particular Buddhist idea, unless that theologian was borrowing not only the specific idea but also an aura of authority, an authority that of course would be compromised if it were realized that the idea in question failed to stand authoritatively for the tradition within its own historical context.

Once again, I am trained on the postorientalist's target. But I must halt this overarching methodological criticism here, for to go any further would be to disqualify Altizer's invocation of Buddhism altogether. Instead, respecting the integrity and importance of his thought within its own sphere, I would like to reflect further on what Altizer's engagement with Buddhist thought actually accomplishes for his own theology. I will also gesture toward certain central issues to which a modern Buddhist theologian—if such an animal ever appears on our screen—will need to respond, issues that are germane to much of Western thinking about Buddhism in our epoch.[11] In this way I might even further the very dialogue that, despite its pitfalls, Altizer divines to be so providential.

## GOING TO EXTREMES

In rendering Buddhism a partner in his project to make the reversal of nihility—and the death of God—ingredient in a new birth of the Kingdom of God, Altizer goes much further than merely to fetishize as our savior the religion that we fear we can understand the least. Altizer actually studies this mysterious oriental shadow, to make it *not* other to him. And here as the logic of dialectical incorporation proceeds, Altizer finds that Buddhism indeed has important convergences with Christianity. Altizer decided early on, for example, that Buddhism and Christianity were the most ethical religions in the world (*OM* 181). Both also radically reject the conventional world (*OM* 178). And most fundamental of all, both Buddhism and Christianity centrally conceive of a totality (*CJ* 163).

Buddhism's signal totality for Altizer would be its assertion of the empty nature of all things and persons, a hallmark Buddhist doctrine. This universal emptiness must apply even to the buddha as well as to nirvana itself: such a point is made most forcefully in the Mahāyāna Prajñā-pāramitā scriptures. This shocking doctrine suggests to the Christian an impressive ability to tolerate nothingness as integral to the sacred and has been a critical inspiration for theologians such as Altizer to understand Christian notions like the *kenosis*, or self-emptying, of God (cf. *CJ* 179). The Buddhist thorough-going emptiness of selves and subjectivities is also helpful for Altizer's project to interpret the contemporary anonymity of human experience as a radical transformation of Christian self-consciousness (*CJ* 187 ff). Yet another implication of the utter universality of emptiness is the thoroughgoing nonduality in Buddhism, which becomes an essential instruction for Altizer on how to bridge the gap to God in the age of the apocalypse, and to abolish (for the first time) the polarity between humanity and deity (*DH* 179).

And yet Altizer's characterization of the Buddhist doctrine of emptiness is flawed, hijacked to a destination (absolute nothingness) that Buddhists themselves have repeatedly forbidden. Moreover, Altizer's investment in this misreading is itself hard to read, for it appears to be double-edged. At first one gets the impression that Buddhism provides for Altizer's theology a legitimizing, if exotic, analogue—as for example when Altizer suggests that the crucifixion of Jesus was the final enactment of Gautama's dissolution of self (*CJ* 175). But then one discerns that the analogy is not quite complete: the very Buddhist absolute nothingness that was so important to Altizer turns out not to be the right (Christian) kind after all. Instead, the Buddhist doctrine of emptiness is pronounced by Altizer to be a simple nothingness, something quite different from the dialectically realized *kenosis* of the Christian God.

For their own part, Buddhist philosophers have long recognized the susceptibility of the doctrine of emptiness to be confused with what they conceived of as nihilism (*ucchedavāda*), the belief that nothing exists whatsoever, along with a concomitant disbelief in the law of cause and effect, that is, karma, which would destroy any basis for ethical restraint. The distinction between emptiness and nihilism is most especially developed in Nāgārjuna's *Madhyamakārikā* (undoubtedly the classic behind Altizer's picture of Buddhist emptiness, even if he seems to miss this critical point), where the author argues that nihilism is but another form of essentialism and thereby merely the flip side of materialism or eternalism. To negate definitively is effectively to affirm (to negate in this way requires there to be something to negate, and thereby covertly affirms its being). According to this Buddhist logic all essential things are independent and eternal, which means in turn that they can neither change nor interact with anything else. For this reason, the essentially existing thing turns out to be nil. Aspiring to elude capture on these twin horns, Nāgārjuna's notion of emptiness would not then definitively deny the existence of anything, only the existence of its essence, which is to say that all things that are conventionally thought to exist do indeed exist, with the important proviso that this existence is of a different nature than is normally conceived: things exist only relationally, dependently and in context, and most important, empty of essence. The distinction between nihilism and the much more complexly conceived notion of emptiness is a fundamental watershed for Buddhist self-definition, a cutting edge for distinguishing the "right view" from a multiplicity of heterodoxies.

Altizer appears to ignore this very central distinction between emptiness and nothingness in Buddhist thought,[12] insisting that Buddhism's way is "a fully or totally negative way" (*DH* 194). Sometimes he seems to put its emptiness on a par with some of his own most sacred moments of nihility: "Even as Buddhism can know and embody an absolute nothingness as an absolute totality, Eckhart could know the 'lowest point' as that point which impels the Godhead to release the totality of itself, and Nietzsche could know an absolute nihilism as the very arena of the totality of Eternal Recurrence of the Will to Power. At no other points has our history evoked a more total nothingness" (*GG* 148). But more often Altizer invokes his own distinction between two kinds of nothingness—primordial nothingness and actual nothingness—which are surely as central to his entire project as is the one between nihilism and emptiness in Buddhist thought. Now while Altizer's pair is not the same as the Buddhist one, it is interesting to note that both pairs are fundamental to their respective tradition's self-definition. Just as Buddhism's distinction would render Altizer's nothingness tantamount to heresy, Altizer's distinction between primordial and actual nothingness creates the critical site where Buddhism can be roundly excluded from the unique and triumphal revelation of Christianity ("it is exactly that emptiness that our nothingness is not" [GG 150][13]) and its status as the foundation of modernity.

Altizer's two kinds of nothingness are developed particularly clearly in *The Genesis of God* by means of an exploration of the metaphysics of creation and the problem of the relation between being and nothing. The eschatology of *The Descent into Hell* is another defining moment wherein Altizer insists upon the necessity of the actual over the primordial. But the distinction is fundamental for him in so much of his work, certainly as early as his telling book *Oriental Mysticism,* where he lays out clearly the difference between the timeless now of the spirit or logos and the historical and temporally specific reality of the flesh of the son of God (*OM* 180). Most crucially, actual nothingness is the only ground against which actual being can come into existence. In the form of dialectical logic in which Altizer founds his project, the ontological status of what is being negated must match the ontological status of what is being created. And everything must be actual in Christianity for Altizer: negation, creation, identity, the fall, redemption. In order for there to be a true *coincidentia oppositorum,* the opposites that are coinciding must be actual opposites.[14] It is only a real and final and actual fall that can make possible a real and final eschatological redemption.[15] Most important of all, an absolute and actual nothingness is what must be negated in order for there to be the only real kind of creation, that is, the Christian one. "An absolute and once-and-for-all beginning is wholly alien to paganism, and even as such a beginning is wholly absent from all non–Biblical worlds, it is wholly absent from every God or absolute which is not the Creator" (*GG* 19).

The primordial is of course synonymous with the pagan; thence does Buddhism (which, Altizer informs us, knows the past and future to be identical) join the ranks of the pagan for Altizerian Christendom.[16] The problem for Altizer in the pagan or the primordial is not merely that it fails to support the absoluteness of the Christian deity and its actions; more critically, it fails to account for historical reality at all. This is where Altizer's theological project would rejoin secular modernity or even postmodernity. Altizer's actual—be it actual nothingness or actual being—will ultimately be consonant with the stark reality of the secular world, a reality that is at the heart of the real "historical consciousness" so regularly associated with the modern West. For Altizer that historical consciousness owes its rigor and its radicality ultimately to the emblematic Christian crucifixion, and the utter confrontation with the reality of the death of

God, but it happens fully only now, in the modern to postmodern epoch, for the first time in human history.[17]

## THEOLOGIZING HISTORICAL REALITY

This, then, is what Altizer's use of Buddhism accomplishes: it supplies Christianity with an idea, and an inspiring model, of transgression, which nonetheless must be reversed, as surely as the principle of reversal governs all historical movement. Buddhism provides for Altizer a first glimpse of the possibility of how nothingness can be sacred, but the primordial purity of that Buddhist nothingness in the end makes it fall short, still subject to the final clarifications of the Christian actual nothingness, which is fully historical and temporal and thereby able to engage contemporary life much more promisingly by virtue, to wit, of an apocalyptic transformation.

Quite apart from the foregoing critique of the violence such a "primordial nothingness" visits upon the *actual* Buddhist discussions of the historical doctrine of emptiness, we might also notice where Altizer's theology leaves the possibility of a modern Buddhist theology. I would submit that, to the degree that Altizer's theology constructs a Buddhism that is inseparable from the primordial, the perhaps unintended consequence is that the prospect of any such contemporary Buddhist theology is rendered nil. For Altizer, Buddhism becomes in effect a discarded handmaiden who once serviced the now triumphant Christian eschatology.

A modern Buddhist theologian could nonetheless learn from Altizer—for he is surely right on this point—that any religious metaphysics that brackets historical reality and adverts to a timeless swoon will have no purchase on modern intellectual thought. And one hardly needs to be reminded of how commonplace it has been for historians of religion to find in Buddhist metaphysics a fundamental vision of an eternal return. But while Buddhologists have failed to ratify this finding in actual Buddhist thought and have even overtly taken issue with it, the fact that this failure has hardly registered among those who would do comparative religion bears testimony to the recalcitrance of what Steven Collins calls "the myth of the myth of eternal return."[18] And so the question merits further consideration. Apparently Altizer's principal grounds for an assertion such as "Buddhism can know beginning and ending as simply identical, just as Buddhism can know the past and future as identical, and identical because all time is finally an empty time" (GG 17) is that the ultimate emptiness of all things makes all things purely and simply identical. But Buddhists never say that, and it is hard to see why it may be concluded—any more than from the fact that for Christians all things are identical in being the creation of God, or even from the postmodern view that all things are identical in being culturally constructed and relative. If these abstract commonalities do not entail an eternal return it is not clear why the Buddhist one (emptiness) does either.

Again Altizer seems to deliberately ignore his own study of the very Mahāyāna and Mādhyamika sources he draws upon for the notion of emptiness, wherein a distinction between, and yet ultimate identification of "conventional" and "ultimate" truth is elaborately developed. Altizer insists that all that counts for the Buddhist view is the ultimate, when in fact the simplicity of that notion is repeatedly called into question, and those same sources propose with increasing nuance that the ultimate can never stand utterly divorced from the conventional, much less be reified as such. To miss the famously paradoxical context in which, yes, notions such as "the sameness of all things," for example, are developed in the Prajñāpāramitā sutras, and to conclude that this means that all things are the same historically is to miss the very fundamental point these very texts make that the ultimately empty nature of all things cannot simply be asserted and that instead any assertion implies an oversimplification and reification. Hence the method is developed whereby all simple predication is refused, and all simple assumptions are deliberately challenged, in order to deny any final or pure identity or simple coming to rest. Why else would the multiple Buddhist sources that are concerned with such issues be sure to point out that even emptiness itself, along with nirvana and everything else that a simple reading would posit as the ultimate truth, is nothing but a concept whose ultimate existence cannot be asserted any more than can some quotidian fact? Why else would the path of these traditions ask of its adherents such complex tasks as to "absorb yourself in contemplation in such a way that you are released in liberation without abandoning the passions that are the province of the world"?[19]

In resisting Altizer's reading of "Buddhism" I am simply drawing upon the same sources that Altizer himself is indebted to for the doctrine of "the void," the very doctrine that for him becomes emblematic of

Buddhist thought and the eternal return that he discerns therein (cf. *OM* 137 ff). One could also mount a similar critique of Altizer's reading of Buddhism by drawing on other Buddhist sources for another Buddhist doctrine (and here the point is so uncontroversial and general that one can speak fairly univocally). This doctrine concerns the integral relation of metaphysics with some sort of path structure, or praxis as such. Most pertinent is the temporality that such a path entails, which calls into question any simple Buddhist equation, as Altizer would have it, of the is with the is not.[20] No one who has studied Buddhist history can have missed the countless iterations of the recurring "sudden-gradual" debate, certainly throughout Mahāyāna tradition but already discernible in the calming-insight pair in Buddhist soteriology from very early on. Now if any purely sudden position had ever been sustained in Buddhism, it might have provided evidence of an Altizerian primordiality, but as is well known, the complex issue is never settled simply, and certainly the upshot virtually always folds in some kind of gradual process.[21] Such a requirement for process implies a unidirectional movement (witness also the recurrent worry about backsliding in early Buddhist soteriology, which itself betrays the desire for decisive forward movement), as do once-and-for-all realizations at definitive moments of breakthrough on such paths.[22]

The "sudden" enlightenment tradition just referred to is associated not with the Madhyamaka sources that Altizer draws upon, but rather with the "third turning of the wheel" tradition in Buddhism, which does indeed speak of a primordial ground, sometimes cast as a universal "buddha nature" or "womb of the tathāgata." These third-turning sources instruct the aspirant to see through the clouds of samsaric particularity to the pure sky that has always already been there and is more true and real than those illusory clouds. Altizer might indeed find evidence in these scriptures (they include several Mahāyāna sutras, the treatises of Asanga, and some passages in East Asian Ch'an as well as Indo-Tibetan rDzogs-chen and Mahāmudrā) of a Buddhist eternal return. But he would have to grant that this would not be synonymous with the primordial nothingness that he has posited as the essential Buddhist truth. For the classic third turning of the wheel scriptures famously renege on the rigorous emptiness of the Prajñāpāramitā and Madhyamaka; what is primordial is not negative, but positive, and eternal.[23] Moreover, whatever their stand regarding an eternal return, these Buddhist works cannot in any event serve emblematically for Buddhist thought overall, since the idea of the primordial was subject to much criticism in Buddhist philosophical circles historically. It has also been rejected by some of the few examples of whom one might term "Buddhist theologians" in the modern period. This group of Japanese scholars, like their chosen predecessors of "second-turning" persuasion, argues that buddha nature and other kinds of primordial grounds violate what they see as the orthodox Buddhist proscription of essentialism of any kind.[24]

Now if the theological project does indeed entail bracketing historical differences and simply picking whatever group of passages one wants to represent Buddhism as a whole, certainly a promising place to begin to look for a "Buddhist view of time," if one insists on finding one, would be the Buddhist doctrine of impermanence, that pervasive theme in sutras, doctrinal treatises, poetry, autobiography, and so many other kinds of writing throughout Buddhist history and geographical spread. The inexorability of change, flux, the impossibility for anything ever to remain the same: Buddhists of all stripes, even meditators and scholars who subscribe to doctrines of primordial enlightenment, so often grapple in their writings with the sad but undeniable facts of life. One could certainly consider a wide variety of ritual, not to mention biography, poetry, and other kinds of Buddhist literary works, to discover the many ways in which death is *not* finally unreal in Buddhism, as Altizer would have it (cf. *CJ* 172 ff). But even to restrict ourselves to the metaphysical, Nāgārjuna's *Madhyamakārikā*, the very text that informs much of Altizer's reading of the Buddhist conception of time, in my view provides compelling grounds for a metaphysics that can engage real history and real death.[25]

The argument turns again on the twin essentialisms of nihilism and materialism. Contra Altizer, Nāgārjuna shows that to be absolutely present or absolutely absent means that the thing or person in question is absolutely stuck, with no possibility for change of any sort. To be absolutely present, or absent, or absolutely anything implies a finality, an isolation, and a simplicity that belie any possibility of modification or influence from without. Once you are absolutely anything, you cannot ever be anything else; if you do become anything else, you are no longer the same you. This means that whatever "you" means, it must be flexible and only roughly defined: dependent and empty of absolute essence. This reading lands Altizer in precisely the dilemma that he assigns to Buddhist metaphysics. It is Altizer's absolute beginning that can never actually occur. In contrast, it is only when something is relative, in interdependent

relation with the world around it, when it is heterogeneous and not absolutely identified as anything once and for all that it can actually achieve
historical existence. It is only emptiness, as Nāgārjuna shows, that allows
change and causality to operate; if things were not empty—and again,
emptiness means merely that the thing is dependent and empty of essence,
not that it is entirely absent—they could never do anything at all, for to
do or be anything at all is to be in relation to the world around oneself.
And to be in relation to the world around oneself is to be nonabsolute.

## THE MIDDLE WAY OF ETHICS

But let us return to the orientalist dilemma posed at the opening of this
chapter: if it is true that by defining oneself in opposition to an other one
also betrays a repressed desire to become that other, or at least be enhanced
by that other, we might now ask, What are the moments in Buddhist
thought with which Altizer might engage his Christianity after all? I have
already suggested a reading of second turning of the wheel emptiness—
that is, relativity, not nothingness or pure primordial anything—that
could actually serve Altizer well. Another moment in Buddhist history
that one would have expected Altizer to draw upon would have been the
Buddhist tantric tradition. And surely there has never been such a tantric
Christian theologian as Thomas J. J. Altizer, for whom a descent into
Hell is identical to an ascent to Heaven!

But if Altizer did mine the tantric literature for his theology, he
would find himself facing first a formidable obstacle. This is so less because of his metaphysics—the practices of the Buddhist tantras certainly
do turn on a *coincidentia oppositorum*, and a reversal of extremes, although
in the end there must be no absolutes here either—than because of the
ethics, or lack thereof, of his apocalypticism. Although the ethics of the
tantras are themselves suspect, and will surely be subject to much criticism
if this material ever comes to be considered normatively in contemporary
Buddhistic discourse (which has not happened yet[26]), at the very least the
tantras are canny enough to announce that their transgressive teachings
are so radical and dangerous that they must be kept secret, limited to the
small circle of initiates who have had the training required to understand
the shocking recommendations in the proper way. Most simply put, the
first thing that a Buddhist tantric guru (let alone a more conventional
Buddhist teacher) would likely tell Altizer would be to stop writing so

openly about the good news of the apocalypse. His work would be regarded as esoteric, not to be published for public consumption on the fear that it would be misused.

When Altizer envisages how the coming of the Kingdom of God will erase humanity, he means humanity in its fallen form, but his vision is easily read as presaging nuclear cataclysm. Similarly, the shattering of the "thou shalt" that will mark the apocalyptic might mean for Altizer something like what the *Lao tsu* says when it claims that the appearance of the doctrine of humanity signals a decline of the Tao, and therefore advises abandoning sageliness and humanity.[27] But the charged and exalted chaos that Altizer goes on to extol could only have been viewed by most Buddhists—and now I mean not only tantrikas, but also monastics and laymen alike, not to mention most non-Buddhists too!—with grave concern. If Buddhist texts speak of realms of open determination, beyond conceptuality, there is never a valorized notion of chaos as such, especially not a valorized social chaos.

In view of the clear dangers that Altizer's apocalyptic message appears to carry, one is indeed pressed to ask for his ethics, but this is not readily forthcoming. The very notion of ethics seems to imply for him only interim and unsatisfactory—even satanic—measures, ripe for their own transgression, which is the only thing that "could open a way to liberation."[28] For Altizer the true ethics is the deep or pure action of apocalyptic enactment, which is lawless and chaotic, albeit predestined, the assured manifestation of God's will. Altizer does sometimes call this pure action "compassion," which for him is real only when it is synonymous with an interior and kenotic dissolution, or, more classically, the absolute sacrifice of the crucifixion. This absolute self-sacrifice brings on the new creation and is the only moment of true and absolute love.

It is clear enough, then, that Altizer's ethics will be closely analogous to his metaphysics of extreme reversal. But beyond the problematic character of that metaphysics for Buddhist logic as already discussed, the extreme reversal of Altizer will also be seen by Buddhists, who require serious ethical training for radical practice of any sort, to be exceedingly risky. Why would one not expect to see, in fact welcome, the most extreme acts of cruelty, if it is the case that the more real and absolute our depravity, the more complete and real will be the birth of the new world that would follow? Altizer does occasionally suggest a distinction between a reviled simple, pagan evil and the absolute evil that is the valorized apocalyptic.[29] Still, the Buddhist—again, tantrika and monastic alike—who stresses intensive training in mindfulness, control of emotions, and a rigorous course in assimilating theory into habitual schema, would have to ask how, in the absence of any similar course of training in Altizer's system, can the participants in the apocalyptic moment be expected to tell the difference between the two kinds of evil? Missing emotional mindfulness, would there not likely result a confusion if not deliberate conflation of the distinction between the two kinds of negativity, thereby sanctioning a self-serving orgy of indulgence? Lacking any conventional morality or rules, how could such participants recall the philosophical theology they read in Altizer, let alone "remember" it in any deeper Augustinian sense of a memory of the present?[30]

Even the metaphysical issues discussed earlier have entailments in the practical sphere that will distinguish much of Buddhist ethics from that suggested by Altizer's apocalypse. Most important, the radical self-sacrifice that Altizer envisages to be ingredient in apocalyptic love, whereby a real self is absolutely destroyed and a real identity is absolutely transformed (*DH* 199ff), is far too simple to stand as the analogue to Buddhist self-denial, since what is being denied in that case never really existed in the first place.

Such complexity and lack of any pure or absolute reversal ensures a critical difference between Buddhist and what Altizer envisions as Christian ethics. Emotionally, or even aesthetically, the absence of the dynamics of extreme denial means that Buddhist self-sacrifice, as for example in the classic story of the bodhisattva feeding his own body to a hungry mother tigress, inspires not the pathos that Christ's body on the cross does, but rather awe and respect. The buddha-to-be performs the sacrifice willingly; it is a strategic decision, a realization that this gift would constitute the most rational solution to a difficult predicament: the claim to life of the bodhisattva's single body is outnumbered by that of the bodies of the tigress and her family. What is more, the bodhisattva also realizes shrewdly that such a sacrifice would benefit his own spiritual development in the end. The "ultimate offense" of the Christian sacrifice here is mediated by calculation (*CJ* 179).

Not only does the diffidence and complexity of such Buddhist self-denial rule out its becoming a dramatic tragedy or scene of pathos. Concomitant to the proviso that what Buddhist self-annihilation annihilates is an illusion is a tendency to emphasize instead the positive, that is, what is thereby made possible, rather than what has been annihilated as such. Compassion and its accompanying realization of the emptiness of self *en-*

*able*: they enable empathy and a seeing of the situation of others. The model of the bodhisattva Avalokiteśvara is emblematic: he is the one who sees—or in its Chinese transformation, she is the one who hears—the suffering of the world. In the context of ethics, the Buddhist emptiness of self means most saliently a porousness between selves so that subjective positions can be shared. Relieved of obsessing about the welfare of her own self, the bodhisattva can finally perceive others on their own terms, and perceive their suffering, which in turn produces the motivation to help them. But this positivity of compassion remains as complex as the negativity involved in negating that which never existed to begin with. Remaining in the background is always the factor of emptiness, now not only the emptiness of the bodhisattva but also the very suffering of the sentient beings for whom the compassion is felt. This produces a salient dissonance: why be compassionate if what is in need of it is actually an illusion? Hence the famous Prajñāpāramitā trope of the bodhisattva's "armor:" the bodhisattva is said to need strength and determination to proceed with full dedication and energy precisely because of the ultimate emptiness of her object of compassion; the fact that suffering is illusory does not mean that it is absolutely nonexistent, as Altizer might have it, or that it is not painfully experienced *as* real.[31] The suffering is illusory, and yet it is painful: this realization produces perhaps even more compassion than would be felt for metaphysically "real" suffering, because it is ultimately gratuitous and could be avoided.

Here in the dissonance of passionate compassion for empty suffering one might want to discern an affinity with the *coincidentia oppositorum* that is so central to Altizer's apocalyptic. But far from a sensibility of fear and trembling, this Buddhist variety produces rather irony and a seasoned recognition of complexity; the stratagems of the lay sage Vimalakīrti are exemplary.[32] And then there is the critical component of calculation: compassion in Buddhism famously requires "skillful means." The compassionate bodhisattva can hardly be said to stand as a ringing symbol of a travesty or utter unthinkableness such as accompanies the kenotic emptying out involved in the death of a God. Yes, the bodhisattva is emptied out, but he or she is also already thinking strategically about how best to work with the idiosyncrasies of the particular sentient beings to be helped, using any means to his or her compassionate end.

The strategic nature of Buddhist compassion also entails the key dimension of consciousness. This is largely misconstrued by Altizer to consist in a simple dissolution in which there is a mere reversion to a primordial ground, which is contrasted unfavorably with the forward movement of his Christian apocalyptic consciousness (*DH* 203).[33] Actually, Altizer seems to be struggling to articulate the nature of the apocalyptic experience for his own theology and might do well to look more precisely at the range of kinds of consciousness and enlightened awareness defined in Buddhist epistemology, which are distinct from conventional, deluded conceptuality. Altizer is right that for Buddhist soteriology the latter kind must be destroyed "before true reality can become manifest" (*OM* 151), but he might note nonetheless that the emptying out upon the realization of emptiness is not thought to spell a blanking out of subjective experience. Rather, there is extensive exploration in the various schools of Buddhist soteriology of the salvific status—and ethical nature—of what Altizer himself suggestively calls "quite simply consciousness itself" (*CJ* 193).[34]

For most Buddhist systems, this would mean something more than the very general arena of a universal, or anonymous, consciousness to which Altizer has gestured as the ground upon which his Kingdom of God would be built. Above all, if Altizer wants the New Jerusalem to be the eschatological realization of a "primordial ground of nirvana," he ought perhaps to take account of the bliss and knowledge that is an intimate ingredient of such a ground in the particular Buddhist sources that speak of it—even if he first shuddered at these sources' invocation of a primordial ground at all (*DH* 192).[35] Interestingly, even in what Altizer sees as a vision of simple pagan primordiality there are articulated kinds of enlightened consciousness that involve individual discrimination as such.[36] Add to this tradition the tantric Buddhist obsession with an experience of bliss-emptiness, deliberately cultivated as both an enabler and a powerful sign that the final realization has taken place. Such tantric sources can also associate that subjective experience of bliss qua emptiness with the energy driving enlightened compassion, in this way paralleling the third-turning sources which also insist that the moment of enlightened realization is absolutely synonymous with compassion. Some tantric and posttantric Buddhist traditions like rDzogs-chen also theorize how such an enlightened consciousness breaks the boundaries of its own interiority, providing further parallel with Altizer's interest in a consciousness that lacks center or circumference and again suggesting that there are inevitable intersubjective and ethical entailments of these rarefied kinds of conscious moments (*CJ* 193 ff).[37]

What Altizer's apocalyptic compassion could also share especially with a third turning of the wheel enlightened ground is its thorough-going spontaneity.[38] Descriptions of the buddha's spontaneous responsiveness to the needs of sentient beings imply not merely lack of needs on the buddha's side but also a fundamental empathy for the needs of the other. Such spontaneity need not be understood to be mere mechanical reaction. Even an extreme exposition of the effortlessness and nonconceptualized nature of the buddha's compassion as *Ratnagotravibhāga* speaks of the buddha's love and specific knowledge of the dispositions of the various kinds of beings, not to mention the buddha's memory, diligence, and ability to train disciples. Again, *nonconceptual* does not mean unconscious or even wordless; the buddha certainly teaches and regularly makes specific statements about specific individuals.[39] Such nonconceptual spontaneity might indeed be purposeless, as Altizer puts it,[40] if he means by that an absence of reified instrumentality, but for Buddhists, in contrast, such "wishlessness" is rarely a matter of resigning agency simply in favor of a God in whom one trusts (some types of Pure Land Buddhists are the exception), and above all a God who according to Altizer's theology must be utterly unknowable.

The inspiration in which the Buddhist sage puts his trust tends in contrast to be thoroughly knowable, and this is certainly true for the other main Buddhist tradition that is both inspiration and anathema to Altizer, the second-turning tradition of emptiness. There too, even if the final reality is emptiness, that does not mean a pure void of consciousness or agency, let alone lack of social responsibility. Quite the contrary, it is precisely emptiness that would make for a social interdependence, which in turn enables a creative canniness, along with flexibility, receptivity, and, yes, consciousness.[41] Anything else, our polyphonic Buddhist chorus intones, be it full and total presence or full and total absence, will not only be incapable of compassionate activity but will be fully frozen in its tracks.

## NOTES

1. Thomas J. J. Altizer, "Kenosis and Sunyata in the Contemporary Buddhist Christian Dialogue," unpublished manuscript, 1993, 3.

2. Altizer, "Kenosis and Sunyata," 13.

3. Thomas J. J. Altizer, "Emptiness and God," in *The Religious Philosophy of Nishitani Keiji: Encounter with Emptiness*, ed. Taitetsu Unno (Berkeley: Asian Humanities Press, 1981), 77.

4. Thomas J. J. Altizer, *Living the Death of God: A Theological Memoir*, unpublished manuscript, chapter 9.

5. Altizer, "Kenosis and Sunyata," 10.

6. See Altizer, "Emptiness and God"; "Kenosis and Sunyata"; "The Buddhist Ground of the Whiteheadian God"; Thomas J. J. Altizer, "Buddhism and Christianity: A Radical Christian Viewpoint," *Japanese Religions* 9, 1 (March 1976): 1–11.

7. "Although Buddhist religious practice should always be regarded as being more primary than Buddhist philosophy, Mahayana Buddhism can probably be made most meaningful by first examining its philosophy" (*OM* 134).

8. Altizer, "Emptiness and God," 75; "Buddhism and Christianity," 5.

9. For Altizer's awareness of some of these traditions, see *DH* 195. Yet in *CJ* 172 he seems ignorant of basic Mahāyāna notions of the buddha who stays in the world, such as is famously asserted in the *Lotus Sutra*.

10. A brief summary of the myth is provided by John Newman, "Eschatology in the Wheel of Time Tantra," in *Buddhism in Practice*, ed. Donald S. Lopez Jr. (Princeton: Princeton University Press, 1995), 284–89.

11. I do not mean to claim that there has been no modern Buddhist theology at all. Certainly the work of the Kyoto School philosophers counts as that, and there have been a variety of attempts by Western writers, although the latter have largely failed to receive much academic attention to date. A recent book attempts to begin to correct this failure: *Buddhist Theology: Critical Reflections by Contemporary Buddhist Scholars*, ed. Roger Jackson and John Makransky (Surrey, England: Curzon, 2000).

12. With the exception of the occasional moments when he remembers the Buddhist equation of samsara and nirvana, as in *OM* 199.

13. Note however that even in the midst of these very distinctions Altizer seems to vacillate over a suspicion that he cannot hold what he thinks of as Buddhist nothingness and the Christian actual nothingness apart—if they have different etiologies, they may end up as the same thing after all (*GG* 149).

14. This line of thought is examined especially clearly in the first chapter of *GG*.

15. As argued for example in the final chapter of *DH*.

16. Altizer also maintains that for Buddhism no real beginning is possible because there is no actual negation (*GG* 17), while he analogizes the Buddhist circle of pure emptiness to a primordial return (*GG* 20).

17. See the final chapter of *OM*, for example, 158; this point is also implicit in *Living the Death of God*, chapter 9. But confusingly, Altizer nonetheless associates Jesus and true Christianity with world renunciation, a side of Christianity that he readily recognizes in Buddhism as well.

18. Steven Collins, *Nirvana and Other Buddhist Felicities: Utopias of the Pali Imaginaire* (Cambridge: Cambridge University Press, 1999), 234. See also Donald S. Lopez Jr., "Memories of the Buddha," in *In the Mirror of Memory: Reflections on Mindfulness and Remembrance in Indian and Tibetan Buddhism*, ed. Janet Gyatso (Albany: State University of New York Press, 1992), 27 ff., and Janet Gyatso, *Apparitions of the Self: The Secret Autobigraphies of a Tibetan Visionary* (Princeton: Princeton University Press, 1998), 109 ff.

19. Robert A. F. Thurman, *The Holy Teaching of Vimalakīrti* (University Park: Penn State, 1976), 24.

20. When Altizer claims that the Buddha's "original state of perfection . . . is present at all times . . . the essential and integral opposite of what Western Christianity has known as Christ . . . [who embodies] a real and actual movement into death and chaos, and a movement which is itself a once-and-for-all event" ("Emptiness and God," 77), he brackets the repeated insistence in classical Abhidharma soteriology that the key moments of enlightened insight are indeed once and for all and allows instead one tradition, that of "original enlightenment"—and only its most extreme rhetoric, taken out of context to boot—to represent all of Buddhism.

21. A typical example of such a compromise solution is in the teachings of Chinul; see Robert Buswell, *Tracing Back the Radiance: Chinul's Korean Way of Zen* (Honolulu: University of Hawaii Press, 1991).

22. The stream-enterer (*srotāpanna*) is usually considered already to be an irreversible stage. Many of the critical Buddhist discussions of irreversibility center on the "path of seeing," as for example in *Abhidharmakośabhāṣya*, chapter 6.

23. For a philosophical discussion of this move and related sudden–gradual debates, see David Ruegg, *Buddha-nature, Mind and the Problem of Gradualism in a Comparative Perspective: On the Transmission and Reception of Buddhism in India and Tibet* (London: School of Oriental and African Studies, 1989). Some syncretic Indo-Tibetan texts in the rDzogs-chen tradition do speak of a primordial emptiness (*ye-stong*) and could be scrutinized regarding the current issues under discussion, but being syncretic, it is still doubtful that they would yield the pure and simple primordial nothingness that Altizer seeks in Buddhism.

24. *Pruning the Bodhi Tree: The Storm over Critical Buddhism*, ed. Jamie Hubbard and Paul L. Swanson (Honolulu: University of Hawaii Press, 1997).

25. To demonstrate this position precisely in *Madhyamakakārikā* would of course require a lengthy exposition; one place to start would be with the second chapter, on motion, where Nāgārjuna demonstrates in detail why any reified notion of motion or a mover must fail to account for actual motion. For a different attempt to establish Nāgārjuna's recourse to empirical reality, see David J. Kalupahana, *Nāgārjuna: the Philosophy of the Middle Way* (Albany: State University of New York Press, 1986), for example, 88. *Madhyamakakārikā's* commentary *Prasannapadā* also repeatedly reiterates the claim that the argument is founded in empirical reality, for example, in the commentaries on chapters 1 and 15. Ironically, the one Buddhist idea that Altizer thinks might indicate an interest in irreducible historical fact, that is, the Sarvāstivāda theory of "objective immortality," is among the positions repudiated by Mādhyamika philosophers as violating empirical reality: see "The Buddhist Ground of the Whiteheadian God," and *OM* 135 ff.

26. This is not quite accurate, for Miranda Shaw's *Passionate Enlightenment: Women in Tantric Buddhism* (Princeton: Princeton University Press, 1994) does aspire to such a role, but this book in my view is so flawed theoretically, not to mention weak in its scholarship of the tradition on which it purports to draw, that it cannot be taken seriously.

27. Altizer, *Living the Death of God*, chapter 9; *Lao Tzu* 18 and 19.

28. Altizer, *Living the Death of God*, chapter 9 (a similar point is made in chapter 5).

29. Ibid., chapter 5.

30. Augustine, *De Trinitate*, XIV, 11.

31. Edward Conze, *The Perfection of Wisdom in Eight Thousand Lines* (Bolinas: Four Seasons Foundation, 1973), 90.

32. Robert A. F. Thurman, *The Holy Teaching of Vimalakīrti* (University Park: Pennsylvania State, 1976).

33. See also *CJ* 181 and the distinction between a Buddhistic dissolution and Christian disenactment of consciousness in *GG* 149.

34. A key passage indicating why consciousness can never be absolutely destroyed according to Altizer's own system is *GG* 145: "Now if a negative center of consciousness is a self-lacerating center, a center of consciousness which continually and compulsively assaults itself, that internal and interior assault is a necessary and inevitable response to a pure negativity which is fully present at that center."

35. A classic source for third turning of the wheel notions of an enlightened primordial ground is *Ratnagotravibhāga*, trans. Jikido Takasaki, in *A Study on the Ratnagotravibhāga (Uttaratantra)* (Rome: Istituto Italiano Per il Medio ed Estremo Oriente, 1966).

36. *Pratyavekṣaṇājñāna.*

37. On the issue of interiority versus exteriority of consciousness in Buddhist descriptions of enlightenment, see Janet Gyatso, "Healing Burns with Fire: The Facilitations of Experience in Tibetan Buddhism," *Journal of the American Academy of Religion* 67, no. 1 (1999): 113–47.

38. Suggestive reflections on the spontaneity of a pure act are broached in *Living the Death of God*, chapter 9.

39. Paul J. Griffiths, *On Being Buddha: The Classical Doctrine of Buddhahood* (Albany: State University of New York Press, 1994), 161–63, discusses third-turning passages that state that the buddha "teaches nothing at all," largely overlooking the nuance of the critique of the ontological status of the referent of words, quite predictable in a Buddhist context, but certainly not equivalent to any simplistic assertion that the buddha has no semantic content in mind when he speaks. There would be no surprise if the claim is that the buddha has an object in "mind" and simultaneously sees its ultimate emptiness.

40. Altizer, *Living the Death of God*, chapter 9.

41. For Mādhyamika ethics and associated states of consciousness and knowledge, see *Madhyamakāvatāra*, trans. C. W. Huntington Jr., *The Emptiness of Emptiness: An Introduction to Early Indian Mādhyamika* (Honolulu: University of Hawaii Press, 1989).

CHAPTER 10

⤚⤙

# The Negative Task of Parable

*Reading Kafka through the Prism of Altizer's Thought*

WALTER A. STRAUSS

The title of one of Thomas Altizer's books, *Total Presence* (1980), is felicitous in a special way: it seems—at least to me—to suggest Altizer's essential presence. This presence, originating in a dialectic between oriental (Buddhistic) mysticism and biblical eschatology and seasoned by Blake, Nietzsche, and Eliade, it moves toward a reconsideration of the situation of God—a resurrected God—within a potentially new theological order, the nature of which will reveal itself, in Altizer's subsequent books, as apocalyptic. If this evaluation is correct, then *Total Presence* is crucial for a definition of the theology of the post-Christian world, a project on which I think Altizer has been embarked for some forty years and which still commands closest attention and demands our most serious reflection. In *Total Presence* we witness not only Altizer's deepening sense of the divine, but we have also for the first time, in clear demarcation, a sense of the vast cultural regions in which Altizer has been living all his life. Not merely are there the preoccupations with the great achievements of literature: these investigations will assume their full stature in *History as Apocalypse* (1985) as profound inquiries into the nature of the Western epic imagination from Homer to the "apocalyptic" Joyce of *Finnegans Wake*. There are also probing comments on Proust and Kafka; and over and beyond literature, we are given splendid insights into the cultural and theological resonances of Bach, Beethoven, and Mozart,

as well as of Leonardo da Vinci, Michelangelo, Rembrandt, and twentieth-century abstract painting. Could one conclude that Altizer's testimony in *Total Presence* is also a homage to the Western artistic intellect,
offered to us by a mind whose love is not only the love of religion but also
the works of the creative imagination, the secular parallel of religion, from
the Greeks to our own times: a comprehensive labor of multiple love?

One of the fundamental considerations in *Total Presence* has to do
with parabolic language. The book's keynote is the theological problem
of speech; the opening paragraph is a fine example of Altizer's elevated
theological discourse:

> Nothing is more distinctive in the biblical tradition or traditions
> than the centrality therein of Word and speech. Whether in its
> enactment of Creation, of Covenant, of Torah, of Messiah, of
> Wisdom, or of Kingdom of God, we may observe here the pri-
> macy of speech but also the ultimacy or finality of speech. Noth-
> ing truly parallel to this ultimacy and centrality of speech may be
> found in other mythical and religious traditions, except for its
> prefigurations in the ancient Near East and its later expressions
> in Judaism, Christianity, and Islam. India and China embody re-
> verse parallels to this primacy of speech, for here silence and
> emptiness effect and express a comparable primacy and finality.
> While speech cannot be said to be primal or ultimate in the
> Greek religious and mythical traditions as such, it is so in the
> Homeric epics and in Greek tragedy, and the historical coming
> together classical culture and the Bible in Christendom can give
> us a decisive clue to the unique identity and the role of literature
> in the Western tradition. Nothing comparable to Dante, Milton,
> or Blake may be found in non-Western literary traditions, for
> nowhere else is God, the sacred, or the ultimate fully spoken,
> nowhere else is it truly realized or actualized in language itself.
> Here God is not simply the object of speech, but the subject of
> speech as well, a subject which the Christian identifies as the
> Word of revelation. (*TP* 1–2)

The argument insists that (at least in Christian hermeneutics) the
prophetic oracle is central to the Bible and that the God of the Bible is
not only a revealed God but also a revealing, that is, a *speaking* God. Parable is its characteristic speech, especially in the gospels, where in all like-

lihood the closest approximation is the voice of Jesus in the parabolic language that marks the synoptic gospels. Parable, according to Altizer, has no meaning outside of itself: it reaches beyond metaphor or allegory and focuses on the enactment that it presents (rather than represents):

> Parable, or pure parable, is present only in its enactment, only in its telling or saying. Therefore, it can pass into writing with a loss of its original immediacy, a loss which occasions a reversal of itself, a reversal effecting its fall into the language of simile and metaphor, a fall culminating in its full reversal in allegory. Writing stills the sound of speech by breaking up and dismembering a vertical immediacy into a horizontal presence. Then vertical presence recedes behind and before the impacting center of voice and in that expanding horizon an immediate identity passes into simile and metaphor. Nevertheless, a tension is present in most or all of the synoptic parables which gives witness to this process of dismemberment and reversal, a tension which is most evident in the chasm which opens up between the story or antistory of the parable and the allegorical interpretation which is sometimes present in the synoptic text. It is precisely in this tension that the original intention of the parable becomes manifest. (*TP* 4)

This perspective enables us to see with greater clarity the significant difference between metaphor, symbol, and allegory by examining the tension between vertical immediacy and horizontal (metonymic) narrative.

This distinction between parable and story/myth is important as well as suggestive. It suggests a confluence between the two types of reality analyzed by Erich Auerbach in *Mimesis*: the narrative patterns growing out of Homer's epics on the one hand and the internalized dimension in the Old Testament on the other. A point of juncture is Dante's *Commedia*, where the two narrative modes intersect, horizontally and vertically. And the *Commedia* can also be seen as a crossroad between epic poetry and symbolic poetry. Altizer himself has traversed these regions in his *History as Apocalypse*. For the present moment it may suffice to call attention to the fact that in the lyric poetry of French symbolism language once again tries to recapture as fully as possible the vertical dimension of speech by means of the symbol, as in Baudelaire's sonnet "Correspondances," where man is seen as moving about in a "forest of symbols":

*Comme de longs échos qui de loin se confondent*
*Dans une ténébreuse et profonde unité*

[Like long echoes which melt in the distance
Into a shadowy and profound unity]

Altizer notes the grand tension between parabolic and mythical language in the sense that both myth and parable establish a nexus between human and cosmic identity.

> Yet that continuum is horizontal in myth, it stretches out into a visionary plane, whereas it is immediate and vertical in parable. Myth distances both the speaker and the hearer from the moment or center of voice, a distance expanding into the horizon of vision. But parable contracts attention into the presence or moment at hand, a presence whose very immediacy resists and opposes the horizontal movement of vision. Pure parable embodies an auditory as opposed to a visual presence, an immediate sounding which commands and effects a total attention. One hears a parable, and does so even in reading, for parable sounds or speaks an immediate presence. (*TP* 5–6)

The parable gives evidence to our human capacity to stand in wonder before the numinous presence; it is not an accident that the verb "astonish" is related to "thunder." The word "myth" relates to telling, it is concerned with the elaboration of the power to narrate. Its dimensions are time and space in which the tale deploys itself: wonderment opens the way to curiosity, to astonishment. The parable exists in the moment, without time and space, more like an epiphany.

Altizer's distinction between parable and myth, between vertical and horizontal enactment of speech can shed light on Kafka's work. Here we have a writer, situated outside the Christian world (yet at the same time marginally within the Jewish world) who reclaims parabolic language in his fictional language and who as a result of personal and cultural agonies was also tempted by an attraction to the theosophical and ecstatic dimensions of Jewish Kabbalah: a writer for whom tradition (that is, Kabbalah) requires innovation and transformation.

Kafka's absolute dedication to literature ("I am literature and nothing but literature") is constantly threatened by the errancy of language, *our* language: it remains a blunted instrument that can be used for groping, never for grasping. That is the very point of the archetypal Kafkan parable entitled "On Parables," which reads like a midrash, a scriptural gloss or commentary, on everything that Kafka wrote between 1912 and his death in 1924.

> Many complain that the words of the wise are always merely parables and of no use in daily life, which is the only life we have. When the sage says: "Go over," he does not mean that we should cross to some actual place, which we could do anyhow if the labor were worth it; he means some fabulous yonder, something unknown to us, something that he cannot designate more precisely either, and therefore cannot help us here in the very least. All these parables really set out to say merely that the incomprehensible is incomprehensible, and we know that already. But the cares we have to struggle with every day: that is a different matter. Concerning this a man once said: Why such reluctance? If you only followed the parables you yourselves would become parables and with that rid of all your daily cares.
>
> Another said: I bet that is also a parable.
>
> The first said: You have won.
>
> The second said: But unfortunately only in parable.
>
> The first said: No, in reality: in parable you have lost.[1]

Within this parable the direction, "Go over," so common to the language of transcendence, implies the very act of transiting; Kafka converts this age-old reference into something fabulous and unknown and immeasurable. So we can say that this archetypal Kafkan fable is about the incommensurability of truth and life, resulting in incommunicability, and about the suspension between truth and lying. Yet parable is the only language available to the seeker after the recondite truth, the voice concealed within the silence.

Thus Kafka can be located in a succession reaching from the legal and prophetic tradition of the Hebrew Bible through the gospels to the midrashic practices of the Talmudists and the Kabbalists, but with an all-important difference: Kafka's new Kabbalah is neither mystical nor does it contain a hermetic revelation: it remains "fabulous," pure fiction, parable.

To come back to the parable "On Parables," Kafka's perennial paradox is how to decipher the undecipherable. The great stumbling-block for Kafka is the remoteness of authority, the immense distance between the authoritative texts and our own time. It is as if our capacity for understanding the old texts had deteriorated and the key to decipherment been forgotten. Not even translation is possible, and any attempt to do so ends in misconception and finally loses itself in nebulous incomprehension.

> Everything fell into place for him for the task of construction. Foreign workers brought the marble blocks, trimmed and fitted to one another. The stones rose and placed themselves according to the measuring motions of his fingers. No building ever came into being as easily as did this temple, or rather, this temple came into being the way a temple should. Except that, out of spite or in order to desecrate or to destroy it completely, instruments evidently of outstanding sharpness had been used to scratch on every stone—from what quarry did they originate?—for an eternity outlasting the temple, the clumsy scribbles of senseless children's hands or possibly the entries of barbaric mountain dwellers.[2]

The "new" construction consists of old building blocks carrying an illegible message of mysterious and presumably destructive significance, for all eternity.

A description of this process of deterioration and devaluation is comically and absurdly outlined in Kafka's story "The Giant Mole," which involves a "magical" sighting of a somewhat monstrous animal and the subsequent misprisions and theoretical distortions that occur *after* the event, by individuals who were not witnesses. Not only does the story describe the generational distortions of an event (even if it is magical) but the interplay of egotism and rivalry on the part of the interpreters of that event): interpretation that becomes increasingly subjective and self-serving, and thereby absurdly meaningless.

Kafka illustrates for our time what happens to a sacred text in which the actual words have become blurred while the interpreters continue to elaborate more and more fanciful exegeses. In terms of the hermeneutical traditions inherent in Judaism, Kafka is delineating the absurdity of midrash without *peshat*: *peshat* aims at establishing the literal meaning of scripture; midrash is the discovery of meaning other than literal in the

Bible interpretation. The two methods are obviously complementary; yet in Kafka *peshat* is impossible or at least unattainable, and thus midrash is always beside the point. Thus in Kafka interpretation one is constantly circumnavigating a missing text, and human error is the source of a failure to preserve and maintain continuity with a scriptural tradition.

All of Kafka's writing from 1912 on until his death in 1924 is an unfolding of this insight into the modern human predicament. Its first striking articulation occurs in the well-known parable "Before the Law," the centerpiece of *The Trial*. The man from the country (alluding to the Hebrew expression *am ha'aretz*, "ignorant country bumpkin") seeks to gain access to the Law, which remains inaccessible to him because of the guardian who seemingly prevents the man's entry, and therefore the man from the country spends his entire time waiting. At the end of his life he finally *sees* the radiance emanating from the Law, but then it is too late. The universe of Kafka is fully outlined here: the supplicant, the mandate to seek the Law, the inability to understand and overcome the distance between the self and the Law, that is, the persistence of obstacles that prevent access or encounter. This same pattern is reiterated in various forms in all sorts of stories: "The Great Wall of China," "The Burrow," and finally in *The Castle*. In "The Great Wall of China," however, we have an important variant, a tiny opening in this apparently impregnable fortress. The parable "A Message from the Emperor" illustrates a potential way out—or better, a way in. Altizer's characterization of parable is splendidly applicable here; as a matter of fact, this parable is the direct enactment of parabolic speech, that is to say, in a meaningful silence. It is revealed that the emperor has a last message directly intended for you, whispers it to a messenger who sets out immediately to deliver it. But he cannot traverse enormous spaces, the virtually infinite distance between the palace and you living in the provinces: "Nobody could fight his way through here, least of all one with a message from a dead man.—But you sit at your window when evening falls and dream it to yourself."[3] One needs to add here that the spoken communication does indeed reach you, the recipient, but not as speech itself but as some kind of inward intuition: vertically, so to speak, rather than horizontally. Kafka's world is one of shattered communication, one in which the Word can no longer be heard but only imagined.

Thus, Kafka's interest in a "new Kabbalah" is meaningful as an attempt to mend the "broken vessels" of Kabbalistic theosophy. This strange and startling phenomenon in Kafka's thought begins with a self-critique dated February 25, 1918. After deploring "the lack of ground underfoot," he goes on to say:

> I have vigorously absorbed the negative element of the age in which I live, an age that is, of course, very close to me, which I have no right ever to fight against, but as it were the right to represent. The slight amount of the positive, and also of the extreme negative, which capsizes into the positive, are something in which I have had no hereditary share. I have been guided into life by the hand of Christianity—admittedly now slack and failing—as Kierkegaard was, and have not caught the hem of the Jewish prayer shawl—now flying away from us—as the Zionists have. I am an end or a beginning.[4]

The previous paragraph is one of the clearest indications of the fact that Kafka's self-imposed mission is grounded in his Jewishness, anchored, so to speak, in his uprootedness; it parallels the decline of Christianity and is thus completely representative of the religious vacuum of the civilized and urbanized West. In one of his aphorisms he reaffirms this position: "To do that which is negative is yet our task; that which is positive has already been given to us."[5] That is what the Kabbalah also had done seven centuries earlier: it had taken Jewish "tradition"—mainly Rabbinic and Talmudic, with some admixture of more recent Hellenistic Neoplatonism and Near Eastern Gnosticism—and proposed to reaffirm it in a new way, with the techniques of a mystical hermeneutic that, perhaps without fully intending to be radical, went counter to the legalistic pronouncements of the rabbinical schools. Apparently Kafka thought that the advent of Zionism had delayed a reappraisal and a revitalization of Jewish identity. And it seems reasonably clear that Kafka sees his "negative task," the articulation of the "negative element of the age in which I live" as a literary and spiritual task, one that would reassemble the shattered fragments into a new yet traditional whole, a meeting ground of writing and scripture ("Schrift"). As he declared in that same diary entry of January 16, 1922: "All such writing is an assault on the frontiers; if Zionism had not intervened, it might easily have developed into a new secret doctrine, a Kabbalah. There are intimations of this. Though of course it would require genius of an unimaginable kind to strike root again in the old centuries, or create the old centuries anew and not spend itself withal, but only then to begin to flower forth."[6]

The task is stupendous: it is an ongoing exploration into something barely knowable, hardly attainable. Kafka's lament runs thus:

> Writing denies itself to me. Hence plan for autobiographical investigations. Not biography but investigation and detection of the smallest possible component parts. Out of these I will then construct myself, as one whose house is unsafe wants to build a safe one next to it, if possible out of the material of the old one. What is bad, as if in the midst of building his strength gives out and now, instead of one house, unsafe but yet complete, he has one half-destroyed and one half-finished house, that is to say, nothing. What follows is madness, that is to say, something like a Cossack dance between the two houses, whereby the Cossack goes on scraping and throwing aside the earth with the heels of his boots until his grave is dug out under him.[7]

No wonder Kafka's perpetual theme since "In the Penal Colony" remained that of exploration and investigation, as is seen in his final works, "The Investigations of a Dog," "The Burrow," "The Hunger Artist," and *The Castle*. The temptation in those works is to pursue some sort of activity as an unending quest without hope of completion. The parable "The New Advocate" introduces us to a mock-heroic Dr. Bucephalus who once was the battle horse of Alexander the Great but who has now become a member of respectable and genteel society: "So perhaps it is really best to do as Bucephalus has done and immerse oneself in law books. In the quiet lamplight, his flanks unhampered by the thighs of a rider, free and far from the clamor of battle, he reads and turns the pages of our ancient tomes."[8] But there is also a parable that describes the dilemma of weariness as a true image of human impotence. Kafka takes the myth of Prometheus and makes it into a paradigmatic parable:

> There are four legends concerning Prometheus:
>     According to the first, he was clamped to a rock in the Caucasus for betraying the secrets of the gods to men, and the gods sent eagles to feed on his liver, which was perpetually renewed.
>     According to the second, Prometheus, goaded by the pain of the tearing beaks, pressed himself deeper and deeper into the rock until he became one with it.

According to the third, his treachery was forgotten in the course of thousands of years, the gods forgot, the eagles forgot, he himself forgot.

According to the fourth, everyone grew weary of the groundless affair. The gods grew weary, the eagles grew weary, the wound closed wearily. There remained the inexplicable mountain crag. —The legend tries to explain the inexplicable. Since it comes out of a ground of truth, it has to end in the inexplicable.[9]

Across the quadruple inconclusive midrashim Kafka locates the true meaning in the very ground out of which the parable arose, as if to say that the mystery had better be stated directly and confronted directly, that by indirections we do not really find directions out. It is this enigma that surely drove Kafka to a quest for a new kabbalistic method. Moshe Idel notes that in the loss of a sense of personal mysticism only stories—parables?—are possible.

Franz Kafka's *Before the Law* is an instructive example of the last remnants of Jewish mysticism operating in a world in which the confidence of man's acts has disintegrated. Since the man from the country is still aware of the mystical radiance that comes from the Law,

> Kafka's Law . . . is intended for everyone who dares, but the loss of self-confidence, faith and energy leaves man with only the capacity to tell mystical stories about an impersonal, fascinating world that, according to Kafka, is *ex definitio* [sic] beyond his reach. All that remains is the awareness that "a radiance streams immortally from the door of the Law." Is not the basic kabbalistic metaphor for the mystical dimension of the law, *Zohar*—radiance? Does not the *Zohar* use the metaphor of entering a palace in order to reach the Law itself, not merely viewing its radiance from the outside?[10]

If Altizer's observations on parabolic speech and on Kafka's renewal of the parable are instructive and thought-provoking, his observations on modern literature in general are equally trenchant. For example, on the subject of the renewal of the Orphic in the literature of the late nineteenth and early twentieth centuries, especially in the guise of French symbolist poetry and its international aftermath, particularly Rilke, Altizer observes:

> Nothing is more significant about modern Orphism than its creation of a new speech and language, thereby it decisively differs from ancient Orphism, and thereby it realizes a new Orphic immanence which is the consequence of a uniquely modern descent into death and nothingness. Modern writing itself is here identified as a fundamentally Orphic writing, and therefore of the transmutation of silence into song, and of our dark center into radiance.[11]

The occasion for this remark is a theological summation of my study *Descent and Return*,[12] which highlights the poetry of Mallarmé and Rilke as an apotheosis of a modern Orphic dispensation. Despite the fact that an Orphic grasp of the poet's commitment to the world subsists into the present epoch (Maurice Blanchot, Wallace Stevens), there has been a countervailing force in literature that appears to spell the end of Orphism. Such is probably the position of Kafka in the spectrum of twentieth-century literature. Kafka can be seen not only as an upside-down Talmudist-Kabbalist, but as a continuation as well as a reversal of the prophetic tradition of ancient Israel. Altizer observes cogently that "nothing is more dramatic in ancient prophecy than the Israelite prophets' struggle against the prophetic call, a struggle most manifestly present in the Book of Jeremiah, and a struggle which is reenacted by Kafka himself. Kafka's dread of writing can be no less than this."[13]

The problem in Orphism may be understood as a tension between the prophetic and the priestly function of the poet as he conceived his mission throughout the nineteenth century, from romanticism through symbolism. The function of the poet is vigorously defined by poets such as Shelley, Novalis, Hugo, and many others. By the time Baudelaire arrives, at midcentury, the poet dons priestly robes; ultimately Mallarmé becomes the high priest of symbolism. The tension between prophet and priest is political as well as spiritual: on the one hand, there is an urge to reform or to rebel (Hugo, Rimbaud) and to carve out radical forms of belief (Blake); on the other hand, one finds a ritualized conservatism, a call for spiritual renewal and transformation (Mallarmé, Valéry, Eliot). Rilke leans more toward the prophetic and for that reason may be the "pure" Orphic of the modern world. In any case, the results of the "priestly" Orphism of Mallarmé and the "prophetic" Orphism of Rilke

are convergences of opposites, in which the regeneration of man, cosmos, and poetic speech are affirmed. In his first Orpheus sonnet, Rilke's
singer ascends out of silence and creates audition:

> *Da stieg ein Baum. O reine Übersteigung!*
> *O Orpheus singt! O hoher Baum im Ohr!*
> *Und alles schwieg. Doch selbst in der Verschweigung*
> *Ging neuer Anfang, Wink und Wandlung vor.*
>
> *Tiere aus Stille drangen aus dem klaren gelösten Wald . . .*
> *. . . . . . . . . . . . . .*
> *                    Und wo eben*
> *Kaum eine Hütte war, dies zu empfangen,*
> *. . . . . . . . . . . . . .*
> *da schufst du ihnen Tempel im Gehör.*

> [A tree arose. O pure transgression!
> O Orpheus sings! O high tree in the ear!
> And everything grew still. And yet in this silence
> New beginnings, signs and changes came into being.
>
> Animals, moved by silence, flocked out of the clear serene forest
>                     And where not even
> A hut existed to receive all this,
> . . . . . . . . . . . . . .
> You created temples for them (the animals) in their hearing.][14]

Such a transformation does not occur in Kafka. As Altizer observes, in
this case, "the prophetic descent issues in no resurrection or rebirth, and
the return from the descent is not into a radiance but rather into an all
too human world, and a world now even darker and more terrible for
the prophet as a consequence of his prophetic call."[15]

The resulting revelation in Kafka is an epiphany of silence, that strange
silence of the Sirens in Homer's *Odyssey*, which Kafka imagines paraboli-
cally as the equivalent of singing. Odysseus, chained to the mast and his
ears filled with wax, imagines that the Sirens' silence is their song and thus
passes beyond them unscathed. "But they—lovelier than ever—stretched
their necks and turned, let their frightful hair openly flutter in the wind
and extended their claws freely on the rock. They no longer wanted to

seduce, they only wanted to seize for as long as possible the radiance from Odysseus' great pair of eyes."[16] And there is a sly appendix to this parable. Perhaps Odysseus, sly fox that he was, knew perfectly what was going on. "Perhaps," says Kafka, "he had truly noticed, although human understanding can no longer grasp it, that the Sirens were silent and offered to the Sirens and the gods the above-mentioned illusory event, so to speak, as a shield."[17] By means of this clever stratagem, Kafka intimates that this whole set of events to elude or defy destiny goes beyond human comprehension.

That silence is in search of an Orphic radiance. It is not that the possibility of radiance has totally disappeared; we have seen that here and on rare occasions a Zoharlike illumination is perceptible from the Law. But, as Altizer puts it, worldly glory has vanished.

> In Kafka, all worldly radiance has . . . disappeared, and so much so that no other radiance is visible or audible, thus necessitating a new silence, and a new silence which speaks the name of God. But that silence is just as forceful, at least for us, as is the prophetic utterance of the divine Name, and even as the prophetic oracles evoke and embody the divine presence as does no other writing, so Kafka's writing evokes and embodies a divine absence and silence as does no other writing in our world.[18]

This decline of the Orphic reaches into the second half of our century in the deconstructive fictions of Samuel Beckett, in which the images of total fragmentation, of aporia, of total silence have invaded the act of thinking and writing so that only a series of desperate formal and symmetrical constructions inhabit a world of emptiness and chaos. And in the work of the remarkable poet Paul Celan the Holocaust has destroyed human poetic discourse (as it used to exist), along with human life and dignity. In the poem "Fadensonnen," threadlike suns (all that is left of solar radiance) hover over a black desert:

| | |
|---|---|
| *Fadensonnen* | Thread-like suns |
| *über der grauschwarzen Ödnis.* | above the grey-black void. |
| *Ein baum-* | A tree- |
| *hoher Gedanke* | high thought |
| *greift sich den Lichtton: es sind* | finds the light's note: there are |
| *noch Lieder zu singen jenseits* | still songs to sing on the other side |
| *der Menschen.* | Of human beings.[19] |

Here it is as if the "high tree in the ear" of Rilke's sonnet, rising and lis-
tening to the Orphic music, attempted to render the tone or note (as if
on a violin's fingerboard) of light itself, light that has not totally faded
from consciousness, so that a future Orphic may even be envisaged.
What may be the theological implications of the final statement: there
are still songs to sing *on the other side* of human beings? *What* other side?
Does it exist at all? Or not yet?

Altizer's fullest conflation of theology and literature is to be found in his
masterful study *History as Apocalypse* (1985). Here Altizer undertakes no less
than a history of Western consciousness and self-consciousness from archaic times through modernity and postmodernity. He uses the epic tradition of Western literature—Homer to Joyce—to present the grand
drama and spectacle of consciousness finding its voice, its identity, and articulating the psychological-anthropological vision of the great epochs of
the past three thousand years. This is accomplished through an astonishing
display of historical, artistic, and philosophical knowledge and informed by
a theological vision that guides the reader from the earliest times to a
dawning of a new apocalypse. In brief, it is an experience both hypnotic
and shattering for the reader, whose powers of imagination and synthesis
are severely tested. *History as Apocalypse* has some similarities with Erich
Auerbach's great *Mimesis*, which is a comprehensive examination of representations of reality from Homer and the Bible to Virginia Woolf.[20]
    Yet this comparison also brings out an important difference in
method between Auerbach and Altizer. Auerbach's procedure is to ex-
tract significant social and historical and aesthetic insights from carefully
chosen examples of literary representations of reality, encompassing a
tension between "inner" and "outer" realities and their myriad interac-
tions. Altizer's way is that of sweeping assertions and generalizations that
hold the texts in a kind of suspension for intellectual scrutiny, but the
texts are seldom treated in any sort of detail. Although Altizer shows a
prodigious grasp of literary and theological characteristics, he is also a
discriminating observer of the important works of art that foreshadow or
usher in a transformation of consciousness: from the Lascaux caves and
Greek sculpture to a persuasive discussion of the Gothic immediately
prior to Dante's time, and finally he rings in analogies between Joyce and
modern painting. A statement such as "[I]t is also possible to employ

Gothic art as a way into the original meaning of the theological language of Aquinas" is as profound as it is illuminating (*HA* 106). For Altizer, the study of theology requires a full encounter with the history of culture, centered in the arts and literature; only in this way, in such conjunctions, can the drama of human consciousness be authentically presented. Consequently, if Altizer's thought—which is a clearly defined and yet passionately articulated vision—is built upon a comprehensive mode of understanding theology, history, and the arts, some way is needed to harness these diverse areas of cultural knowledge into a conceptual framework that does justice to the multiplicity of his insights.

There are, it seems to me, two possibilities. The more important one would interpret literature (or the arts) in terms of theological concepts or criteria, yet in cultural (not in doctrinal) terms. The model for this is Altizer's *History as Apocalypse*. The other option is to seek out literary forms and patterns (rather than meanings) that can be illuminated by theological notions, in the way in which the present essay attempts to do with Kafka. This method is more in tune with literary hermeneutics that focus on detail.

Perhaps the two approaches can be brought together by someone whose commitment to literary detail and to a cultural synthesis is both vital and provocative. The fact that Altizer has provided others with the challenge and the means to undertake such tasks is not the least evidence of his stature as a major cultural thinker of our epoch.

## NOTES

1. Franz Kafka, *Parables and Paradoxes,* ed. Nahum N. Glatzer, multiple translators (New York: Schocken, 1961), 11.

2. Ibid., 47; translation slightly modified.

3. Ibid., 15.

4. Franz Kafka, *Dearest Father: Stories and Other Writings* (New York: Schocken, 1954), 100.

5. Ibid., 37 (aphorism 27).

6. *The Diaries of Franz Kafka 1914–23*, ed. Max Brod, trans. Martin Greenberg and Hannah Arendt (New York: Schocken, 1949), 202–03.

7. Kafka, *Dearest Father*, 350.

8. Franz Kafka, *The Complete Stories*, ed. Nahum N. Glatzer, multiple translators (New York: Schocken, 1971), 415.

9. Kafka, *Parables and Paradoxes*, 83; translation slightly modified.

10. Moshe Idel, *Kabbalah: New Perspectives* (New Haven: Yale University Press, 1988), 271.

11. Thomas J. J. Altizer, "A Contemporary Quest for a New Kabbalah," in *Essays in European Literature for Walter A. Strauss*, ed. Alice N. Benston and Marshall C. Olds (Manhattan, Kansas: Studies in Twentieth Century Literature, 1990), 230.

12. Walter A. Strauss, *Descent and Return: The Orphic Theme in Modern Literature* (Cambridge: Harvard University Press, 1971).

13. Altizer, "A Contemporary Quest," 231.

14. From Rainer Maria Rilke, *Sämtliche Werke*, vol. 1 (Frankfurt: Insel-Verlag, 1956), 731; translation mine.

15. Ibid.

16. Walter A. Strauss, *On the Threshold of a New Kabbalah: Kafka's Later Tales* (New York: Peter Lang, 1988).

17. Kafka, *Parables and Paradoxes*, 91; translation slightly modified.

18. Altizer, "A Contemporary Quest," 231.

19. Paul Celan, *Poems: A Bilingual Edition*, ed. and trans. with introduction by Michael Hamburger (New York: Persea Books, 1980), 182–83; translation slightly modified.

20. Erich Auerbach, *Mimesis: The Representation of Reality in Western Literature* (Princeton: Princeton University Press, 1953).

CHAPTER 11

❧❧

# In the Wasteland

*Apocalypse, Theology, and the Poets*

DAVID JASPER

Voice speaks. And when it speaks, and as it speaks, it
embodies itself.

—Altizer, *The Self-Embodiment of God*

This sentence from a book that Thomas J. J. Altizer himself believes
is his best, and is certainly one of his most introspective and theologically mature works, will form the beginning and ending of
this chapter. *The Self-Embodiment of God* has been described by Altizer as
a gratuitous gift, the result of a long and deep struggle, and it is perhaps
for this reason that its reader—though this is also true of most of his writing—must transcend the author himself, enacting a genuine communion
that is nothing short of a liturgical experience. This may well explain why
a critical reading of Altizer's work is so difficult, perhaps ultimately impossible: certainly it evokes a religious reading that, at best, is participatory
or even celebratory, rather like his own readings of poets such as Blake or
Dante. To read is to speak, which becomes a self-embodiment realized in
a silence that is the heart of prayer and celebration. Around these words,
perhaps in the form of a meditation, this chapter will move.

185

The themes of Altizer's writing are remarkably consistent over some forty years, though they are deepened through the development of a style that is itself profoundly poetic and a real self-enactment of the word. In his 1963 essay "America and the Future of Theology" Altizer wrote of America as a desert "shorn of the vegetation of history. But a desert can also be a way to the future" (*RT* 31). This cultural desert becomes the wilderness where we have our beginning and our ending and where is found our true self. In between there is the distraction of speech, against which, paradoxically, the poets write and from which, in Altizer's vision, theology must flee toward a profound isolation that is its heart. In the same essay he writes that "theology must cultivate the silence of death. To be sure, the death to which theology is called is the death of God" (*RT* 30). Apart from this the Word becomes simply words in a babble of confusion that only the radical, apocalyptic Jesus can save us from in the pure *coincidentia oppositorum* that neither the church nor Christendom have ever acknowledged. This is most deeply pursued in Altizer's recent book, *The Contemporary Jesus* (1997), which can be read, in some ways, as a working through of the central passage in his early essay "William Blake and the Role of Myth" (1965): "Of course, Blake belongs to a large company of radical or spiritual Christians, Christians who believe that the Church and Christendom have sealed Jesus in his tomb and resurrected the very evil and darkness that Jesus conquered by their exaltation of a solitary and transcendent God, a heteronomous and compulsive law, and a salvation history that is irrevocably past" (*RT* 182). Theology must turn toward the future in a move that lies at the heart of liturgical celebration and cultivate an isolation that—like that of the Desert Fathers—is deeply communal, unlike the terrible solitariness of the transcendent God of Christendom. It is also a move at one with the poets who live alone in the babble of our confusions yet, like the aged Coleridge on Highgate Hill, sustain within their word the vision that to all others may seem defeat and despair. He wrote at the end of his tragic life:

> All Nature seems at work. Slugs leave their lair;
> The Bees are stirring—Birds are on the wing—
> And Winter slumbering in the open air,
> Wears on his smiling face a dream of Spring!
> And I, the, while, the sole unbusy Thing,
> Nor honey make, nor pair, nor build, nor sing.

Yet well I ken the banks, where Amaranths blow,
Have traced the fount whence streams of Nectar flow.[1]

Amaranths are the immortal flowers of Greece, which bloom in paradise
for poets and artists. And Coleridge, like Altizer himself, was a preacher,
though both had left and been rejected by their pulpits, yet remaining so
in their poetry and their word.

"Resurrection is the voice of speech only when that voice is actual
as silence, only when the voice of speech has passed into silence."
These words of Altizer in *The Self-Embodiment of God* lie at the heart
of the nature of prayer and are realized as closely as anything in the silence experienced at the center of the Eucharist that *is* the moment of
resurrection even and only in the event of Christ's passion and death.
But they are also the expression of a deep Christian poetics that recognizes the true poet as one who actually overturns the language that sus-
tains the enterprise of theology and effects what Altizer calls a "fully
kenotic" or self-emptying theology. We move here on the boundaries
of a silence that, like Augustine in *The Confessions* (Altizer's "favorite
theological book"[2]), opens our ears and eyes to the profound dichotomy between nature and grace. The true poet, who is the heretic
knowing the depths and utter solitude, overturns theological discourse
in a move, repeatedly made and rarely heard, and makes possible the
survival of a Christianity that the traditon would call, at best, "post-
Christian," but a Christianity rejected by Christendom itself. In philosophical terms probably only Hegel (whose huge shadow stretches
across everything that Altizer has written) has given us the opportunity
of a language that can project theology into a genuine future, though in
the succession of epic poets at least from Dante is given us a true adumbration of it. In recognition of this I will employ the term "true
poet," acknowledging Altizer's own writing as within this poetic tradition and as a poetics that yearns in its very language for a "total presence," which is, in fact, nothing other than true prayer—a voice of
silence experienced as such an intensity that it is everything and nothing. Such total presence in Altizer's theology is a suspension that explains his profound acknowledgement of Dante's vision of Purgatory,
the place (which is no place) where opposites meet and the possibility
is held out of redemption and purification. It is, for me, best realized in
romantic poetry again by Samuel Taylor Coleridge—a poet whom Altizer has not referred to, but with whom he shares many of his deepest

insights and poetic realizations. In 1817, Coleridge wrote a fragment of verse, which he entitled "Limbo," presumably writing of himself:

> With scant white hairs, with foretop bald and high,
> He gazes still—his eyeless face all eye;—
> As 'twere an organ full of silent sight,
> His whole face seemeth to rejoice in light!
> Lip touching lip, all moveless, bust and limb—
> He seems to gaze at that which seems to gaze on him!

This moment of silence, wholly embodied in language, is a total presence, the meeting of opposites, in which the poet finds in absolute solitude a pure vision, which in a recent unpublished essay written in honor of Patrick A. Heelan, Altizer has meditated upon through the visual poetics of another preacher, Vincent van Gogh. Van Gogh's tragic last letter to his brother, written in July 1890, sums up the work of a true theologian and poet in a cry of dereliction that is deeply christocentric, its final terrible question prompted by the moment when we truly "see," and seeing is utterly extinguished in the realization of St. Paul's words on "the image of the invisible God" (Colossians 1: 15).[3] "Well, my own work, I am risking my life for it and my reason has half foundered owing to it—that's all right—but you are not among the dealers in men so far as I know, and you can choose your side, I think acting with true humanity, but what's the use?"[4] This is the van Gogh whose last self-portrait painted in Paris Altizer has described as "the very face of death," yet a transfiguring embodiment in which life and death are truly indistinguishable, "for death in being truly embodied, thereby ceases to be death alone, ceases to be sheer nothingness, but becomes instead an embodied nothingness or an embodied death, and thus a death actually occurring."[5]

In these moments the task of the theologian is radically transfigured, for it has abandoned the language of theology as it has always been understood and finds itself only in the deep experience of the poet, and beyond that in a vision in which, we might say, the invisible proceeds up into the visible; a necessary death, which alone precedes resurrection. The artist and the poet has always known this intense moment, which is the end of all speech. In this same essay, "Van Gogh's Eyes," Altizer traces this abysmal light back to the Scrovegni Chapel frescoes of Giotto, painted in about 1305, in which one of the most profound paintings is the *Lamentation over the Dead Christ*, a revolutionary work in the history of Christian art. Here all is concentrated upon the gaze, and above all the gaze of the grieving mother looking straight into the face of her dead son, taking her whole being from his eyes, which are themselves lifeless yet full of life, in a moment of utter grief, which leaves her "nowhere reflected but in the pupils of the eyes of God,"[6] and God is dead. Altizer claims that van Gogh was the first painter fully to envision the absolute darkness of the Godhead itself—but Giotto also knows this darkness, as did Meister Eckhart, another preacher, who, in his great sermon "Qui audit me," affirms, "Man's last and highest parting occurs when, for God's sake, he takes leave of God." Surely no one knows this more than the Mary of Giotto's fresco, and it is of this abyss that Altizer speaks in his book *Total Presence* (1980), for only in this total presence does language move into silence, and only thus can the language of Jesus himself be recovered. Only then is it possible to think God without any conditions, to think beyond Being without any pretence at an inscription of God or any description of him as Being. Only then can we realize how dehumanizing has been almost all theology in the Christian tradition, precisely because, as Ray L. Hart argues, of its preoccupation with God in a way that only God can be preoccupied with himself.[7]

Here, indeed we truly discover the being of God when God is not being God. Giotto knows this, and so does van Gogh, though it cost him his life, and before that his sanity. But another modern poet, never referred to by Altizer, finds this again in a contemplation that is deeply religious yet utterly unmoved by the discourse that is the realm of theology and the Church. The title of Yves Bonnefoy's most startling collection of poems is *Ce qui fut sans lumière* (*In the Shadow's Light*) (1987). Bonnefoy is fascinated by the coincidence of light and darkness—of darkness *in* light and light *in* darkness. His poem "Dedham, vu de Langham" is a profound meditation on the work of John Constable, and in particular the painting of September 1802, usually entitled simply *Dedham Vale*. In a remarkable way, Bonnefoy realizes in words a picture that lies peacefully beyond language, capturing like so many of Constable's greatest works a moment in time that becomes eternal in the held image of the painting. (The original title of Constable's most famous painting, *The Haywain*, was *Landscape: Noon*, is a visual "spot of time" and as much a painting of a moment as a pastoral scene). Words are absorbed into the silence of the image, yet the painter needs the poet to capture the instant of vanishing into eternity.

*On pourrait croire*
*Que tout cela, haies, villages au loin,*
*Rivière, va finir. Que la terre n'est pas*
*Même l'éternité des bêtes, des arbres. . . .*

[You might think that
The whole scene, the hedges, the distant villages,
The river, was about to vanish. That the earth
Was not even the eternity of the flocks and trees. . . .][8]

Then as we move between word and image, Bonnefoy introduces from this silence the sound of music—another deep theme in Altizer's work, which resonates with a harmony found in the coincidence of opposites—a death into new and creative life. Altizer has written that music is the only art "in which the sacred is truly universal, and so much so that it is extraordinarily difficult to discover a genuine music which is genuinely profane."[9] Bonnefoy writes of Constable the artist:

*Tu as vaincu, d'un début de musique,*
*La forme qui se clôt dans toute vie.*

[You vanquished
With the beginnings of a music
the form which is the dead face of all life.][10]

Thus music brings life—just as the angel announces to Hagar the well in the desert that gives her life. Constable's painting is usually thought to be based on Claude's *Hagar and the Angel*, a biblical story (see Genesis 21:19) that fascinates Bonnefoy with its theme of life given out of death and rejection:

*Peintre de paysage, grâce à toi*
*Le ciel s'est arrêté au-dessus du monde*
*Comme l'ange au-dessus d'Agar quand elle allait,*
*Le coeur vide, dans le dédale de la pierre.*

[Thanks to you, landscape painter,
The sky has paused above the world
As did the angel above Hagar when she went
With empty heart, into the labyrinths of stone.][11]

In this wasteland where the angel appeared to Hagar, which is also the lush Vale of Dedham, the word moves into image in the silence that is the fullness of speech, and this is the birth of music. It is from this wasteland that Altizer, in self-confessed isolation (theology is never, properly, merely written, but lived within), speaks in *The Self-Embodiment of God* and *The Contemporary Jesus*, with an intensity that comes as close as anything in contemporary writing to an apocalypse of the word, moving through language as only true poets have done. This apocalypse is also at the heart of liturgy, though a primitive liturgy far from contemporary liturgical practice within the church, which has forgotten the apocalyptic prayer that is most truly the language of Jesus. Altizer has acknowledged his own debt to the liturgical scholar Dom Gregory Dix, and in particular his great book *The Shape of the Liturgy* (1945), written in the darkest days of modern European history. Early in his account of the Eucharistic Prayer, Dix gives close attention to words in I Corinthians 11:25, "Do this in remembrance (*anamnesis*) of me." Referring back to the earliest Roman tradition in Justin and Hippolytus, Dix writes of the "active sense . . . of 're-calling' or 're-presenting' before God the sacrifice of Christ, and thus making it here and now operative by its effects in the communicants . . . the eucharist is regarded both by the New Testament and by the second century writers as the *anamnesis* of the passion, or of the passion and resurrection combined."[12] In the anamnesis of the Eucharist, the moment of the passion is not merely commemorated as an act in history but is realized actually within the utterance and present act of the Eucharistic prayer. It is this presenting, or "presencing" of the sacrament as an apocalyptic enactment (a ground underplayed in Dix's account of the liturgy) that is fully realized in the heretical imagination of the poets in whom language becomes a genuine *kenosis*. That is, language is fully found only in a self-emptying and therefore in the silence that lies at the heart of the celebration of the sacrament, that is a reversal, in the death of God, of everything, and an apocalyptic moment beyond anything realized within the church, its liturgy, or its formularies. Altizer finds it most radically in Joyce's *Finnegans Wake*, writing,

> If *Finnegans Wake* is our most imaginative text which is simultaneously a liturgical text, only here does our uniquely Western liturgy undergo a full imaginative metamorphosis, and even if the awe and sublimity of the Mass now passes into a cosmic ribaldry, there an ultimate transgression occurs, and one inverting

and reversing the Eucharist, as the language of the Roman Rite becomes the very opposite of itself in *Finnegans Wake*. (GG 133)

The *Wake* continuously enacts a death that is an awakening, a sacrifice that is deeply worshipful precisely in its glorious profanity, so that finally, "I sink I'd die down over his feet, humbly dumbly, only to washup," and in this ending is the beginning, "A way a lone a last a loved a long the" . . . "riverrun, past Eve and Adam's . . ."[13] Here the "fall" of the opening page of the *Wake* is a reinvention of Blake's vision in which the fall is all,[14] an absolute *felix culpa*, the true moment of creation and an absolutely apocalyptic moment of reversal of all history.

It is this moment that is disastrously refused by Klee's "Angelus Novus" in the celebrated ninth of Walter Benjamin's *Theses on the Philosophy of History*, as it flees backward into the future, driven by the storm that we have called "progress."[15] This deeply profane, deeply liturgical moment is known only to those whom Altizer has called "radical" or "spiritual" Christians, those who, like Blake and Joyce, celebrate a death that is also the genesis of God. This genesis can only be in and through the absolute *kenosis* or self-emptying of God and always an anamnesis of the moment of dereliction recognized in the words of the true poet: "My God, my God, why have you forsaken me?" (Mark 15:34; Matthew 27:46), or van Gogh's cry, his last written words before his suicide, "What's the use?"

Here we recognize Altizer's long obsession with the theology of Karl Barth, and Barth's cry for a "theology of freedom" that looks ahead and strives forward, and his acknowledgment of the apocalyptic Christ. In his book *Genesis and Apocalypse* (1990) Altizer affirms:

> Perhaps the deepest theological response to Nietzsche's vision of eternal recurrence was the *Church Dogmatics* of Karl Barth, the first theology which was a theology of the Church and only of the Church, and thus the first Christian theology which effected or intended a total disjunction or chasm between the Church and history, for it was the first theology created in full response to the historical realization of the death of God. (*GA* 149)

I have long realized that Barth's theology, first articulated in the horror of the Great War of 1914–1918 in the *Römerbrief* (still, I believe, the most profound theological meditation of the modern period), can be fully understood only within a reading of Dostoevsky and Kierkegaard, and also of Joyce and Kafka, and against the vision of Mathias Grünewald's "Crucifixion" in the Isenheim altarpiece,[16] where the words of the evangelist, as he holds his book, are fulfilled and silenced in the finger pointing to the terible figure hanging on the cross. This is a moment of absolute isolation, a *coincidentia oppositorum* that is at the same time a celebration and a true anamnesis.

That is, when we speak of the *celebration* of the Eucharist, which is also the ultimate risk, we use the word in its primary sense of performing an action appropriate to the occasion, or the celebration of a past event by a festival.[17] Such festivities are only found, paradoxically, in the deepest solitude, in the deepest darkness where is affirmed the No which evokes a Yes, the last word of Joyce's great epic *Ulysses*. It is in the insistence of this that Altizer remains a preacher—along with van Gogh, Barth, Blake, and the poets. Blake, in his "Memorable Fancy" in *The Marriage of Heaven and Hell* (1790–93), walks among the fires of hell, delighted with the enjoyments of genius, which to angels look like torment and insanity, for Blake, like Nietzsche, knew well the ecstasy of "liberation occasioned by the collapse of the transcendence of Being, by the death of God" (*RT* 116).

## A CONCLUDING NARRATIVE

The eyes of humanity first looked into the accursed glass of vision in that moment in Eden when Adam and Eve, having eaten of the fruit, realize that their eyes are opened and see that they are naked, and seeing themselves, they cover up their nakedness and are found by God cowering in the bushes for shame. This is the first moment of human self-consciousness, when the human gaze looks reflectively into its own subjectivity and the long process of human history is born, which culminates for us in the Enlightenment obsession with the self, beginning with Descartes, an obsession that becomes a sickness unto death, until postmodernity asks the inevitable question, Who comes after the subject?[18] Was this, after all, the question from which Adam and Eve were hiding—though theology has traditionally constructed a different drama? But as we now acknowledge the deconstruction of the structures and values of the self as sustained by modernity, may we now at last be realizing the paradoxical possibility that the moment of fall allowed, for the first time, a loss of that very self that is prompted by the reflective gaze—an absolute loss that is, at the same time, the moment of profoundest creativity. Then paradise lost becomes the moment of creation in a coincidence of opposites that Blake acknowledges most deeply in Milton and that lesser poetic spirits such as Andrew Marvell feared would bring about the ruin of sacred truths.[19]

Among our contemporary theologians, Thomas Altizer has most courageously acknowledged this dark moment of deepest creation. He has preached this with a consistency and an insistence throughout his career in a word that is itself an overcoming of the deep and deadly dualism within the Christian tradition and an apocalypse that is a recovery of John 1:1 and a pure theology that escapes all the tricks of the theologians into an absolute presence and a silence of prayer that is nothing less than God. Such speech is a poiesis (following 1 Corinthians 11:24), an enactment: "It is enacted in the dawning of the actuality of silence, an actuality ending all disembodied and unspoken presence. Then speech is truly impossible, and as we hear and enact that impossibility, then even we can say: 'It is finished'" (*SEG* 96).

## NOTES

1. For a commentary on this late sonnet, see Richard Holme's remarkable second volume of his life of Coleridge, *Coleridge: Darker Reflections* (London: HarperCollins, 1998), 546–47.

2. An acknowledgment made in his "Living the Death of God: A Theological Memoir," unpublished manuscript.

3. For further commentary see Jean-Luc Marion, *God without Being*, trans. Thomas A. Carlson (Chicago: Chicago University Press, 1991), 17.

4. *The Letters of Vincent van Gogh*, ed. Mark Roskill (London: Fontana, 1983), 340.

5. Thomas J. J. Altizer, "Van Gogh's Eyes," in *Hermeneutic Philosophy of Science, Van Gogh's Eyes, and God: Essays in Honor of Patrick A. Heelan, S.J.*, ed. Babette E. Babich (Dordrecht: Kluwer Academic Publishers, 2002), 393–402.

6. Austin Farrer, *A Celebration of Faith*, ed. L. Houlden (London: Hodder & Stoughton, 1970), 122.

7. Ray L. Hart, *Unfinished Man and the Imagination* (Atlanta: Scholars, 1985), 38.

8. Yves Bonnefoy, *In the Shadow's Light*, trans. John Naughton (Chicago: Chicago University Press, 1991), 93.

9. Altizer, "Living the Death of God," chapter 2.

10. Bonnefoy, *In the Shadow's Light*, 93.

11. Ibid., 95.

12. Dom Gregory Dix, *The Shape of the Liturgy* (Westminster: Dacre, 1945), 161.

13. James Joyce, *Finnegans Wake* (London: HarperCollins, 1994), 628, 3.

14. "In the light of Blake's vision, the fall is all, and, dialectically, the very fullness of his vision derives from the totality of its fallen ground: vision cannot reverse all things unless it initially knows them in a fallen form" (*RT* 172).

15. Walter Benjamin, *Illuminations,* trans. Harry Zohn (London: Fontana, 1973), 249.

16. Karl Barth writes in the *Römerbrief* : "Jesus would not be the Christ if figures like Abraham, Jeremiah, Socrates, Grünewald, Luther, Kierkegaard, Dostoevsky remained, contrasted with Him, merely figures of past history, and did not rather constitute in Him one essential unity" (*The Epistle to the Romans*, trans. from the sixth edition by Edwyn C. Hoskyns [Oxford: Oxford University Press, 1933], 117).

17. See P. F. Bradshaw, "Celebration," in *The Eucharist Today*, ed. R. C. D. Jasper (London: SPCK, 1974), 131–32.

18. This was the question answered by Jean-Luc Nancy in 1986 as follows: "One of the major characteristics of contemporary thought is the putting into question of the instance of the 'subject,' according to the structure, the meaning and the value subsumed under this term in modern thought, from Descartes to Hegel, if not to Husserl. The inaugurating decisions of contemporary thought . . . have all involved putting subjectivity on trial" (*Who Comes After the Subject?* ed. Eduardo Cadava, Peter Connor, and Jean-Luc Nancy [New York and London: Routledge, 1991], 5).

19. [T]he Argument
    Held me a while misdoubting his Intent,
    That he would ruine (for I saw him strong)
    The sacred truths to Fable and old Song.

(Andrew Marvell, "On Mr. Milton's *Paradise Lost*," in *The Poems of Andrew Marvell*, ed. Hugh Mcdonald [London: Routledge & Kegan Paul, 1969], 64.)

# CHAPTER 12

# Kenosis

ALPHONSO LINGIS

In every generation there is a compulsion, in people of robust health, to go wander in regions of polluted air and water, meager food, filth, and disease. There is a compulsion to go to regions inhospitable to human life—jungle and desert and tundra, extreme altitudes and polar icescapes. There is a compulsion to go dwell among the plague ridden, where there are lepers and where vast numbers of people are HIV positive. There is a compulsion in the body to strip itself of its comforts and protective carapace and know how much solitude, boredom, anxiety, and how much discomfort, exhaustion, and pain it can endure. This is the compulsion of Prince Siddhartha to leave his palace and never return; the compulsion of backpackers, explorers of jungles, deserts, polar icecaps, the oceans; aid workers in refugee camps; and war correspondents.

There is an official discourse about warriors in times past and about soldiers today: that they go off to war out of a radiant commitment to the justice of their society, which is being attacked or is attacking an unjust society, out of a personal commitment to an honor that will be on them even if they are massacred, and in quest for glory. But in our century the literature of war narrates only the laying waste to territories and habitats, the slaughter of noncombatants, and extremes of physical exhaustion, filth, and carnage—of the victors as of the defeated. If in our time such literature has been permitted, what it recounts has always been recounted by those returning from war. Those who go off to war have not blinded themselves to what awaits them. Have not the extremes of physical abjection, misery, and agony exerted a strange power of attraction on them?

There is a compulsion to go where the forces of destruction ferment, where natural and cosmic forces drive madness and crime, the compulsion of pathologists, psychoanalysts, prison guards; the compulsion of mafiosos, street gangs, and solitary dreamers. For such people to stay in the safe and hospitable places, the hygienic places, where the air is clean, the water purified, and the food nutritious and abundant is to skim over reality. Thought too is driven by an excessive compulsion and is itself an excess over and beyond perception. Thought pushes ever further into the maelstrom of ignorance. We anticipate the coming consignment of all the psychology, economics, and physics of today to the merely literary status that the science of the Middle Ages has for us. We anticipate the coming consignment of all we know to ignorance and superstition. Thought negates the identities of all that is named.[1] There is a compulsion in thought to think of degeneration, defeat, and death, of chaos, catastrophe, and apocalypse. Thought is seeing what exceeds the possibility of seeing, is seeing what is intolerable to see, what exceeds the possibility of thinking.

> Philosophy, as I have hitherto understood and lived it [Nietzsche wrote], is a voluntary quest for even the most detested and notorious sides of existence. From the long experience I gained from such a wandering through ice and wilderness, I learned to view differently all that had hitherto philosophized: the *hidden* history of philosophy, the psychology of its great names, came to light for me. "How much truth can a spirit *endure*, how much truth does a spirit *dare*?"—this became for me the real standard of value. Error is *cowardice*—every achievement of knowledge is a consequence of courage, of severity towards oneself, of cleanliness towards oneself—Such an experimental philosophy as I have lived anticipates experimentally even the possibilities of the most fundamental nihilism; but this does not mean that it must halt at a negation, a No, a will to negation. It wants rather to cross over to the opposite of this—to a Dionysian affirmation of the world as it is, without subtraction, exception, or selection.[2]

## VISION AND IMAGINATION

This occurred in the spring of 1951 [Thomas Altizer writes], when I was almost twenty-five years old and a theology student at the University of Chicago, a period of immense turmoil for me, when I was not only visited by deep depression but locked into a genuine isolation, and again and again as I walked to campus over the Chicago midway I would acutely experience deep tremors in the earth, tremors threatening to open up into the depths below, where I would be consumed by a threatening abyss. This was my condition when one night as I was struggling with a recurrent insomnia, I suddenly awakened as though from a deep sleep, and awakened with a full vision, a vision paradoxically of darkness itself, a pure darkness, and yet one wholly luminous in that very darkness, and so luminous that I could see the very face of this darkness, a face that I could only know and name as Satan. Nor did I simply see this Satan, for this was a seeing in which I was consumed, I could actually experience myself as being drawn into the very body of Satan, one which I could experience as an ultimate bonding, a horrible but ineradicable union, and one which I have subsequently known as changing my life forever.[3]

Vision designates one of the five senses. But in current usage, the term "vision" preeminently designates the vision of visionaries—of Milton, Blake, Joyce, Gandhi, Che Guevara, Nelson Mandela.[4] It also designates the acheronian visions of Dante, Hieronymus Bosch, Louis-Ferdinand Céline, and Jean Genet. The thought that sees what exceeds the possibility of seeing, that sees what is intolerable to see, what exceeds the possibility of thinking, is vision. The visions of visionaries are vast and astounding, far exceeding the radius accessible to ordinary sight and exceeding the predictable.

Thomas Altizer is a visionary thinker. His is a thought that issues from visions, that elaborates, that consecrates the visions of visionaries. His own thought issues from a vision of his own—a vision of Satan that marked his life.

The vision of the prophet, the epic poet, and the great historical figure is not simply the overarching conceptual framework that guides his thought and action; it is a *vision*. Since the first epistemologists of modern times, this vision of visionaries has been assimilated to imagination. *Imagination* has served as a cover term for so many disparate things—the afterimages persisting on the eye, monocular images, the imagos that structure perceptions and memories, the imagination of imaginative variation and projections and models, dreams, the archetypes in dreams but also in waking perception and discourse, the fantasy of wish fulfillment, hallucination, the imagination of plastic artists, poetic imagination, the creative imagination of productive thinking, the mythical and religious imagination, and the visions of seers and visionaries. The use of the terms *image* and *imagination* to designate any kind of representation, which use we find in seventeenth-century epistemology, is still current in ordinary language. But psychoanalysis has pulled 'imagination' over toward 'fantasy,' the infantile belief in the omnipotence of thought, wish fulfillment. And literary criticism has pulled 'imagination' over toward 'fiction,' in which any resemblance to real persons and facts is unintended and purely coincidental. Imagination retains a relationship to visual perception; to imagine is to visualize. Auditory, tactile, and gustatory imagination have remained marginal to the discussion of imagination.

Psychology and the philosophy of mind have generally taken imaginative visualizing to be derivative of perceptual vision. If vision is seeing what is there, what is given, if it is intentional and receptive, then the visions of the productive imagination cannot really be simply a creative projection of the mind itself. In our dreams, Merleau-Ponty wrote, it is debris from the perceived world we still see. "During the dream itself, we do not leave the world behind: the dream-space is segregated from the space of clear thinking, but it uses all the latter's articulations; the world obsesses us even during sleep, and it is about the world that we dream." Dreams, hallucinations, erotic obsessions, and psychedelic intuitions "endeavour to build a private domain out of fragments of the macrocosm. . . . The most advanced states of melancholia, in which the patient settles in the realm of death, and, so to speak, takes up his abode there, still make use of the structures of being in the world, and borrow from it an element of being indispensable to its own denial."[5]

Immanuel Kant recognized an essential function of the imagination in every mind that is both receptive and active, both empirical and theoretical, both a perception of what is given and a conceptualizing and reasoning about what is given. For there is a fundamental nonconformity of our concepts to our perceptions: our concepts are abstract and universal, but our percepts are particulars. An imagination supplies schemas that make the application of concepts to percepts possible. The schemas share with percepts a sensuous materiality; they share with concepts a generality; they are general images. This "transcendental" imagination productive of schemas turns out to be reproductive: imagination produces these schemas by generalizing images of things seen and recalled from memory. An imagination that produces images to conform with concepts for which no percepts had been given only produces transcendental illusions. Martin Heidegger saw that the production of schemas for our concepts works by synthesizing past with present and with future. There is at work in it a power to envision the future and retain the past and extend the present with them and from them. The "transcendental imagination" is, Heidegger declares, this very temporalizing power in us. But Heidegger's explanation leaves aside visualization; his imagination is peculiarly nonimagistic. And indeed, the thrust of Heidegger's interpretation is to reduce the separation between understanding and imagination. The understanding does not produce its universal concepts (as a priori forms) for which then the imagination would supply general images. If the imagination is a synthesizing, or synopsizing, activity, and if this activity is more fundamentally the unfolding of a field of time where the future gives direction and the past momentum to the present, then this activity is also the activity that produces transtemporal forms, that is, concepts.

Slavoj Žižek argues that "obsessed as he is with the endeavour to synthesize, to bring together the dispersed manifold given in intuition, Kant passes over in silence the opposite power of imagination emphasized later by Hegel—namely, imagination qua the 'activity of dissolution,' which treats as a separate entity what has effective existence only as a part of some organic Whole."[6] "Imagination," Žižek says, "stands for the capacity of our mind to dismember what immediate perception puts together, to 'abstract' not a common notion but a certain feature from other features. To 'imagine' means to imagine a partial object without its body, a colour without shape, a shape without a body: 'here a bloody head—there another white ghastly apparition.'"[7] But Hegel has characterized understanding also as the power of the negative, which separates, abstracts or extracts, elements from the living whole of experience, setting them up as concepts, that is, fixed and inert determinations. Thus Žižek too posits an essential affinity between imagination and understanding.

## THE VISION OF VISIONARIES

How inadequate are all this epistemology and transcendental phenomenology for understanding the visions of visionaries and seers! Vision is
the distance sense, and the visionary vision sees what lies beyond the
horizons of sight. What is visual in the vision of a visionary is not so
many fragments recalled from the daytime empirical perception. The vision of a visionary is not just reproductive, and not just reproductive and
generalizing. The force of vision in him is not a force that dismembers
and dissolves what perceptual vision encounters as organic wholes—
although it is a force that breaks through the whole fabric of what is given
in ordinary and pragmatic sight. Far from fabricating out of fragments of
the macrocosm a private domain in which the individual can take up his
or her abode, the vision of the visionary opens upon immense spaces
inhabited by vast populations of human and extrahuman beings.

'Vision' designates both the faculty of sight and that which is seen.
The terminology of literary analysis acribes visions—especially those that
we have to acknowledge in the works of Dante, Milton, and Blake—to
creative imagination. But in the experience of the visionary, the vision—
that which is seen—is given, imposed on him. His faculty of seeing is in
a state of utter passivity. His seeing is ecstatic *kenosis*, self-emptying. He is
in thrall to the vision before him. To no longer consign the visions of
visionaries to imagination and understand them, we need a phenomenology of perception that no longer ascribes certain visual appearances to
the thing itself and others to the fabricating powers of the mind.

Something that is real and seen with ordinary sight is visible in a wave
of time and a field of extension, sending echoes and heralds of itself back
into the past and into the future. A house that is real and seen projects its
appearances across different perspectives, in different atmospheres, and on
the surfaces of our sensibility. A tree sends shadows off itself and halos over
itself. A river forms a screen and a phosphorescent veil over the rocks
below. A cliff face forms a screen over itself; it doubles up into a facade. A
fox glimpsed in the forest generates phantasmal reflections of itself, refracts
off hints and lures, and leaves traces.

Something that is real and seen also projects its form into us as an or-
ganizing diagram for our sensory-motor forces. To see it is to orient our
receptive surfaces and our limbs to it and to know how to reach for it and
handle it. And things are not only structures with closed contours that
lend themselves to manipulation and whose consistency constrains us.

They lure and threaten us, support and obstruct us, sustain and debilitate us, direct us and calm us. They enrapture us with their sensuous substances and also with their luminous surfaces and their phosphorescent facades, their halos, their radiance, and their resonances.

The vision of visionaries is not simply a creative imagination that draws lines and colors them in the emptiness outside the radius of what ordinary sight can see. What is seen in visionary vision bears with it the evidence of reality. As when in ordinary perception the overcast skies and the bleak desolation of wastelands weigh on us, the immense distances and depths seen in visions make themselves felt, as what has to be endured. The vision requires courage, the courage that confronts hard reality; it is pusillanimity that discredits it in the name of quotidian reality. Remote distances and vast depths intensify with their light all things visible to perception. And they attract and weigh on our emotional forces.

There is a naive picture of visions empowering, transfiguring, glorifying the visionary. But that which is seen in the vision besets the visionary, who is passive before it; it invades him, occupies him, emptying him of what he thought he had and was. And in this *kenosis* it could be that it is the abyss and pure darkness that is seen.

It is the distances and the lower depths themselves that make themselves visible and exert their vertiginous attraction on backpackers, explorers, aid workers, war correspondents, soldiers, street gangs, solitary dreamers, and Prince Siddhartha. How facile to ascribe these to morbid fixations, to individual and social pathologies. The acheronian visions of Dante, Hieronymus Bosch, Louis-Ferdinand Céline, and Jean Genet demonstrate the presumptuousness and superficiality of such explanations.

The psychoanalytic theory of introjection argues that fantasies are not simply the carefree emanations of an unoccupied mind; from infancy fantasizing is driven by the force of reality. This theory can help us understand the risks the visionary runs in exposing himself to what is seen in his vision.

In the days, weeks, and months of infant life, an infant's body parts are progressively animated, become mobilizable, are integrated. The infant progressively takes over the inner space of his body, which becomes more and more distinct and separate from the arms and body of his mother and from outlying things that have places of their own. But then, according to psychoanalysis, the infant begins to introject objects from the outside world into his body space. It is not simply that sounds reverberate and colored patterns hover in the inner space of his body; whole objects are felt to have invaded that space. The concept of 'introjection'—a stronger notion than 'receptivity'—implies that the bringing of outside things inside his body is an action of the infant himself, and psychoanalysts attribute a protective function to it: the infant defends himself against the diffuse pressure of the environment by detaching some object from it, bringing it inside, occupying himself with it and closing himself against the rest.

The infant feels himself and the body space he has progressively taken over to be porous and vulnerable. What is called infantile fantasies are not the gratifications of wish fulfillment; they contain the original sense of infantile psychic and bodily vulnerability. In infantile and adult "fantasizing" there is exposure of one's innermost space to alien objects that break through the walls of one's substance, invade it, occupy it, make it suffer. In the visions of visionaries these alien objects can come with their own fields from remote distances—and the empty abysses themselves can invade. In the operation of introjection the infant is also masochistically making himself vulnerable to the alien force of what he introjects, making himself suffer. In his and in the adult's "fantasies," as in the vision of visionaries, there is a kind of ecstatic pain. The sight of the old man, the diseased man, and the corpse did not make Prince Siddhartha shut himself behind the gates of his palace but led him forth to wander the world.

## VISIONARY LITERATURE AND THEORY

Although the essential of a vision is in the silent, silencing epiphany, most of what we know as visions comes to us from texts—from sacred writings, epic poets, mystic writings, cosmic literature, and world-historical orations. There is a language, then, that conveys vision—epic, prophetic, visionary language. There is also a presence of language in the vision itself—invocation and appeal. The visionary calls upon a nonhuman Other, an Interlocutor. The incantatory force of his voice is cast in ritual formulas and repetitions; his own individual voice is enveloped and lost in anonymous chants. Very often his voice calls up visible beings who have voices, and who may be only voices. And in the measure that mythic, mystical, epic, or prophetic language is composed, it elucidates the open dimensions, paths, and signposts of the vision for the visionary.

The visionary language then communicates the vision. It does not simply communicate to us concepts whose consistency and coherence graph the space of a vision that is the visionary's alone. Already the marvel of all language is that words spoken to us put us in touch not with images or concepts of things in the mind of the speaker, but with the things themselves which he has seen and which we can see. The visionary language *makes us see* what the visionary has seen. But for us to see what the visionary has seen is for a visionary to awaken in us. It is indeed a visionary in us that alone makes contact with the visions in visionary literature and receives from them the visions the writers have received. Thomas Altizer affirms that it is through knowing a primal vision of one's own time and world that one can open one's own vision to the infinitely deeper vision of our great visionaries."[8]

Seeing is believing. Phenomenology names a movement in philosophy that binds speculative thought to experience. Experience is conceived more broadly than the experimental observations formulated mathematically, verifiable and repeatable, that count as experience in the sciences. But there is certainly a primacy accorded to perception and on what is common, and not idiosyncratic, in our perceptions. Phenomenology as a discourse, a descriptive discourse, can communicate what is common in perceptual experiences. Among our five senses, there is, in our species of primate, a primacy of vision. Phenomenology recognizes a primacy of the life world, the natural world. Its world is not a spectacle; phenomenology recognizes a primacy of the everyday world, the practicable world. Phenomenology was heralded, at the beginning of the twentieth century, as a radical and revolutionary new philosophy. But Heidegger, and before him Husserl, found themselves citing phenomenological accounts of things and events in Plato and Aristotle. Was not phenomenology the core of every discourse that we recognized to be philosophy?

The vision of visionaries is not that of common experience; instead visionaries are extraordinary, extraordinarily individual. The visions of visionaries are world-historical and cosmic, opening upon time and space more vast than that of the everyday practicable world. The content of these extraordinary visions is communicated in the mythic language of Gilgamesh, the *Rig Veda*, and the mystical language of Plotinus and John of the Cross. It is communicated in the epic poetry of Homer and Milton and William Blake and the magic realism of Gabriel García Márquez. It is communicated in the prophetic language of Simon Bolivar and Che Guevara, Martin Luther King Jr. and Nelson Mandela.

Thinking, in systematic language, about what is given in visions is what Thomas Altizer identifies as theology.

Western theology had been tied up with metaphysics. Metaphysics had distinguished the finite sphere of the empirically given with infinite space-time beyond it. Theology then was conceived as a discourse about the infinite beyond, outside of the empirical experience the sciences or phenomenological philosophy discuss. Modern sciences project the empirical universe itself to be open, set in infinite dimensions of time and space. This discovery of the infinity of the universe "brought to an end every real distinction between the heavens and the earth" (*GA* 165). They extend their explorations and their methods into the heavens, the infinite space-time that had been the reserve of theology. But theology had also a positive object of study: God. Today, Altizer observes, there is no positive discourse about God. "Just as there is virtually no major twentieth century philosophical language about God, our truly major twentieth century imaginative language and imagery about God is a truly negative one, and even our major theological language is never actually affirmative in speaking of God and of God alone."[9] The theology that had been structured by the metaphysical opposition of a finite empirical world and an infinite space-time beyond, the realm of a God positively characterized is no longer possible. Theology today for Altizer is a thinking about what is seen in the visions of visionaries and what is said in their mythic, mystic, epic, and prophetic languages. Theology takes the visions of visionaries to be experiences of historical events. It is thus distinguished from literary criticism, which takes the works of Dante, Blake, Kafka, and Joyce to be literature, products of the imagination, fiction.

The visionary theology Altizer promotes is "an empirical theology, a theology recording actual vision, and one only possible by way of opening one's own vision to the infinitely deeper vision of our great visionaries, and it is even possible to test or possibly to verify such an empirical theology by attempting to correlate it with the primal vision of one's own time and world."[10] A thinking that takes the visions of visionaries to be experiences is confirmed by a vision that thinker himself has had. Visionary theology is a systematic discourse, but it can only be the work of visionaries.

> No writing as such rivals the deep and ultimate authority which is present in true epic, an ultimate authority which is undeniable, or undeniable in terms of the revolutionary historical transformation which it either embodies or effects. The Christian epic alone is exterior and interior at once, and the transformations

which are realized in its narrative movement are simultaneously realized in the interior of its reader, so that the reader is called to actually enact that which is read; and that enactment is a primary source of the authority of the epic. So it is that the Christian epic is a form of the eucharist or the mass, and there is a 'real presence' in that epic which is a eucharistic presence, and a eucharistic presence which is a eucharist consecration. (*GA* 172)

No one is more reticent than visionaries before the necessity to speak of their visions, to hold them to be authentic visions. Yet the visionary finds that "to refuse this experience would be to refuse my deepest center, or to refuse that center which I have been most deeply given, and one apart from which my life and work would be unreal."[11]

## SATANIC VISION

Milton's and Blake's visions arose both from the experience of revolutionary modern science and from the revolutionary economic, social, and political transformations of their time—from the experience of violent revolution, the English, American, and French Revolutions. Blake, and more explicitly Hegel, saw in the French revolution on the one hand the emergence of a universal consciousness, a consciousness of universal humanity in the affirmation of liberty, equality, and brotherhood. But at the same time this consciousness is a consciousness of the death of God and of all forms of authority, a consciousness of "the impersonal actuality of death" (*GA* 164).

The twentieth century has been a century of utterly unparalleled carnage. Genocide—the annihilation of a whole people whatever they have done or not done—has been pursued against one people or another every year for sixty years, and the most technologically advanced societies have constructed thermonuclear arsenals, which already are capable of destroying all that human history and civilizations have achieved. The twentieth century has known an experience of radical evil, but there is not in the sciences nor in phenomenological philosophy a comprehensive account of this experience. The experience of radical evil is, however, the center in visionary writers such as Kafka, Beckett, and especially Joyce. "Nowhere else is there such a deep divorce between thinking and imagination in our world."[12]

We cannot truly or deeply enter our world apart from a vision of radical evil. "Concretely, this can be observed in the very vacuity and hollowness of our language of Yes-saying and Yes-saying alone, or a Yes-saying occurring apart from the deepest No-saying, or apart from absolute abyss or absolute chaos."[13] Vision for us is inevitably a vision of the abysses of evil. "All of us, even if only implicitly or indirectly, have known visions of Satan, and known them when we are most fully awake, or most fully open to the world itself."[14]

For Altizer, Christianity has a particular place among all the visionary discourses, and a particular relevance today, in that it uniquely presents a vision of radical evil. "Jesus named Satan more fully and more continually than any previous prophet, and the New Testament is unique in the world's scripture by way of its continual calling forth of damnation and Satan."[15]

But the abyss is not an immemorial depth of nothingness. It exists as a event—depicted in the Christian vision as the fall of Satan and also as the passion and death of Christ. The fall is not simply the effect of an external cause. Altizer thinks of it as a kenotic self-emptying. The abyss of hell is not pure negativity, for Satan is depicted there as reigning in majesty. The fall of Satan is his descent to earth. "Satan undergoes a kenotic voyage from Hell to earth where he kenotically empties himself into a serpent" (*GA* 162). Parallel with this, Christ undergoes a kenotic voyage from heaven to earth, where he kenotically empties himself of his Godhead and undergoes passion and death. Altizer finds fully expressed in Blake the vision of the coinciding of Christ with Satan.

Altizer understands this self-emptying of Satan and of Christ as Hegel and Blake understood the self-emptying in the mind of God: "Evil is the withdrawal into self-centeredness, a withdrawal which *from the beginning* occurs in the 'externalization' and 'alienation' of the divine Being, for Absolute Being becomes its own 'other,' and thereby it withdraws into itself and becomes self-centered or 'evil'; but this is that self-alienation which yields to death, a death which is the death of the abstraction or alienation or 'evil' of the divine being" (*GA* 169).

These ontological events—or cosmic events, since as events they must be conceived as occurring in time, or giving birth to time—are also inner events of human existence. And this, Altizer says, is distinctive to the Christian epics. Unlike other ancient and modern epics, "the dramatic action of the Christian epic is cosmic and interior at once" (*GA* 162). There is then a kenotic self-emptying within the human soul. Self-emptying is a free and individual act (*GA* 164).[16]

This Christian theology has itself emptied out in our time.

> Never before has man been so totally immersed in a profane consciousness; neither classical Confucianism nor the Olympian religion of ancient Greece was so decisively turned away from the transcendent and the holy, and today we can only wonder at the natural piety of the Stoic and Epicurean schools, to say nothing of the dismay and skepticism with which the contemporary sensibility must inevitably react to the call of the higher expressions of mystical sanctity for an identification with the finitude and the transiency of the world.

But, Altizer affirms, "we must remain closed to a positive vision of the sacred insofar as we accept the destiny of our history." "Realizing as we must that every original symbol of the sacred has disappeared in our darkness, we must be open to a dialectical metamorphosis of the sacred, a kenotic transformation of the sacred into the profane, an historical epiphany of the broken but triumphant Body of Jesus in a totally fallen human hand and face" (*NA* 216-17).

The sacred is in decomposition. The sacred *is* in decomposition. The Christian vision shows the kenotic self-emptying of Satan, of Christ, of God. Altizer's radical theology tells of the kenotic self-emptying of the Christian theology, the Christian epic, and the Christian vision itself. But it is this very kenotic self-emptying that is the sacred.

The compulsion of backpackers; explorers of jungles, deserts, the polar icecaps, and the oceans; aid workers in refugee camps; and war correspondents, though the suspicion of morbidity and masochism is already there, can still be accommodated within a radiant positivist ideology of health, power, and self-realization. But the speeches, statues, and memorials honoring warriors and soldiers seem to us but cant declaimed by old men who stayed in the safety of chanceries, bunkers, and the inner offices of banks. The compulsion of pathologists, psychoanalysts, prison guards, of mafiosos, street gangs, and solitary dreamers, is consigned to sociopathology. Religion itself is discredited as subservience, servility, resentment. But the Christo-Satanic epic casts these kenotic compulsions as events in a cosmic and ontological vision, events that bear witness to the sacred.

# NOTES

1. "Hearing hears silence whenever and wherever it actually hears, whenever and wherever it is actual and real. Indeed it then hears silence to the extent that it hears, as its own act of hearing now empties every presence of all that identity which is embodied in speech. All identity then progressively becomes drawn into the actual silence of self-identity, as the realization of that self-identity now actually and actively unsays all the naming of speech" (*SEG* 87).

2. Friedrich Nietzsche, *The Will to Power*, trans. Walter Kaufmann (New York: Random House, 1967), §1041.

3. Thomas J. J. Altizer, "A Vision of Satan" unpublished manuscript.

4. Altizer locates the moment when Greek sculptors gave vision to their works. This vision was from the first visionary vision. The Diskobolos is "a total body because it wholly consumes all attention in its presence. That total absorption of attention is the realization of the birth of vision, of a pure vision, a vision which is totally immanent vision, and a vision which is wholly focused upon the pure immediacy of an instantaneous moment" (*HA* 23).

5. Maurice Merleau-Ponty, *Phenomenology of Perception*, trans. Colin Smith (London: Routledge & Kegan Paul, 1962), 293.

6. "The human being is this night, this empty nothing, that contains everything in its simplicity—an unending wealth of many representations, images, of which none belongs to him—or which are not present. This night, the interior of nature, that exists here—pure self—in phantasmagorical representations, is night all around it, in which here shoots a bloody head—there another white ghastly apparition, suddenly here before it, and just so disappears. One catches sight of this night when one looks human beings in the eye—into a night that becomes awful" (G. W. F. Hegel, "Jenaer Realphilosophie," in *Frühe politische Systeme* [Frankfurt: Ujllstein, 1974], 204; Donald Phillip Verene, *Hegel's Recollection* [Albany: State University of New York Press, 1985]).

7. Slavoj i ek, *The Ticklish Subject* (London: Verso, 1999), 29, 30.

8. Altizer, "A Vision of Satan," 6–7.

9. Ibid., 7.

10. Ibid., 6–7.

11. Ibid., 4–5.

12. Ibid., 2.

13. Ibid., 11.

14. Ibid.

15. Ibid., 12.

16. "Each fall is a consequence of a free and individual decision and will" (*GA* 166).

# A Response

## Thomas J. J. Altizer

A genuine response to these truly challenging essays may well be beyond the power of this theologian, and it is certainly not possible here to engage them with the fullness that they demand, so only an all too limited response will now occur. Perhaps what is most challenging here is the question of the very possibility of theology today, and while only Taylor resolutely denies this possibility, all of the chapters speak in a language well beyond our existing theological languages, and thus place in question not only those languages, but the very possibility today of theological language itself. If I am simply and only a theologian, I just thereby am open to the gravest challenge, a challenge occurring here, and hopefully one that can open a new theological language for me, and thereby a genuine theological transformation.

Such a transformation occurs in Ed Casey's chapter, and occurs through a deep and even dialectical polarity between a metaphysical theology and an incarnational theology, yet here theological thinking as such is truly disguised, which is not to say that it is absent, an absence impossible in this enactment. Now an incarnational theology fully disenacts and disembodies every possible metaphysical theology, one occurring not only in a deconstruction of metaphysical thinking, but also in a full resolution of that thinking itself, a resolution realizing a "body" that is the very opposite of any ontological identity, and yet a "body" that is a final consequence of metaphysical thinking itself. Hence the ending of metaphysics is the fulfillment of metaphysics, as most purely enacted in

Hegel's *Science of Logic*, and while Hegelian thinking is alien to Casey, dialectical thinking is not, even if it is camouflaged. That camouflage is manifest in the theology here called forth, and perhaps most so in what Casey understands as "body," a body fully incarnate in "flesh," and a "flesh" that is here and now and nowhere else. This is the context in which he issues his deep challenge to my theology: Is this a theology that disembodies "flesh," a disembodiment that could only be a reversal of genuine incarnation, and hence a theology in servitude to that which this theology itself knows as Satan? Yet underlying this challenge is Casey's conviction that only a primordial body could be an apocalyptic body, for only a primordial body could truly become incarnate, with the apparent consequence that "flesh" is a true dissolution of consciousness and history, a dissolution that is a resurrection of the primordial itself. Is such a theological movement finally a renewal of the absolutely primordial Godhead, a renewal only possible through the ending of theology, or the ending of everything that we have actually known as God?

Hart is now our foremost theologian of primordial Godhead, yet this is only possible through his voyage into the Nothing, a Nothing apart from which Godhead would be wholly indeterminate and unmanifest, and thus a Nothing at the center of every possible actualization of the Godhead. For Hart, pure Godhead cannot be manifest, a manifestation or actualization occurring in the genesis of the Creator, now the nihil is internal to God or the Creator, and this is the very point at which Hart can say farewell to all Neoplatonisms, for now Godhead is manifest as a "Godhead against God." Yet Hart would appear to remain within the horizon of Neoplatonism in knowing an eternal creation and an eternal genesis of God, thereby presuming a fundamental distinction between eternal creation and temporal creation, although he is silent about the role of the nihil in this distinction. Is the nihil born in the birth of the temporal, and if that is a necessary birth for the very actualization of the Godhead, does it necessarily realize an ultimate chasm or dichotomy between Godhead and God, and is this a dichotomy that we inevitably know in anything that we can apprehend as redemption? Whereas a pure or purely indeterminate Godhead is wholly beyond all possible suffering, there is an ultimate suffering of the Creator, and one only redeemable in the suffering of the creature. The Christian knows this suffering or passion to be absolute in the Crucifixion, but is the Christ of Passion the redeemer of the Creator, and the Christ of Glory the reflection of the Godhead and not the Creator? Does not an ultimate distinction between eternal creation and temporal creation entail this conse-

quence, but can a purely primordial Godhead be known to wholly and finally perish in the Christ of Passion, a perishing that is the perishing of all
possible eternal creation, and precisely thereby a total realization of the
temporal creation or of genesis itself?

It cannot be denied that a deep rebirth of Neoplatonism has occurred in recent thinking, and even in our most avant garde thinking, as
most purely and most profoundly embodied in Levinas, who finally ends
every thinking that is not a thinking of primordial Godhead. Now if my
theology can be known as our fullest apocalyptic theology, it is all too
natural to contrast this theology with the thinking of Levinas, for this is
a contrast that can draw forth the ultimate distance or the ultimate opposition between primordial Godhead and apocalyptic Godhead. While
the approaches of D. G. Leahy and Edith Wyschogrod are very different,
they are alike in apprehending a chasm between Levinas and Altizer, and
not simply because the latter is the weaker thinker, but far more so because the thinking of Levinas makes an apocalyptic thinking absolutely
impossible. Perhaps this is the point at which Levinas most deeply differs
from Heidegger, and not only from Heidegger but from the whole tradition of modern German philosophy, a philosophy giving birth to a
purely apocalyptic thinking, and even if the primordial thinking of Heidegger is a reversal of this thinking, it nevertheless remains in genuine
continuity with its apocalyptic origins. Now such origins are wholly dissolved with everything that Levinas understands as the Infinite, an infinite that is the primordial Godhead, and if it is Levinas alone who can
know primordial Godhead as the origin of Ethics, this is an Ethics
wholly other than every ethics, and one that can be known only through
the dissolution of every philosophical ethics, and every historical ethics
that is independent of the Torah.

It is Wyschogrod rather than Leahy who is truly loyal to Levinas, but
unlike Levinas her mind is genuinely open to opposition, as opposed to
Levinas she can think the most ultimate heterodoxy, and perhaps most
clearly so in her voyages into my thinking. I must confess that she opens
vistas in my thinking that were unknown to me, as she does here in her
understanding of the Christ of Passion as a primordial passion, and one
even present in the immediacy of an unformed and primordial matter.
While she attributes such an understanding to me, I cannot recognize it as
such, but I can sense that this might well be yet another point at which my
thinking is incomplete or unfulfilled, and perhaps most unfulfilled in my
understanding of the Crucifixion. Now if Crucifixion truly is Apocalypse,

and Genesis itself is finally Apocalypse, what are the consequences there-from for our understanding of matter and of the body? Does this open the possibility of a matter that is prior to the creation, and not that matter which Greek philosophy knows as *hule*, but rather a matter that is insepa-rable from both crucifixion and apocalypse? And is this the very matter that is glorified in resurrection, and not a resurrection that is a resurrec-tion of glory, but far rather a resurrection that is the resurrection of the "flesh?" Is that glorified "flesh" a truly primordial matter, but a primordial matter inseparable from crucifixion and apocalypse, and precisely thereby inseparable from genesis itself?

Leahy is now our primal apocalyptic thinker, and yet an apocalyptic thinker who has entered into an ultimate encounter with our most purely primordial thinker, Levinas, an encounter that is certainly not a dialectical encounter, but one issuing in a new understanding of Levinas. This fully calls forth the truly radical thinking of Levinas, and in this essay one making possible a realization that Levinas and Altizer are genuine opposites, but whereas Levinas's project is truly real, Altizer's project if only in this perspective can be known as being simply impossible and most clearly so in calling forth an "absolute actuality sans actuality." If Al-tizer can know God's affirmation of his death as his very own, a death that is the final realization of Godhead itself, that death is inseparable from the advent of an apocalyptic nothingness, and one that is itself ful-filled in the advent of our world. Yes, that world is an actual apocalyptic nothingness, and an apocalyptic nothingness that is an absolutely new nothingness, now our own consciousness is no more, or is no more in its deepest ground, for now self-consciousness is absolutely exiled from itself. If this is realized by the reversal of the priority of interiority to ex-teriority, that is an apocalyptic realization, and if only Altizer's "absolute foolery" can know this as an apocalyptic consummation, this is not the end of eternal recurrence; it is far rather the final realization of that eter-nal recurrence that is the very reversal of eternal return. That is a rever-sal that begins with the prophetic revolution of Israel, a revolution wholly alien to Levinas, and wholly alien to every truly primordial thinker; hence it is invisible in every genuine Neoplatonism, but inevitably present in all truly apocalyptic thinking and vision.

It is Walter Strauss who most deeply initiated me into Kafka, that Kafka who has most clearly and most decisively recorded our apocalyp-tic nothingness, and most purely so in his parabolic writing, a parabolic writing that is the first actual renewal of the parabolic language of Jesus, and most manifestly so in its apocalyptic ground. Kafka's writing is perhaps most deeply parabolic when it is seemingly free of the genre of the parable; then writing itself is immediately present, and if Kafka could know that presence as an ultimate curse, then parable does exist in what Strauss calls forth as a moment without time or space, but if only thereby it is totally present. Kafka is our purest witness to the total presence of an eternal damnation, and if thereby an epiphany of an absolute silence occurs, that is a deafening epiphany, and deafening not as a primordial chaos, but as an apocalyptic and purely incarnate chaos. Strauss can know parable as the only language for the voice concealed within this silence, but thereby a total silence becomes hearable, and hearable through that voice that is the voice of silence.

David Jasper is the only priest in this company and the only one who here explicitly speaks of prayer, but now prayer can only be silence, and if he can know total presence as true prayer, thereby he can know pure theology as the absolute presence and silence of prayer. Yet that is a prayer impossible apart from an absolute loss, an absolute loss knowable in prayer as a moment of profoundest creativity, for that is a loss that is continually renewed in the Eucharist, a Eucharist that is an anamnesis of Christ's passion and death. The breaking of the body of Christ in the Eucharist is the renewal of absolute loss, and if that breakage here issues in the real presence of resurrection, that is the real presence of total presence, and a total presence that is an apocalyptic presence. The truth is that we have no full theology of the Eucharist, perhaps because we have no full theology of prayer, and if a theology of prayer is what is most missing in our theological world, perhaps nothing else could be a more decisive witness to the death of God in our theology itself.

Carl Raschke can know a deicide that has been committed by the masses. Now for the first time deicide is universally embodied, and an absolutely new realism is at hand, as God's death has ended "representation." For the death of God abolishes every boundary between immediacy and mediacy, between *ousia* and parousia, and between temporality and eschatology or apocalypse. The time of the death of God is the time of dismemberment and sacrifice, but now a universal sacrifice and dismemberment, a sacrifice renewing the sacrifice of Christ, although now that sacrifice occurs in the brute actuality of our new world. Raschke can know this sacrifice as a Dionysian sacrifice, an overcoming of every possible dualism, and if only thereby a renewal of the Crucifixion itself, as an infinite divine presence is overcome once and for all.

If this ushers in the Age of the Spirit, Alphonso Lingis is yet another witness to that Spirit, and is so even as a philosophical thinker, a thinker who can know that thought itself finally negates everything that is named, and if genuine thinking exceeds the very possibilities of thinking, if only thereby it establishes the possibility if not the necessity of ultimate vision. Perhaps no other philosopher has so fully drawn forth the radical evil of the twentieth century, an evil that Lingis has traveled to the ends of the earth to encounter, for evil as evil is purest in its primordial form, and is truly invisible even if all-pervasive in our civilization. And if the genuinely sacred has now wholly decomposed in that civilization, it can now only openly be encountered in those societies most distant from that civilization, but then darkness itself becomes visible, and most visible in that universal sacrifice or universal mass that Lingis has again and again unearthed. Is that a truly Dionysian sacrifice, and is it, too, a renewal of the Crucifixion, and a renewal of that crucifixion that is crucifixion alone?

A genuine Buddhism would appear to be most distant from that crucifixion, but it is nevertheless possible that a pure crucifixion may well be more fully present in Buddhism than in any manifest form of Christianity, for if crucifixion is finally resurrection, and not a resurrection in the beyond but far rather a resurrection of the "flesh," then a Buddhist realization of a pure emptiness that is all in all as an absolutely liberating totality could be a realization of a crucifixion that is resurrection itself. Janet Gyatso rightly observes that Tantrism is missing from my apprehension of Buddhism, even if she can identify me as a Tantric Christian theologian, but a Tantric theologian who refuses the esoteric path of genuine Tantrism, and if I can only understand Buddhism from a Christian perspective, and thus must miss its own integral center, my real purpose here is an employment of a Buddhist horizon as a way to a total transformation of Christian theology. Inevitably, I must therefore be closed to a genuinely or purely Buddhist nothingness or emptiness, but must any truly contemporary understanding of that emptiness be likewise so closed, and if Gyatso can refuse the Kyoto School as a genuine expression of Buddhism, is it Buddhism itself that she would apprehend as making a contemporary Buddhist theology impossible? No doubt this impossibility is far purer in Buddhism than in Christianity, but in this perspective we can see that the theology that we have known in the Western world is truly unique, and perhaps most unique in its understanding of Godhead itself, a Godhead that unlike *sunyata* calls forth its own actual opposite or its own integral other, an otherness realizing a uniquely Western Angst and a uniquely Western Nothing.

Mark Taylor can know my thinking as being haunted by the impossibility of theology, a theology impossible today as it has never been so before, an inevitable consequence of the death of God, and if my theology refuses this consequence, that is yet another sign of the final death of theology. There can be little doubt that the twentieth century has been obsessed by death as has no other historical world, a death that is truly all in all; thereby it can be understood as a renewal of primitive Christianity, or a renewal of a Christianity ultimately centered in the Crucifixion. Taylor's own theological work is a genuine expression of that Christianity, and if he is now impelled to reverse his own theological thinking, is that because we have now entered an absolutely new world that is liberated from the ultimacy of death? Is that the new world realizing our theological language as a language that is now and perhaps always has been past? And is this above all manifest in a contemporary America, and in an American society and culture that Altizer abhors, and if Altizer is a theologian who could never be an American, is it precisely thereby that he is disengaged with the world? No, I could never accept Andy Warhol as a genuine much less a revolutionary artist. Is this itself a decisive sign of my alienation from the real world, or from our real world? Is all theology truly alienated from this world, and is this also and perhaps above all true of a theology of absolute death that is precisely thereby a theology of absolute life, or a theology of the death of God that is a purely apocalyptic theology and even thereby a theology of absolute resurrection? Is all such language and thinking now infinitely distant from us, and therefore truly dead and buried, or is ours a new death calling for an absolutely new language, and, yes, an absolutely new theological language?

Brian Schroeder's thinking of absolute atonement is a voyage into that new death, a death that can only truly or fully be understood by knowing the self-sacrifice of God, a self-sacrifice that in being the reversal of genesis is absolute apocalypse itself. Perhaps Schroeder is most original here in understanding the self-sacrifice of God as the realization of the absolute responsibility of God, a responsibility inseparable from an absolute atonement, which itself is a kenotic transfiguration of the Godhead. Only that transfiguration makes possible an absolute atonement, an atonement realizing a *coincidentia oppositorum* between the Godhead and its own inherent opposite, and in this absolutely kenotic act Godhead itself is manifest and real as "nothingness." If it is only Christianity that

knows that Nihil, it is only Christianity that knows the self-sacrifice of
the Godhead, or knows that sacrifice as actuality itself. But Schroeder's
deeper project is the calling forth of an apocalyptic ethics, an ethics embodying absolute responsibility, a responsibility in which a primordial
and an apocalyptic ethics coincide. Hence Schroeder embraces the dar-
ing project of uniting Levinas with an ultimately radical theology, one
merging a preprimordial and anarchic past with an apocalyptic future
that is here and now, and that alone can make possible an absolute responsibility for us. That responsibility is a total freedom, and one only
made possible by the death of God, for it is the *kenosis* or the self-sacrifice of God that is the ultimate ground of that freedom embodied in an
apocalyptic ethics, one wherein God's absolute responsibility becomes
our own.

Now if Schroeder can know that all ethics is now empty and illusory
apart from the death of God, this condition is a consequence of our nihilism, a new nihilism embodying a new absolute alterity. But that alterity makes possible a new truly affirmative will to power, as now a
self-emptying power becomes an absolute power for us, for this is an
apocalyptic will to power, and one that is a concrete and actual expression
of absolute atonement. That atonement is the only possible expression of
ethics after the death of God, and if absolute atonement is absolute *kenosis*, that is the very *kenosis* that is the center of an apocalyptic ethics, a center that is the full and final embodiment of the self-sacrifice of God.
Hence responsibility now can only be an absolute responsibility, and if this
is the very responsibility that was inaugurated by Jesus himself, and one
consummated in the crucifixion of Jesus, it is by embodying that crucifixion that we become absolutely responsible, a responsibility that at
bottom is an absolute atonement.

Lissa McCullough is a theologian deeply committed to an absolutely
new theology, one reflected here in her calling forth of the total act of
God, an act that is the irreversible sacrifice of the pleroma of the Godhead, and all events whatsoever are grounded in the totality of this act.
This is the sacrifice actually embodied in the death of God in the Crucifixion, a death that is a pure and total passion, but that is the passion that
is the deepest ground of existence itself. Godhead itself is only embodied
through death, one originating in the sacrifice of the primordial pleroma,
and one consummated in the Crucifixion, but it is precisely the very perishing of God that is the resurrection of God, and a resurrection occurring "in our very flesh." McCullough can capture the systematic core of

my theology more effectively than I can myself, and here she can know the self-negation of God as an apocalyptic *coincidentia oppositorum*, as one realizing an absolute affirmation of the world and the flesh, and that is the very affirmation in which the perishing of God becomes the resurrection of the body, a resurrection that is apocalypse itself.

Yet the ultimate ground of this resurrection is that genesis that *is* apocalypse, an absolute act that is an absolute disenactment, and a disenactment or reversal of primordial Godhead itself. This is that absolute death occurring in the absolute act of genesis, an absolute death that alone is the source and ground of an absolute life or an absolute actuality, and if that life is finally the resurrection of the body, that body is an apocalyptic body, or the body of an absolutely new apocalyptic Godhead. Hence genesis, or an absolute beginning, is not only the genesis of God, but finally the apocalypse of God, and that genesis is inseparable from that apocalypse, or absolute beginning is inseparable from absolute ending. So absolute beginning is the beginning of the passion of God, a passion that McCullough can know as a sacrificial exile of God from God, an exile alone actualizing the liberating release of omega from alpha, or of apocalyptic Godhead from primordial Godhead. If this exile is an absolute "self-othering" of God from God, it precisely thereby is an ultimate fall of the Godhead, but a liberating fall culminating in the redemption or atonement of Godhead itself. And that redemption *is* resurrection, and a resurrection of the body that is the resurrection of the "flesh," a flesh that is the very flesh of Christ, or the flesh of that crucifixion that *is* resurrection. Finally, that flesh is our very own, or our very own when we exist in Christ, or exist in that apocalypse of God that is resurrection itself.

Once again "flesh" becomes primal in the discourse of this volume, and even if "flesh" appears to be the most immediately meaningful of all theological symbols, in this discourse it is the most elusive and baffling of all such symbols, and perhaps most so when it is associated with anything that we can literally or empirically know as flesh. Is that why resurrection is such a controversial category in modern theology, and in modern biblical scholarship as well, just as it is equally baffling in modern literary language, and so much so that our literary criticism and scholarship virtually ignores every theological meaning of resurrection? Is it possible that we are more deeply alienated from "flesh" than we are from Godhead itself? And are we most deeply alienated from "flesh" in being alienated from body itself, and not simply from our own immediate body, but from a primordial body that is our own original body?

Perhaps the most radical thinking about primordial body occurs in Lurianic Kabbalism, a Kabbalism ultimately grounded in Tsimtsum, an original withdrawal or contraction of the Godhead, which makes possible the creation. This is immediately followed by the "Breaking of the Vessels," a cosmic and universal disruption, which is necessary to make possible a cleansing or purification of the elements of evil in the Sefiroth or that whole realm of divinity underlying and grounding the creation. This is an ultimate and ontological crisis, and ever since that primordial act, all being is in exile, an exile that will only be resolved by that Tikkun that is the restitution or reintegration of the original whole. Now the advent of primordial space is accompanied by a flowing of the divine light into that space, and the first being that emanated from this light is Adam Kadman or a primordial humanity, and Adam Kadman is nothing but a configuration of the divine light that flows from the essence of the Godhead or En-Sof into the primeval space of the Tsimtsum. The body of this original humanity is a divine and cosmic body, and it is destined to effect that Tikkun, which is the salvation of totality itself.

While Lurianic Kabbalism is a deeply esoteric way, its symbolic depths entered the Western imagination, or at least are fully paralleled therein, giving us not only Milton's Christ but Blake's Albion and Joyce's Here Comes Everybody. Here, a universal humanity is not only a divine and cosmic humanity, but one undergoing an ultimate fall or eternal death, a death and fall absolutely necessary to effect a transfiguration of a wholly fallen totality, and a transfiguration occurring in the body or "flesh" of this universal humanity. Hence this primordial body is a truly fallen body, or is the consequence of an ultimate and absolute fall or exile, but only this exile makes possible an absolute transfiguration, and an absolute transfiguration occurring in the very actuality of body or "flesh" itself. Hence primordial body is fallen and redemptive at once, or "flesh" and Spirit simultaneously, and if this primordial body is original body itself, that body is a body of transfiguration, and a transfiguration of ultimate contraries or opposites into an absolutely new and finally apocalyptic body, which is not only the resurrected body, but a resurrected totality, or that totality that is absolute novum.

In the New Testament, it is Paul who speaks most forcefully and continually of "flesh" (*sarx*), a "flesh" that is pure sin, and is only manifest as such as a consequence of the Crucifixion, an apocalyptic crucifixion ushering in the new aeon or the new creation. It is noteworthy that in Paul's ecstatic celebration of the resurrection in I Corinthians 15 it is only a "spiritual" body and not a fleshly body that is triumphantly resurrected, for when the last trumpet sounds, our perishable body will put on imperishability, and this mortal body must put on immortality. At no other point is Paul's understanding of grace so deeply pagan, and this is the understanding that soon dominated the greater body of Christianity, not truly being reversed until the full advent of the modern world. But then it is reversed only by the most radical expressions of Christianity, and never fully reversed in any orthodox form of Christianity, and even if historical scholarship can demonstrate the deep dichotomy between the resurrection of the body and the immortality of the soul, no orthodox theology has yet resolved this dichotomy. Indeed, flesh itself is a truly elusive theological category, being at once the body of sin and the site of resurrection, a flesh that is simultaneously the body of Satan and the body of Christ, and if thereby flesh is an ultimately dichotomous theological category, it has only been resolved as such in our deepest and most radical vision.

The dichotomy between "flesh" and Spirit is at the very center of Paul's thinking, just as it is in every genuinely apocalyptic thinking. Here "flesh" is the true opposite of Spirit, but it is an opposite absolutely transfigured in apocalypse itself, an apocalypse in which Spirit is all in all only as a consequence of a total and final transfiguration of "flesh." Is that a transfiguration not only foreshadowed but made possible by genesis itself, and if genesis is finally an apocalyptic genesis, is "flesh" itself a consequence of that genesis, a flesh that is finally incorporated into an apocalyptic totality, but is so incorporated only as a consequence of an absolute transfiguration? Here, the very image of the Body of Christ is all too significant, for that is an image of primordial Logos and apocalyptic body at once, an apocalyptic body that is all in all and all in all as that primordial ground that is the source of all and everything, for this image truly conjoins an absolute beginning and an absolute ending or absolute transfiguration, so that thereby genesis and apocalypse are clearly united. But can that body be a body of sin and a body of grace at once. Is it a body that is inevitably and necessarily a body of sin as the atoning victim, and as such a body that is absolutely guilty? Only the Crucifixion makes manifest an absolute guilt, but that very manifestation or actualization is inseparable from the full and final advent of the new creation, a new creation that is an absolute transfiguration, and an absolute transfiguration of that old creation, which is "flesh" itself.

This is a "flesh" that is an absolutely transfigured flesh in the Body of Christ, but is that a transfiguration of primordial body, and of that primordial body that is the consequence of absolute beginning? The prologue to the Fourth Gospel enacts the primordial Logos as the very agent of creation, and this is the Logos that became "flesh," and if that flesh is the ultimate destiny of the Logos, is this a destiny already enacted in genesis itself, and enacted in that act that is the absolute act of creation? While virtually all theology knows the act of creation as an absolutely sovereign act, is it simultaneously an absolutely kenotic or self-emptying act, and is this absolutely necessary if its ultimate end is redemption itself, and a redemption that is the absolute transfiguration of "flesh"? This is a redemption that every orthodox Christianity refuses, and every Gnostic Christianity as well, for it is a redemption that is a transfiguration of flesh itself, and of that flesh or body that is "here and now and nowhere else."

Thereby body itself becomes a total presence, a total presence that is a total body, but is a total body only as an absolutely transfigured body, or that body of Christ that is the absolutely transfigured body of Satan. But it is flesh itself that is so transfigured, and that flesh that is immediately here and now, yet in this perspective that flesh is truly here and now only as a consequence of this transfiguration, a transfiguration that is not only the consequence of incarnation, but *is* incarnation itself, is the embodiment of "flesh" itself. Yet that flesh that is sin itself is that flesh that is most distant from us, or most alien to us, for even if the body of sin is seemingly an immediate body, at bottom it is an infinitely distant body, and not because it is infinitely distant from "soul," but far rather because it is infinitely distant from every possible true immediacy. A Pauline dichotomy between law and grace is illuminating here, a law that is the absolutely imperative and a grace that is the absolutely indicative, a law that is absolutely alien and distant and a grace that is totally present, the one impelling an absolute bondage and the other calling forth an absolutely new freedom, but a freedom only possible when an ultimate bondage is finally ended. A Pauline freedom from the "law" is thereby a freedom from the "flesh" of sin, and a flesh that is "flesh" precisely because it is disincarnate, so that original sin can here be understood as the advent of disincarnation, or the advent of the "spiritual" itself. This is just what Barth understands as religion in his revolutionary commentary on Paul's Epistle to the Romans, and thereby we can understand religion or the "spiritual" as disincarnation, but a disincarnation that is the advent of a wholly fallen flesh, or that flesh that is the body of sin.

Now this is the very body of sin that undergoes an absolute reversal in the Crucifixion, but is that a reversal of anything that we can understand as primordial body, or anything that we can envision as original body? Now if an absolute genesis or an absolute beginning is the inauguration of that creation that is finally redemption, and the body of that redemption is an absolutely transfigured body, then that transfigured body could be an absolutely transfigured primordial body, and even an absolutely reversed original body. Otherwise redemption could not be actual and real, or absolutely actual and real, and here that primal Christian symbol of *felix culpa* is illuminating, for if the fall is the fall of body itself, and the fall of primordial body, it is a fall finally culminating in an absolutely transfigured body, an absolute transfiguration only possible as a transfiguration of a fallen body, and thus that fall is necessary to transfiguration itself, or to an absolute transfiguration. Hence creation is finally inseparable from fall, or is inevitably destined to fall, but that fall is a *felix culpa* and is so to make possible an apocalyptic or total redemption, a redemption that is the redemption of a wholly fallen body. Hence the redeeming or the atoning body of Christ is an absolutely guilty body, but as the body of Christ it is simultaneously an absolutely gracious body, and only the *coincidentia oppositorum* of an absolutely guilty body and an absolutely gracious body makes possible what we can know as redemption.

Thus "flesh," and a wholly fallen flesh, is inseparable from an absolutely gracious body or flesh, and therefore "flesh," too, is a *coincidentia oppositorum* and is the dialectical coincidence or union of absolute bondage and absolute liberation, or of an absolutely alien "law" and an absolutely apocalyptic grace. Then immediacy itself becomes an ultimate mystery, an immediacy that is at once an absolutely alien and an absolutely liberating immediacy, but thereby we can understand the necessity of an ultimate descent, and of an ultimate descent into the body itself. Apart from such a descent, we can only know our body as an ultimately dichotomous body, one fully manifest in what we can know and experience as our most immediate body, a body here and now and wholly elsewhere simultaneously, or a body fully incarnate and fully disincarnate at once. Hence the incarnation that we can know, or the bodily incarnation immediate to us, is present and absent at once, and totally present and totally absent simultaneously, a simultaneity that is "flesh" and Spirit at once, and only thereby are we now actual as and in our bodies. From that perspective, the promise of an ultimate body is an ultimate illusion, but so likewise the judgment that we are only a fallen body is a fully comparable illusion, but these illusions can be dissolved by way of an ultimate descent into the body, and even if this descent can be known as a descent into Hell, it is just thereby an ascent into Heaven, and into that Heaven that is an absolutely transfigured Hell.

All too significantly, there is nothing more minimal in the great body of historical Christianity than an enactment of Christ's descent into Hell, if only thereby Christ's ultimate movement is here known as an ascent into Heaven, a Heaven that is the absolute opposite of Hell, and an eternal life that is the absolute opposite of eternal death. So, too, it is only in Christianity that the body itself is known as a body of sin. No other tradition has known such an ultimately alien chasm between body and grace, or such an ultimate distance between a resurrected or redeemed body and our actual or immediate bodies. It is also revealing that the ultimate heretics in Christianity are either those committed to a total dissolution of the body or those committed to an apocalyptic transfiguration of the body, and if it is heterodoxy that most deeply calls forth orthodoxy, Christian orthodoxy has called forth a mystery of the body rivaled by no other tradition, a mystery of the body even greater than the mystery of God. This is why we are more manifestly alienated from "flesh" than we are from Godhead itself, but is that alienation a consequence of the uniquely Christian God, that God who is absolute sovereignty and absolute transcendence alone, and whose redemptive act can actually be known only as an absolutely judgmental act? Is it possible that it is the very enactment of the uniquely Christian God that has realized the ultimate mystery of our bodies, a mystery of the body inseparable from an ultimate alienation from the body, and an alienation from the body that is a uniquely Christian eternal death?

Here, the very advent of a new postmodernity is truly illuminating, an advent accompanied by a comprehensive renewal of orthodox Christianity and of religion itself, and an advent embodying a truly new and far more comprehensive emptiness of the body, as for the first time body itself is inseparable from an all too actual emptiness, and a body that can only actually be known as a total exteriority. While it is true that our deeper prophets foresaw this destiny, just as a late modern literature and art could enact it, such an ultimate epiphany is nevertheless defying contemporary understanding, and there is no more difficult or daunting challenge today than is a voyage into that new body that is engulfing us. Could this occur by way of a quest for primordial body, and not a primordial body that is an unfallen body, but rather a primordial body that is a truly fallen body, and fallen if only because of its ultimate destiny, a destiny that is an apocalyptic transfiguration, and thus an ultimate realization of primordial body itself? Is it actually possible to think or even to speak of primordial body? True, we have been given ultimate visions of primordial body, and even given them in the late modern world, but is such vision possible today? Perhaps the ultimate emptiness of our present condition could make possible such a vision, but this is not a challenge to an elite few; it is rather a challenge to us all, and just as each of us has been hurled into a condition of ultimate emptiness, each of us must find a way through that emptiness, and perhaps by way of discovering primordial body itself.

Certainly a primordial body that is an ecstatically joyous body is deeply alien to us, and so, too, is a primordial body that is a whole and integral body, or a primordial body that is a wholly innocent and unfallen body. While we can entertain images of such a body, these can only be illusory images to us, and illusory if only because of the emptiness of our new bodies, bodies inseparable from a total exteriority, and a truly new exteriority, an exteriority that is a consequence of the very reversal of our interiority. It is also possible to know such an exteriority as a consequence of an ultimate judgment, but once such a judgment has occurred, there can be no return to a body innocent of that judgment, and thus no return to a primordial innocence. Not only is every innocence an innocence lost, just as every paradise is a paradise lost, but in our new perspective we can know every body as a body lost, as body is now inseparable not only from an ultimate emptiness, but from an ultimate abyss as well, an abyss that for the first time can immediately and universally be known. The new passivity of postmodernity is a decisive sign of this abyss, a passivity that is not only a passivity of the spirit but a passivity of the body, too, a passivity inseparable from our new emptiness, a new emptiness that is a consequence of a new exteriority, and a new bodily exteriority, an exteriority internally embodying a total exteriority. Is that very exteriority a new way for us into primordial body, and into a primordial body that is a totally exterior body, a body that *Finnegans Wake* can enact as "Here Comes Everybody," but that only in our new world is manifest to everyone?

Now if it is possible for us to know primordial body as an exterior body, is it possible to know that body as a consequence of fall, and a fall that is an inevitable realization of genesis itself? If genesis is the consequence of the self-negation, or the self-emptying, or the self-sacrifice of the primordial pleroma, as I maintain in my later work, then a primordial body issuing therefrom could only be a self-alienated or self-divided body, a body that is body and antibody at once, or for-itself and against-itself simultaneously. In this perspective, there can be no actual body, or actual human body, apart from such self-division or self-alienation, and hence no human body that is simply a natural body, or that is only a literal or empirical body. The Christian tradition can know a dichotomy between body and soul as a consequence of the fall. In the ancient form of that tradition only the body is truly mortal, hence its alienation from the soul, and its primal identity as "flesh." The resurrection could never be a resurrection of that flesh, but only the resurrection of a new "spiritual body," a spiritual body that is the very opposite of the physical body, as first proclaimed by Paul (I Corinthians 15:35–56). If this is the tradition that has engendered our deepest hatred of the body, it is also one that is open to the deepest reversal of that hatred, and only such a reversal could make possible an opening to a primordial body that is the very seed of an apocalyptic transfiguration.

Yet if that resurrection occurs only through crucifixion, and through the crucifixion of a real and actual body, that is the crucified body that becomes the resurrected body, a crucified body that is finally the body of us all, and if apocalyptic body is all in all, it is so not as a "spiritual body," but as a transfiguration of the deepest actuality of the body itself. Such an actuality could only be potentially present in primordial body, a body that has not yet undergone an ultimate passion and death, for ultimate death occurs only in the Crucifixion, but apart from an ultimate actualization of primordial body the Crucifixion could not be actually real, could not actually be crucifixion. Dialectical theologians have known that the resurrected body is not an empirical body, or not a body that empirically can be known, but so, too, the primordial body is empirically unknown, but it is all too real as an ultimate ground of the body, and an ultimate ground of that body that is a fully human body, or that body that we most immediately know. And if we know a body that is our own and not our own at once, or a body that is center and periphery simultaneously, such a body is impossible apart from primordial body, a body that is the consequence of an absolute genesis or an absolute beginning, and an absolute beginning that is inseparable from an absolute or apocalyptic ending. But an apocalyptic ending is not the ending of the body; it is far rather its absolute transfiguration, a transfiguration in which primordial body is finally apocalyptic body, but only through that absolute death that is absolute transfiguration.

If we do not yet know a resurrected body, or do not do so either fully or decisively, we can know a crucified body, and can know the full actuality of that body, and most clearly know it in the ultimate suffering of the body of humanity, a suffering that can be known as a renewal of the Crucifixion. But if it is a renewal of the Crucifixion it is a renewal of the passion of God, a passion inseparable from an apocalyptic transfiguration, a transfiguration only possible through the death of God, or only possible through an absolute self-emptying or self-sacrifice of the Godhead, a sacrifice that is the sacrifice of the Crucifixion, and a crucifixion that is itself the consequence of an absolute genesis or an absolute beginning. But if the Crucifixion is the most ultimate realization of the body itself, it is so only as an absolute breaking of the body, a breaking that is renewed in the Eucharist, and comprehensively embodied in the most ultimate suffering of the body of humanity, then body as body is absolutely real, and finally real only as the body of Christ. This is certainly not the "spiritual body" of Christ, not a mystical body that is an other-worldly body, it is the very reversal of every possible other-worldly body, indeed, a reversal ending every other-worldly body, a reversal that is the totality of incarnation, and only thereby the totality of resurrection itself. Yes, we can only know resurrection as crucifixion, but thereby we do know resurrection, and know a resurrection that is the resurrection of the body, and thereby know incarnate body itself.

If that body is the very body of the Godhead, it is the consequence of the total act of God, the consequence of God's own absolute self-negation, a kenotic self-negation that is an absolute atonement, and the absolute atonement of Godhead itself. Only that atonement finally ends every trace or echo of a primordial plenum, an ending that is the advent of absolute apocalypse, and an absolute apocalypse that is fully incarnate, and fully incarnate in and as body itself. Now if that body is an atoning body, and a body atoning "flesh" and Spirit simultaneously, that simultaneity is an absolute transfiguration of the body, a transfiguration that is the resurrection of the body, and a resurrection occurring "in our very flesh."

# Thomas J. J. Altizer

⁓⁓

# Comprehensive Bibliography

### Compiled by Lissa McCullough

## BOOKS

*Oriental Mysticism and Biblical Eschatology.* Philadelphia: Westminster, 1961.

*Mircea Eliade and the Dialectic of the Sacred.* Philadelphia: Westminster, 1963; reprint, Westport, CT: Greenwood Press, 1975.

*Radical Theology and the Death of God*, with William Hamilton. Indianapolis: Bobbs-Merrill, 1966.

*The Gospel of Christian Atheism.* Philadelphia: Westminster, 1966.

*The New Apocalypse: The Radical Christian Vision of William Blake.* East Lansing: Michigan State University Press, 1967; reprint, Aurora, CO: Davies Group, 2000.

*The Descent into Hell: A Study of the Radical Reversal of the Christian Consciousness.* Philadelphia: Lippincott, 1970; reprint, New York: Seabury, 1979.

*The Self-Embodiment of God.* New York: Harper & Row, 1977; reprint, with an introduction by Jacob Neusner, Brown Classics in Judaica. Lanham, MD: University Press of America, 1985.

*Total Presence: The Language of Jesus and the Language of Today.* New York: Seabury, 1980.

*History as Apocalypse.* Albany: State University of New York Press, 1985.

*Genesis and Apocalypse: A Theological Voyage toward Authentic Christianity.* Louisville: Westminster John Knox, 1990.

*The Genesis of God: A Theological Genealogy.* Louisville: Westminster John Knox, 1993.

*The Contemporary Jesus.* Albany: State University of New York Press, 1997.

*The New Gospel of Christian Atheism.* Aurora, CO: Davies Group, 2002.

*Godhead and the Nothing.* Albany: State University of New York Press, 2003.

*Living the Death of God: A Theological Memoir.* Unpublished manuscript.

*The Apocalyptic Trinity.* Work in progress.

## BOOKS EDITED

Coeditor, with William Beardslee and J. Harvey Young. *Truth, Myth, and Symbol.* Englewood Cliffs, NJ: Prentice-Hall, 1962.

Editor, *Toward a New Christianity: Readings in the Death of God Theology.* New York: Harcourt, Brace & World, 1967.

Coeditor, with David Ray Griffin, *John B. Cobb's Theology in Process.* Philadelphia: Westminster, 1977.

Series editor with James O. Duke, Studies in Religion series, Crossroad Press and Scholars Press, 1978–1981.

## CONTRIBUTIONS TO BOOKS

"The Religious Meaning of Myth and Symbol," in *Truth, Myth, and Symbol,* ed. Thomas J. J. Altizer, William A. Beardslee, and J. Harvey Young. Englewood Cliffs, NJ: Prentice-Hall, 1962, 87–108.

"The Death of God and the Uniqueness of Christianity," in *The History of Religions: Essays on the Problem of Understanding,* ed. Joseph M. Kitagawa. Chicago: University of Chicago Press, 1967, 119–41. Simultaneously printed as chapter 1 of *The Gospel of Christian Atheism.*

"The Significance of the New Theology," in *The Death of God Debate,* ed. Jackson Lee Ice and John J. Carey. Philadelphia: Westminster, 1967, 242–55.

"Theology and the Contemporary Sensibility," in *America and the Future of Theology,* ed. William A. Beardslee. Philadelphia: Westminster, 1967, 15–31.

"Thomas J. J. Altizer" and "Discussion," in *The Altizer-Montgomery Dialogue: A Chapter in the God Is Dead Controversy.* Chicago: Inter-Varsity Christian Fellowship, 1967, 7–18, 57–96.

"The Sacred and the Profane: A Dialectical Understanding of Christianity," in *Philosophy and Religion: Some Contemporary Perspectives*, ed. Jerry H. Gill. Minneapolis: Burgess, 1968, 161–72. Reprinted from Altizer and Hamilton, *Radical Theology and the Death of God*, 140–55.

"An Inquiry into the Meaning of Negation in the Dialectical Logics of East and West," in *Religious Language and Knowledge*, ed. Robert H. Ayers and William T. Blackstone. Athens: University of Georgia Press, 1972, 97–117.

"Method in Dipolar Theology and the Dipolar Meaning of God," in *Philosophy of Religion and Theology* [no editor]. Chambersburg, PA: American Academy of Religion, 1972, 14–21.

"Eternal Recurrence and Kingdom of God," in *The New Nietzsche: Contemporary Styles of Interpretation*, ed. David B. Allison. New York: Dell, 1977, 232–46.

"A Holistic, Non-alienated Theologian" and "Spiritual Existence as God-Transcending Existence," in *John B. Cobb's Theology in Process*, ed. David Ray Griffin and Thomas J. J. Altizer. Philadelphia: Westminster, 1977, 1–4, 54–66.

"Demythologizing as the Self-Embodiment of Speech," in *Orientation by Disorientation: Studies in Literary Criticism and Biblical Literary Criticism Presented in Honor of William A. Beardslee*, ed. Richard A. Spencer. Pittsburgh: Pickwick, 1980, 139–50.

"History as Apocalypse," in *Deconstruction and Theology*, ed. Carl A. Raschke. New York: Crossroad, 1982, 147–77.

"A New History and a New but Ancient God? A Review-Essay," in *Eric Voegelin's Thought: A Critical Appraisal*, ed. Ellis Sandoz. Durham: Duke University Press, 1982, 179–88. Reprinted from *Journal of the American Academy of Religion* 43, no. 4 (December 1975): 757–72.

"Theology as Reflection upon the Roots of Christian Culture," in *The Vocation of the Theologian*, ed. Theodore W. Jennings Jr. Philadelphia: Fortress, 1985, 135–42.

"Satan as the Messiah of Nature," in *The Whirlwind in Culture: Frontiers in Theology*, ed. Donald W. Musser and Joseph L. Price. Bloomington, IN: Meyer Stone Books, 1988, 119–34.

"Emptiness and God," in *The Religious Philosophy of Nishitani Keiji*, ed. Taitetsu Unno. Berkeley: Asian Humanities Press, 1989, 70–81.

"Nietzsche and Biblical Nihilism," in *Nietzsche and the Rhetoric of Nihilism: Essays on Interpretation, Language and Politics*, ed. Tom Darby, Béla Egyed, and Ben Jones. Ottawa: Carlton University Press, 1989, 37–44.

"The Beginning and Ending of Revelation" and "Reply: The Self-Realization of Death," in *Theology at the End of the Century: A Dialogue on the Postmodern*, ed. Robert P. Scharlemann. Charlottesville: University Press of Virginia, 1990, 76–109, 130–35.

"Buddhist Emptiness and the Crucifixion of God," in *The Emptying God: A Buddhist-Jewish-Christian Conversation*, ed. John B. Cobb Jr. and Christopher Ives. Maryknoll, NY: Orbis, 1990, 69–78.

"A Contemporary Quest for a New Kabbalah," in *Essays in European Literature for Walter A. Strauss*, ed. Alice N. Benston and Marshall C. Olds. Manhattan, KS: Studies in Contemporary Literature, 1990, 229–37.

"Total Abyss and Theological Rebirth: The Crisis of University Theology," in *Theology and the University: Essays in Honor of John B. Cobb, Jr.*, ed. David Ray Griffin and Joseph C. Hough. Albany: State University of New York Press, 1991, 169–84.

"The Theological Conflict between Strauss and Voegelin," in *Faith and Political Philosophy: The Correspondence between Leo Strauss and Eric Voegelin, 1934–1964*, trans. and ed. Peter Emberley and Barry Cooper. University Park: Pennsylvania State University Press, 1993, 267–77.

"God as Holy Nothingness," in *What Kind of God? Essays in Honor of Richard L. Rubenstein*, ed. B. R. Rubenstein and M. Berenbaum. Atlanta: Scholars Press, 1995, 347–56.

"The Apocalypse of the Spirit," in *Dissent and Marginality: Essays on the Borders of Literature and Religion*, ed. Kiyoshi Tsuchiya. Hampshire, England: Macmillan, 1997, 29–44.

"Contemporary Christian Radical Theology," in *Radical Theologians in Conversation*, ed. Dan Cohn-Sherbok and David A. Hart. England: Cassell Press, 1998.

"Kenosis and Sunyata in the Contemporary Buddhist-Christian Dialogue," in *Masao Abe: A Zen Life of Dialogue*, ed. Donald W. Mitchell. Boston: Charles E. Tuttle, 1998, 151–60.

"The Otherness of God as an Image of Satan," in *The Otherness of God*, ed. Orrin F. Summerell. Charlottesville: University Press of Virginia, 1998, 206–15.

"Modern Thought and Apocalypticism," in *Encyclopedia of Apocalypticism,* vol. 3, *Apocalypticism in the Modern Period and the Contemporary Age,* ed. Stephen Stein. New York: Continuum, 1998, 325–59.

"The Holocaust and the Theology of the Death of God," in *The Death of God Movement and the Holocaust: Radical Theology Encounters the Shoah,* ed. Stephen R. Haynes and John K. Roth. Westport, CT: Greenwood, 1999, 17–23.

"The Self-Saving of God," in *The Blackwell Companion to Postmodern Theology,* ed. Graham Ward. Oxford: Blackwell, 2001, 427–43.

"Van Gogh's Eyes," in *Hermeneutic Philosophy of Science, Van Gogh's Eyes, and God: Essays in Honor of Patrick A. Heelan, S.J.,* ed. Babette E. Babich. Dordrecht: Kluwer Academic Publishers, 2002, 393–402.

"Crucifixion and Apocalypse," in *Mélanges en l'honneur d'André Gounelle à l'occasion de son 70e anniversaire,* ed. Marc Boss and Raphaël Picon. Paris: Van Dieren, 2003.

"The Sacred Vision of a Solitary Voyager," in *Encounters with Alphonso Lingis,* ed. Alexander E. Hooke and Wolfgang W. Fuchs. Lanham, MD: Lexington Books, 2003, 43–50.

"The Primordial, Godhead, and Apocalyptic Christianity," in *Theology in Global Context: Essays in Honor of Robert Cummings Neville,* ed. Amos Yong and Peter Heltzel. New York and London: T & T Clark, 2004.

## JOURNAL ARTICLES

"Religion and Reality," *Journal of Religion* 38, no. 4 (October 1958): 251–62.

"The Romantic Achievement of Sigmund Freud," *Emory University Quarterly* 14 (October 1958): 171–83.

"Science and Gnosis in Jung's Psychology," *Centennial Review* 3, no. 3 (Summer 1959): 304–20.

"The Religious Foundations of Biblical Eschatology," *Journal of Religion* 39, no. 4 (October 1959): 263–73.

"Demythologizing and Jesus," *Religion in Life* 29, no. 4 (Fall 1960): 564–74.

"The Influence of Nietzsche upon Contemporary Thought," *Emory University Quarterly* 16, no. 3 (Fall 1960): 152–63.

"The Challenge of Modern Gnosticism," *Journal of Bible and Religion* 30, no. 1 (January 1962): 18–25.

"Mircea Eliade and the Recovery of the Sacred," *Christian Scholar* 45, no. 4 (Winter 1962): 267–89.

"Nirvana and Kingdom of God," *Journal of Religion* 43, no. 2 (April 1963): 105–17. Reprinted in Martin E. Marty and Dean G. Peerman, ed., *New Theology*, no. 1. New York: Macmillan, 1964, 150–68.

"A Theonomy in Our Time?" review article on Paul Tillich, *Christianity and the Encounter of the World Religions,* in *Christian Scholar* 46, no. 4 (Winter 1963): 356–62.

"America und die Zukunft der Theologie," *Antaios* 5, no. 5 (January 1964): 424–36; translator unknown. Original English version, "America and the Future of Theology," in Altizer and Hamilton, *Radical Theology and the Death of God,* 9–21.

"Theology and the Death of God," *Centennial Review* 8, no. 2 (Spring 1964): 129–46. Reprinted in Altizer and Hamilton, *Radical Theology and the Death of God,* 95–111.

"Creative Negation in Theology," *Christian Century* 82 (July 7, 1965), 864–67.

"William Blake and the Role of Myth in the Radical Christian Vision," *Centennial Review* 9, no. 4 (Fall 1965): 461–82. Reprinted in Altizer and Hamilton, *Radical Theology and the Death of God,* 171–91.

"The Shape of a Radical Theology," with William Hamilton, *Christian Century* 82 (October 6, 1965).

"Word and History," *Theology Today* 22 (October 1965): 380–93. Reprinted in Altizer and Hamilton, *Radical Theology and the Death of God,* 121–39.

"Theology's Response to the Challenge of Secularism," *Centennial Review* 11, no. 4 (Fall 1967): 474–82.

"Catholic Philosophy and the Death of God," *Cross Currents* 17 (1967): 271–82.

"Amerikas Schicksal und der Tod Gottes," *Antaios* 9, no. 5 (January 1968): 483–99; translated by Reinhard Wonneberger. English version unpublished and unavailable.

"Radical Theology and Political Revolution," *Criterion* 7 (Spring 1968): 5–10.

"Imagination and Apocalypse," *Soundings* 53, no. 4 (Winter 1970): 398–412.

"Dialectical vs. Di-Polar Theology," *Process Studies* 1, no. 1 (Spring 1971): 29–37.

"The Dialectic of Ancient and Modern Apocalypticism," *Journal of the American Academy of Religion* 39, no. 3 (September 1971): 312–20.

"Religion Conquering Itself," review article on Louis Dupré, *The Other Dimension: A Search for the Meaning of Religious Attitudes,* in *Journal of Religion* 54, no. 1 (January 1974): 86–92.

"The Buddhist Ground of the Whiteheadian God," *Process Studies* 5, no. 4 (Winter 1975): 227–36.

"A New History and a New but Ancient God? A Review-Essay," *Journal of the American Academy of Religion* 43, no. 4 (December 1975): 757–72. Reprinted in *Eric Voegelin's Thought: A Critical Appraisal,* ed. Ellis Sandoz. Durham: Duke University Press, 1982.

"Buddhism and Christianity: A Radical Christian Viewpoint," *Japanese Religions* 9, no. 1 (March 1976): 1–11.

"The Apocalyptic Identity of the Jew," a review article on Terrence Des Pres, *The Survivor,* and Edmond Jabès, *The Book of Questions,* in *Journal of the American Academy of Religion* 45, no. 3, Supplement (September 1977): L: 1055–73.

"Overt Language about the Death of God," a self-review of his own books in retrospect, *Christian Century* 95, no. 21 (June 7–14, 1978): 624–27. Continued in "Altizer on Altizer," *Literature and Theology* 15, no. 2 (June 2001): 187–94.

"Mircea Eliade and the Death of God," *Cross Currents* 29, no. 3 (Fall 1979): 257–68.

"Nirvana as a Negative Image of God," *Zero: Contemporary Buddhist Life and Thought* 2 (1979): 88–99. Reprinted in *Buddhist and Western Philosophy,* ed. Nathan Katz. New Delhi: Sterling, 1981, 18–29.

"The Anonymity of God," *The University of Dayton Review* 14, no. 3 (Fall 1980): 17–26. Reprinted in *Is God God?* ed. Axel D. Steuer and James Wm. McClendon Jr. Nashville: Abingdon, 1981, 19–35.

"Ritual and Contemporary Repetition," *Dialog* 19 (Fall 1980): 274–80. Published simultaneously under the title "Literature and Rite," *The University of Dayton Review* 14, no. 3 (Fall 1980): 41–51.

"The Apocalyptic Identity of the Modern Imagination," in *The Archaeology of the Imagination,* ed. Charles E. Winquist. *Journal of the American Academy of Religion Thematic Studies* 48, no. 2 (June 1981): 19–29.

"Revelation and the Hermeneutical Spiral," in *Unfinished . . . : Essays in Honor of Ray L. Hart*, ed. Mark C. Taylor. *Journal of the American Academy of Religion Thematic Studies* 48, no. 1 (1981): 99–109.

"Paul and the Birth of Self-Consciousness," *Journal of the American Academy of Religion* 51, no. 3 (September 1983): 359–70. Reprinted as chapter 4 of *History as Apocalypse.*

"The Atheistic Ground of America," *Anglican Theological Review* 71, no. 3 (Summer 1989): 261–72.

"Is the Negation of Christianity the Way to Its Renewal?" *Religious Humanism* 24, no. 1 (Winter 1990): 10–16.

"Hegel and the Christian God," *Journal of the American Academy of Religion* 59, no. 1 (Spring 1991): 71–91. Revised and published as chapter 2 of *The Genesis of God.*

"Tragedy and the Genesis of Nothingness," *Sophia* 33, no. 1 (March 1994): 1–13.

"The Contemporary Challenge of Radical Catholicism," *Journal of Religion* 74, no. 2 (April 1994): 182–98.

"The Challenge of Nihilism," *Journal of the American Academy of Religion* 62, no. 4 (Winter 1994): 1013–22.

"Russia and Apocalypse" (published in Russian), trans. Yuri R. Selivanov, *Issues of Philosophy* 7, Russian Academy of Sciences, Moscow (1996): 110–26. English version unpublished.

"Apocalypticism and Modern Thinking," *Journal for Christian Theological Research* 2, no. 2 (1997). Online journal: http://www.apu.edu/~CTRF/jctr. html; INTERNET.

"Nietzsche and Apocalypse," *New Nietzsche Studies* 4, no. 3/4 (2000–2001): 1–13.

"Absolute Nothingness and Taylor's Imagology," *Journal of Cultural and Religious Theory* 2, no. 2 (April 2001). Online journal, ISSN: 1530-5228: http//www.jcrt.org/archives/02.2/altizer.shtml; INTERNET.

"Altizer on Altizer," a self-review essay, *Literature and Theology* 15, no. 2 (June 2001): 187–94.

## BOOK REVIEWS, BRIEF ARTICLES, INTRODUCTIONS, AND RESPONSES

Review of C. F. Kelley, *The Spirit of Love: Based on the Teachings of St. Francois de Sales,* in *Journal of Religion* 31, no. 4 (October 1951): 306.

Review of C. G. Jung, *Psychology and Alchemy,* in *Journal of Religion* 34, no. 3 (July 1954): 222–23.

Review of C. G. Jung, *The Practise of Psychotherapy,* in *Journal of Religion* 35, no. 1 (January 1955): 53–54.

Review of Winston L. King, *Introduction to Religion,* in *Journal of Religion* 36, no. 3 (July 1956): 196.

"Incarnation," in *A Handbook of Christian Theology*, ed. Marvin Halverson and Arthur A. Cohen. New York: Meridian, 1958, 186–88.

Review of Mircea Eliade, *Birth and Rebirth: The Religious Meanings of Initiation in Human Culture,* in *Journal of Religion* 40, no. 2 (April 1960): 131–32.

Review of Roger Caillois, *Man and the Sacred,* in *Journal of Religion* 40, no. 2 (April 1960): 132.

Review of Arthur A. Cohen, *The Natural and the Supernatural Jew,* in *Journal of Religion and Health* 2 (July 1963): 348–50.

"A Comment on 'Teaching World Religions,' by W. L. King," in *Journal of Bible and Religion* 32, no. 1 (January 1964): 23–24.

Review of Owen Barfield, *Worlds Apart: A Dialogue of the 1960s,* in *Journal of the American Academy of Religion* 32, no. 4 (October 1964): 384–85.

"Still Burning Bright," review of Jean H. Hagstrum, *William Blake: Poet and Painter, An Introduction to the Illuminated Verse,* in *Christian Scholar* 48, no. 2 (Summer 1965): 165–67.

Review of Seymour Cain, *Gabriel Marcel,* in *Journal of Religion* 45, no. 4 (October 1965): 355.

"Discussion: Responses to Paul Lehmann's 'The Tri-unity of God,'" *Union Seminary Quarterly Review* 21, no. 2, part 2 (January 1966): 207–10.

"A Dialogue with His Audience," an interview, *Barat Review* 2 (June 1967): 71–78.

"Comment," in *World: Vatican II's Constitution on the Church in the Modern World, Part 1: The Church and Man's Calling*, ed. Peter Foote, et al. Chicago: Catholic Action Federations, 1967, 43.

"A Response to Anselm Atkins' Ninety-Five Theses," *Continuum* 6, no. 1 (Spring 1968): 89–92.

Review of Regis Jolivet, *Sartre: The Theology of the Absurd,* and Charles N. Bent, *The Death-of-God Movement,* in *Journal of the American Academy of Religion* 36, no. 2 (June 1968): 162–63.

"Supernaturalism," in *Encyclopaedia Britannica*, vol. 21. Chicago: Encyclopaedia Britannica, 1968: 432.

"Stanley Romaine Hopper's *The 'Eclipse of God' and Existential Mistrust*: A Response Stanley Romaine Hopper," in *The Eastern Buddhist* 3, no. 2 (October 1970), 158–61.

"Comment on Murray Greene, Hegel's 'Unhappy Consciousness' and Nietzsche's 'Slave Morality,'" in *Hegel and the Philosophy of Religion: The Wofford Symposium*, ed. Darrel E. Christensen. The Hague: Martinus Nijhoff, 1970, 147–52.

Responses in *The Theology of Altizer: Critique and Response*, ed. John B. Cobb. Philadelphia: Westminster, 1970, 68–76, 112–24, 138–46, 194–205, 227–33.

Review of Rosemary Radford Ruether, *The Radical Kingdom: The Western Experience of Messianic Hope*, in *Journal of the American Academy of Religion* 39, no. 4 (December 1971): 569.

Review of Jackson Lee Ice, *Schweitzer: Prophet of Radical Theology*, in *Journal of the American Academy of Religion* 41, no. 2 (June 1973): 269–71.

"From Death into Life: Are Theologians Free Simply to *Choose*? A Response to Driver's Challenge," in *Journal of the American Academy of Religion* 41, no. 2 (June 1973): 238–42.

Review of Rubem A. Alves, *Tomorrow's Child: Imagination, Creativity, and the Rebirth of Culture*, in *Journal of the American Academy of Religion* 42, no. 2 (June 1974): 376–78.

Review of Eric Voegelin, *Anamnesis*, in *Journal of Religion* 59, no. 3 (July 1979): 375–76.

Review of Bernd Magnus, *Nietzsche's Existential Imperative*, in *Journal of the American Academy of Religion* 47, no. 4 (1979): 697.

"Foreword," in Mark C. Taylor, *Deconstructing Theology*. New York: Crossroad, 1982, xi–xv.

Review of Frans Jozef van Beeck, *Christ Proclaimed: Christology as Rhetoric*, in *Journal of the American Academy of Religion* 50, no. 1 (1982): 136.

Review of Keiji Nishitani, *Religion and Nothingness*, in *Journal of the American Academy of Religion* 52, no. 1 (March 1984): 198–99.

Review of Susan A. Handelman, *The Slayers of Moses*, in *Religion and Literature* 16, no. 1 (Winter 1984): 73–78.

Review of Samuel C. Heilman, *The People of the Book: Drama, Fellowship, and Religion,* in *Religion & Literature* 16, no. 1 (1984): 79–83.

Review of D. G. Leahy, *Novitas Mundi: Perception of the History of Being,* in *Religious Studies Review* 11, no. 4 (October 1985): 350–52.

"The Triumph of the Theology of the Word," review of Mark C. Taylor, *Erring: A Postmodern A/theology,* in *Journal of the American Academy of Religion* 54, no. 3 (Fall 1986): 525–29.

Review of Mark C. Taylor, *Erring: A Postmodern A/theology,* in *International Studies in Philosophy* 20, no. 1 (1988): 115.

Introduction to D. G. Leahy, "To Create the Absolute Edge," in *Journal of the American Academy of Religion* 57, no. 4 (Winter 1989): 773–79.

Review of Henry M. Rosenthal, *The Consolations of Philosophy,* in *Journal of the American Academy of Religion* 58 (Winter 1990): 725–27.

Review of Mark C. Taylor, *Disfiguring: Art, Architecture, Religion,* in *Theology and Literature* 7, no. 4 (December 1993): 403–05.

"Abe's Buddhist Realization of God," a response to Abe's rejoinder, in *Buddhist-Christian Studies* 13 (1993): 221–22.

Review of Graham Parkes, ed., *Nietzsche and Asian Thought,* in *International Philosophical Quarterly* 26, no. 1 (1994): 130–31.

Review of Stephen Barker, *Autoaesthetics: Strategies of the Self after Nietzsche,* in *International Studies in Philosophy* 27, no. 2 (1995): 111–12.

Review of Michael Allen Gillespie, *Nihilism before Nietzsche,* and Michel Haar, *Nietzsche and Metaphysics,* in *Journal of Religion* 77, no. 2 (April 1997): 328–30.

Review of Peter H. Van Ness, ed., *Spirituality and the Secular Quest,* in *Journal of Religion* 78, no. 2 (April 1998): 336–37.

Review of Charles E. Winquist, *Desiring Theology,* in *International Philosophical Quarterly* 31, no. 4 (1999): 143–44.

Review of Thomas A. Carlson, *Indiscretion: Finitude and the Naming of God,* in *Journal of the American Academy of Religion* 68, no. 1 (March 2000): 160–63.

"D. G. Leahy," in *The Routledge Encyclopedia of Postmodernism,* ed. Victor E. Taylor and Charles E. Winquist. London and New York: Routledge, 2000.

Review of D. G. Leahy, *Foundation: Matter the Body Itself,* in *International Studies in Philosophy* (2004).

Review of Paul J. Levesque, *Symbols of Transcendence: Religious Expression in the Thought of Louis Dupré*, in *International Studies in Philosophy* (2004).

## UNPUBLISHED THESIS AND DISSERTATION

"Nature and Grace in the Theology of Saint Augustine." Master of Arts thesis, University of Chicago, June 1951. 123 pp.

"A Critical Analysis of C. G. Jung's Understanding of Religion." Ph.D. dissertation, University of Chicago, August 1955. 276 pp.

## UNPUBLISHED NOVEL

*Laura: A Portrait of a Saint* (1993).

## UNPUBLISHED MANUSCRIPTS

*Access to these manuscripts may be requested by contacting the author.*

"The Language of Mircea Eliade," presented in the religion department at Emory University, April 1977.

"History and Apocalypse," circa 1984.

"*Finnegans Wake* as Contemporary Expression of Biblical Apocalypse," presented at the Society of Biblical Literature annual meeting, Atlanta, Fall 1986.

"Primordial and Apocalyptic Time," presented at the American Academy of Religion annual meeting, Atlanta, Fall 1986.

"The Silence of God," 1988.

"The Apocalypse of God," retirement lecture presented at State University of New York at Stony Brook, May 1992 (retirement postponed until 1995).

"Russia and Apocalypse," in English, 1992. Russian translation published in *Issues of Philosophy* 7 (Moscow, 1996). Shortened version presented at the American Academy of Religion annual meeting, San Francisco, November 1992.

"Dionysian Theology as a Catholic Nihilism," presented at the American Academy of Religion annual meeting, Washington, November 1993.

"The Satanic Transgression of Crucifixion," written for a volume to appear in England, project later cancelled, 1993.

"Can the Genuinely Christological Be Authentically Theological?" circa 1995.

"A Contemporary Apocalyptic Thinker: D. G. Leahy," a review article on D. G. Leahy, *Foundation: Matter the Body Itself,* January 1996.

"A Radical Theologian's Response to 'The Sea of Faith,'" a response to the Sea of Faith annual conference held in July at Leicester, England, August 1997.

"Blessing the Fall," an essay in honor of Robert Detweiler, November 1997.

"Joyce and the Christian Epic Tradition," presented in absentia at the conference Joyce, Altizer, and the Christian Epic Tradition, Rome, Italy, June 1998.

"A Vision of Satan," January 1999.

"Nietzsche and Apocalypse," fall 2000.

"*Ereignis* and the Nothing," November 2001.

"A New America," a response to the one-year anniversary of 9/11, September 13, 2002.

"Doing Radical Theology," October 2002.

"Foundations of Apocalypticism," October 2002.

"Ancient and Modern Apocalypticism," November 2002.

## SELECTED CRITICAL ASSESSMENTS OF ALTIZER

Borné, Gerhard F. *Christlicher Atheismus und Radikales Christentum.* Munich: Chr. Kaiser, 1979.

Butler, Clark. "Hegel, Altizer, and Christian Atheism," *Encounter* 41, no. 2 (Spring 1980): 103–28.

Cobb, Jr., John B., "Altizer and Christian Theology," *Clio* 16 (Summer 1987): 331–44.

———, ed. *The Theology of Altizer: Critique and Response.* Philadelphia: Westminster, 1970.

Driver, Tom F. "From Death into Life: Altizer Challenged," in *Journal of the American Academy of Religion* 41, no. 2 (June 1973): 229–42.

Feero, Richard L. "Radical Theology in Preparation: From Altizer to Edwards." Ph.D. dissertation, Syracuse University, 1993.

Krieger, Frederick B. "The Curious Theology of Thomas J. J. Altizer," *Canadian Journal of Theology* 13, no. 2 (1967): 86–98.

Leahy, D. G. *Foundation: Matter the Body Itself.* Albany: State University of New York Press, 1996. Cf. pp. 188–251 and 576–628.

Meyer, Eric C. "A Critical Analysis of the Death of God Theology of Thomas J. J. Altizer in Its Origins and Development." Ph.D. dissertation, University of Munster, 1971.

———. "Thomas J. J. Altizer's Construction of Ultimate Reality and Meaning," *Ultimate Reality and Meaning* 1 (1978): 258–77.

Odin, Steve. "Kenosis as a Foundation for Buddhist-Christian Dialogue: The Kenotic Buddhology of Nishida and Nishitani of the Kyoto School in Relation to the Kenotic Christology of Thomas J. J. Altizer," *The Eastern Buddhist* 20, no. 1 (Spring 1987): 34–61.

O'Regan, Cyril. *Gnostic Return in Modernity.* Albany: State University of New York Press, 2001. Cf. pp. 65–76.

Rohmann, Klaus. *Vollendung im Nichts? Ein Dokumentation der amerikanischen "Gott-ist-tot-Theologie."* Zurich: Benziger, 1977.

Smith, F. Joseph. "'God Is Dead'—Philosophical Sources and Themes," *Centennial Review* 11, no. 4 (Fall 1967): 456–73.

Taylor, Mark C. "Altizer's Originality: A Review Essay," *Journal of the American Academy of Religion* 52, no. 3 (September 1984): 569–83.

Winquist, Charles E. "Thomas J. J. Altizer: In Retrospect," *Religious Studies Review* 8, no. 4 (October 1982): 337–42.

# Contributors

THOMAS J. J. ALTIZER is emeritus professor of religious studies at the State University of New York at Stony Brook. He is the author of some fifteen theological works, including *Genesis and Apocalypse* and *The Genesis of God.* His most recently published work is *Godhead and the Nothing.*

EDWARD S. CASEY is Leading Professor of Philosophy at the State University of New York at Stony Brook. The author of numerous books and articles, his most recent works are *Representing Place* and *The Fate of Place.*

JANET GYATSO is the Hershey Professor of Buddhist Studies at Harvard Divinity School. She is currently president of the International Association of Tibetan Studies. The author of *Apparitions of the Self: The Secret Autobiographies of a Tibetan Visionary* and *In the Mirror of Memory: Reflections on Mindfulness and Remembrance in Indian and Tibetan Buddhism*, recently she has been working on Tibetan medical tradition, Buddhist monastic material, and the place of women in tantra.

RAY L. HART is interim dean of the School of Theology at Boston University. A former president of the American Academy of Religion and editor of the *Journal of the American Academy of Religion*, his books include *Unfinished Man and the Imagination* and *Religious and Theological Studies in American Higher Education*. Preoccupied in the past two decades with the apophatic theologies of the West, he is currently at work on a book tentatively titled *God Being Nothing.*

DAVID JASPER is professor of literature and theology and formerly dean of divinity at the University of Glasgow, holding degrees in English from Cambridge University and theology from Oxford University. He is founding editor of the journal *Literature and Theology*. His most recent book is *The Sacred Desert*, and he has also recently edited a reader in religion and literature with Robert Detweiler.

D. G. LEAHY was most recently Distinguished Visiting Professor of Philosophy at Loyola College in Maryland and is the author of *Faith and Philosophy: The Historical Impact, Novitas Mundi: Perception of the History of Being*, and *Foundation: Matter the Body Itself*. He is founder of The New York Philosophy Corporation (http://newyorkphilosophy.org) where he teaches courses on his philosophical work and the history of philosophy.

ALPHONSO LINGIS is emeritus professor of philosophy at Pennsylvania State University. His publications include *Excesses: Eros and Culture, Libido: The French Existential Theories, Phenomenological Explanations, Deathbound Subjectivity, Abuses*, and *Sensation: Intelligibility in Sensibility*. His most recent books are *Dangerous Emotions* and *Foreign Bodies*.

LISSA MCCULLOUGH is assistant professor of religion at Muhlenberg College; she has also taught at New York University and Hanover College. She received her master's degree from Harvard Divinity School and her doctorate in theology from the University of Chicago. Her first book is on the religious thought of Simone Weil, and she is interested in working out a radical theology of the body, among other projects.

CARL A. RASCHKE is professor of religious studies at the University of Denver. A pioneer in postmodern theology, he has published various books and articles on the subject, including *The Alchemy of the Word, Theological Thinking, Fire and Roses, The Engendering God*, "The Deconstruction of God" in *Deconstruction and Theology*, and an article on postmodern theology in *The New Handbook of Christian Theology*.

BRIAN SCHROEDER is associate professor of philosophy and coordinator of Religious Studies at the Rochester Institute of Technology. He is the author of *Altared Ground: Levinas, History, and Violence* and coauthor (in Italian) of *Environmental Thinking: Between Philosophy and Ecology*.

WALTER A. STRAUSS is the Treuhaft Professor of the Humanities, Emeritus, at Case Western Reserve University. His major interests are comparative literature from 1850 to the present, principally European and American, and the relationship of literature to history, philosophy, theology, and the arts. He has published articles on many authors from Dante to Beckett, as well as books on Proust, the Orphic theme, and Kafka.

MARK C. TAYLOR is the Cluett Professor of Humanities and Religion at Williams College and the founder of the Global Education Network. His most recent books include *Confidence Games: Money and Markets in a World without Redemption, Grave Matters, The Moment of Complexity: Emerging Network Culture, Hiding*, and *About Religion*.

EDITH WYSCHOGROD is the J. Newton Rayzor Professor of Philosphy and Religious Thought at Rice University. Her most recent books are *Emmanuel Levinas: The Problem of Ethical Metaphysics* and *An Ethics of Remembering*. Her earlier works include *Spirit in Ashes* and *Saints and Postmodernism*.

# Index